THE DOG OF
THE MARRIAGE

THE COLLECTED STORIES

Amy Hempel

WITH AN INTRODUCTION BY
Rick Moody

Quercus

First published in Great Britain in 2008 by

Quercus
21 Bloomsbury Square
London
WC1A 2NS

A CIP catalogue reference for this book is available
from the British Library

ISBN (HB) 978 1 84724 235 8
ISBN (TPB) 978 1 84724 236 5

10 9 8 7 6 5 4 3 2 1

Printed and bound in Great Britain by Clays Ltd, St Ives plc.

Page 409 constitutes an extension of the copyright page.

To Nan Graham

CONTENTS

On Amy Hempel   xi

REASONS TO LIVE

In a Tub   3

Tonight Is a Favor to Holly   5

Celia Is Back   13

Nashville Gone to Ashes   17

San Francisco   27

In the Cemetery Where Al Jolson Is Buried   29

Beg, Sl Tog, Inc, Cont, Rep   41

Going   53

Pool Night   57

Three Popes Walk into a Bar   63

The Man in Bogotá   73

When It's Human Instead of When It's Dog   75

Why I'm Here   81

Breathing Jesus   85

Today Will Be a Quiet Day   89

CONTENTS

AT THE GATES
OF THE ANIMAL KINGDOM

Daylight Come   101

The Harvest   103

The Most Girl Part of You   111

Rapture of the Deep   123

Du Jour   129

Murder   133

The Day I Had Everything   139

To Those of You Who Missed Your Connecting
    Flights Out of O'Hare   149

And Lead Us Not into Penn Station   153

In the Animal Shelter   157

At the Gates of the Animal Kingdom   159

The Lady Will Have the Slug Louie   169

Under No Moon   171

The Center   177

Tom-Rock Through the Eels   181

The Rest of God   191

TUMBLE HOME

Weekend   199

Church Cancels Cow   201

The Children's Party   203

CONTENTS

Sportsman   209

Housewife   221

The Annex   223

The New Lodger   229

Tumble Home   233

Notes   302

THE DOG OF THE MARRIAGE

Beach Town   305

Jesus Is Waiting   309

The Uninvited   317

Reference #388475848-5   337

What Were the White Things?   343

The Dog of the Marriage   347

The Afterlife   367

Memoir   373

Offertory   375

Notes   404

ON AMY HEMPEL

It's all about the sentences. It's about the way the sentences move in the paragraphs. It's about rhythm. It's about ambiguity. It's about the way emotion, in difficult circumstances, gets captured in language. It's about instants of consciousness. It's about besieged consciousness. It's about love trouble. It's about death. It's about suicide. It's about the body. It's about skepticism. It's against sentimentality. It's against cheap sentiment. It's about regret. It's about survival. It's about the sentences used to enact and defend survival.

In 1985, when Amy Hempel's first collection *Reasons to Live* was first published, we found ourselves in the heady period of the American short-story renaissance. However briefly, it was not only acceptable to write and publish short stories (there were many more venues for them in that bygone time), but it was even possible to sell a few copies of your collection along the way. Some of this had to do with the notable Vintage Contemporaries line of paperback short fiction, which brought us, in its first seasons, such voices as Richard Ford, Jay McInerney, and Raymond Carver. Some of this had to do with the editorial vision of one Gordon Lish, as keen and vigorous a proponent of literary fiction as has existed in the last fifty years. In the course of his ascendancy, he had the temerity of purpose to bring to light writers like Carver, Barry Hannah, Mary Robison, and Amy Hempel, among many others.

I was in graduate school in this heady moment. I was in my second year of graduate school when Hempel's first collection hit shelves (and along with *Self-Help,* by Lorrie Moore, it was one of the books that everyone wanted to read at the time). I was exhibiting symptoms of boredom and impatience with most of the *masculine* examples of contemporary fiction. I couldn't sympathize, finally, with Ford and McInerney characters. I had never punched another man, nor shot a bird from the sky, nor had I fact-checked among the coke-snorting glitterati. And these narratives by male writers seemed to *require* complicity with their larger-than-life protagonists.

Then came the Hempel collection. As with Lorrie Moore, the Hempel stories were urbane, witty, somber, dazzling, oblique, and quietly, desperately heroic. In *Reasons to Live,* one had a sense that the author really *was* trying to use sentences to save lives, because there were so many memorable, quotable sentences hiding in the occasionally inscrutable fragments of life contained therein: "A blind date is coming to pick me up, and unless my hair grows an inch by seven o'clock, I am not going to answer the door." Or: "In the park, I saw a dog try to eat his own shadow, and another dog—I am sure of it—was herding a stand of elms." Or: "Here's a trick I found for how to finally get some sleep. I sleep in my husband's bed. That way the empty bed I look at is my own."

These Hempel sentences, with their longing and their profound disquiet, do not rage or posture the way the men of the minimalist realist period did. They ache. And this ache seems to have everything to do with a rather profound and cruelly underestimated lineage of women writers in North America, writers in many cases much *more* important than their male counterparts, among them Grace Paley, Mary Robison, Alice Munro, Lydia Davis, Joy Williams, Cynthia Ozick, and Ann Beattie.

Well, to put it another way: Hempel, in this first collection, came out from under Paley's skirt, if I can manhandle an Ernest Hemingway reference, but she also became her own thing. Where Paley's voice has everything to do with the New York City of the first half of the twentieth century, and its slangy Yiddishisms, Hempel's voice has something to do with stand-up comedy, contemporary poetry, celebrity magazines, visual arts, the West, and the popular song. (Poetry especially becomes more and more of an influence on her nearly Japanese compaction the further along she goes in her work.)

At the time of publication, *Reasons to Live* was noteworthy for one overpowering story, a story which, at this late date, is known to almost all enthusiasts of recent short fiction, since it is anthologized frequently. The story in question is named "In the Cemetery Where Al Jolson Is Buried." Though the narrative frame of this composition is accessible enough—the narrator tries to buoy the spirits of a dying friend through the distraction of the well-turned anecdote—it's the violations of well-made story structure and conventionally "literary values" that make the story even more lasting: "Make it useless stuff or skip it," the dying friend says at the outset (perhaps a manifesto for Hempel's mulch of popular culture and high literature), and the narrator complies: "Did she know that Tammy Wynette had changed her tune? Really. That now she sings 'Stand by Your *Friends*'? That Paul Anka did it, too, I said. Does 'You're Having *Our* Baby.' That he got sick of all that feminist bitching."

"Al Jolson" is a gem in a volume that while possessed of bounteous moments of transfiguration (I like, for example, the lovely conversation between a father and his children about Jell-O in "Celia Is Back," or Wesley the world-weary comedian in "Three Popes Walk into a Bar") is the *beginning* of a great career rather than its finest hour. I'd go so far as to say that *Reasons to Live* looks like a sweet but quaint memory in the brilliant light of Hempel's next book, *At the Gates of the Animal Kingdom* (1990). It's true that it took Hempel five years to write the 137 pages of the second volume of stories, and it's true that this was actually *fast* for her (*Tumble Home* took seven years, and *The Dog of the Marriage* took eight), but when the results are as pitch-perfect and unforgettable as "The Harvest," or "The Most Girl Part of You," or "Rapture of the Deep," all of them stunners from the second volume, who really gives a shit how long the book takes or whether it's shorter than one of those big encyclopedic tomes that the boys, obsessed with the sound of their own voices, were frequently writing in the same period? When "The Harvest" first came out in Gordon Lish's *Quarterly,* I remember being arrested not only by the broad course of the story (of the narrator's massive car accident) itself, but most especially by the double-space break in the middle, after which the following appeared: "I leave a lot out when I tell the truth. The same when I write a story. I'm going to start now to tell you what I left out of 'The Harvest,' and maybe begin to wonder why I had to leave it out." The narrative then goes on to undercut virtually every trustworthy assertion made in its prior pages, doing a merry dance of destruction on the grave of the realistic fiction, conjuring instead the many illuminating paradoxes of consciousness and identity. Only a scant few works of contemporary fiction have done the same with such grace and style.

By the time *Tumble Home* (1997)—Hempel's third book—emerged into the light of day, the short-story renaissance of the middle eighties was six feet under, and many of the best venues for the publication of this time-honored form were interred in the mausoleum of literary nostalgia. Hempel, like Paley before her, and perhaps in reply to the literary politics of the moment, began to attempt to reckon with longer work. The result was the novella-length title story of her third collection. The leap in mastery, in seriousness, and sheer literary purpose was inspiring to behold.

It's the natural trajectory of a writing career that a writer becomes better at being herself. If Hempel, in *Reasons to Live,* despite her great comic timing and her unflappable need to whistle in the graveyard, had skills most of us will never ever hope to have, the first book nonetheless had certain things in common with the literary zeitgeist of the eighties. Yet in *Tumble Home,* with its obsessive concentration on loss and romantic disaffiliation, with its oblique despair and its brokenhearted comic couplets, Hempel sounds like no one else on earth but Amy Hempel. Hempel the miniaturist. Hempel the enemy of causality. Hempel the cataloguer of phobias. Hempel the animal philosopher. She gave up willful contemporaneity, and instead she allowed the mask of a perfect surface to drop a little bit so that the raw, troubled landscape underneath could rise up in its place.

Which is to say that "Tumble Home," the story, represented a new zenith in a career that already had many, many high points, and if the reading public had, as it does now and again, turned some of its attention away from the implicit challenge of short fiction, not to mention the novella, the loss was theirs. In "Tumble Home," the narrator addresses an absent lover directly, from institutional confines, her tired voice given mainly to the little amusements of her daily life, though much around her is about suffering and the attempt to recover from it: "The other day I was playing Scrabble with Karen. I saw that I could close the space in D-E- -Y. I had an N and an F. Which do you think I chose?" The unspeakable tragedy that is just offscreen in "Tumble Home," a mother's suicide, is of such magnitude that the story is bent by its force, and yet the narrator's insistence on attempting levity in the face of this legacy makes her, and the story itself, that much *more* electrifying: "So a lot of the time it's moisturizers and accessories, physical fitness and hair. And still so many ways to go wrong, as when I said to Chatty, hadn't she colored her hair, and Chatty's frosty reply that she had not *colored* her hair, she had *enhanced* it."

Tumble Home, the book, with its stately and proud first-person narrators, set the bar very high indeed for Amy Hempel. One can think only of the great European voices, of Kleist or Chekhov. And yet *The Dog of the Marriage* (2005), the fourth collection by Amy Hempel, is even better than the other three. It's a triumph, in fact. For the first time, Hempel turns her attention toward carnality, toward sexuality itself, and since the excisions, the margins, in Hempel stories have often been as telling as what occurs within, it must have required significant resolve on her part to allow her characters, for the first time, to take off their clothes.

It's perhaps not unfair at this point to let the reader in on a secret known about the author of these stories, namely that at the time of this composition, Amy Hempel, writer of luminous short fiction, is also embarked on the study of *forensics* at a regional citadel of criminal justice education. When faced with the entirety of the output of Hempel—with the movement of it down through the upper layers of psychology into the mystery of physiognomy—how predictable is this side interest of the author's! One is reminded, for example, of a moment in "Tumble Home": "Not everything I know is something I want to see. Though on highways, and, once, on a mountain road, I have strained to see things I didn't want to see. The worst I ever saw was a body without a head." And there are many such other instances, instances when the body is rent open in the search for identity, the car crash in "The Harvest," the cemetery with the dead baby in it ("The Annex"), and on and on.

That is, Hempel's materialism (another way of saying realism) is manifest in her intense need to attempt to locate identity in the body, to keep prying away at the body to see if the emotions are located in a specific spot therein, no matter how violent or frustrating the endeavor. With Hempel, it's just as in the Enlightenment, an era obsessed with finding the physical seat of the soul: "Look at me. My concerns—are they spiritual, do you think, or carnal? Come on. We've read our Shakespeare. 'There's no art / To find the mind's construction in the face.'" Hempel both wants to *believe* (there is the unbidden tolling of religious language in these stories), and hates the gobbledygook of anything but flesh.

And thus the bedroom. Marriages are relentlessly falling apart throughout *The Dog of the Marriage,* and pregnancies are ending badly, and pets vanish or are killed, and all of this dissolution is intolerable and overwhelming, until we get to the story called "Offertory." Essentially a sequel to "Tumble Home," in which the painter of the earlier novella (the recipient of that narrator's direct address epistle) is here embodied once more in a carnally voracious lover, now directly engaged with the delicate first-person speaker of Hempel's later efforts. He's the lover who would have her tell him stories of her carnal escapades. The narrator, like the author herself, is an adept in the telling, and she provides a wealth of details: "And when

I really could not remember what happened the tenth time, I made something up. I made up something I guessed would be what he wanted. For example, he wanted to know when the husband was with us both at once, whose name did he cry out when he came? He asked for the tenderest time, the most violent time, the most nonchalant time, the classiest time, the first and the last time, all twelve times." Besides being one of the most erotic stories in contemporary literature, "Offertory" is incredibly sad, and very revealing about all the hardship that transpires between men and women. It seems to me that with the possible exception of Mary Gaitskill, no one has written as well about sex and identity in thirty or forty years.

Who is it who writes these stories and makes this brave journey into the forensic psychology of everyday life? She came from Chicago, grew up in the Denver area, had an early life with no shortage of trouble, went to high school in Chicago, went to California to be a journalist, knocked around Haight-Ashbury in the late sixties, couldn't finish school, tried to be pre-med, worked as a veterinarian's assistant. Faced a lot of death in the family. Had a number of automobile accidents. Avoided flying. Put off buying a computer. Later, she was married for a time. She made a living teaching, and spent a lot of time volunteering with seeing-eye dogs. Not a terribly unusual story, as far as American lives go, and the author, who is gracious, self-effacing, and endlessly generous, never advertises much about it.

From such a life comes work that is consonant with what is greatest, what is most inspiring and transportative about the history of literature over the course of the last few centuries. Hempel, I'd argue, knows as much as anyone since Kafka about the tendency of human beings to do much better at dreaming than living. How to explain where these stories come from, short of prying open the writer? If it were Hempel herself trying to answer the question, she would avoid reply, and would come up instead with some howlingly funny line to deflect away the sad fact that some questions are simply unanswerable. The best we can do is to try to keep on living and to take pleasure where it is available, especially, for example, in the pleasure of language. You are about to participate in that particular pleasure, richly.

It's all about the sentences.

—Rick Moody

THE
COLLECTED STORIES
OF AMY HEMPEL

REASONS TO LIVE

IN A TUB

My heart—I thought it stopped. So I got in my car and headed for God. I passed two churches with cars parked in front. Then I stopped at the third because no one else had.

It was early afternoon, the middle of the week. I chose a pew in the center of the rows. Episcopal or Methodist, it didn't make any difference. It was as quiet as a church.

I thought about the feeling of the long missed beat, and the tumble of the next ones as they rushed to fill the space. I sat there—in the high brace of quiet and stained glass—and I listened.

At the back of my house I can stand in the light from the sliding glass door and look out onto the deck. The deck is planted with marguerites and succulents in red clay pots. One of the pots is empty. It is shallow and broad, and filled with water like a birdbath.

My cat takes naps in the windowbox. Her gray chin is powdered with the iridescent dust from butterfly wings. If I tap on the glass, the cat will not look up.

The sound that I make is not food.

When I was a girl I sneaked out at night. I pressed myself

to hedges and fitted the shadows of trees. I went to a construction site near the lake. I took a concrete-mixing tub, slid it to the shore, and sat down inside it like a saucer. I would push off from the sand with one stolen oar and float, hearing nothing, for hours.

The birdbath is shaped like that tub.

I look at my nails in the harsh bathroom light. The scare will appear as a ripple at the base. It will take a couple of weeks to see.

I lock the door and run a tub of water.

Most of the time you don't really hear it. A pulse is a thing that you feel. Even if you are somewhat quiet. Sometimes you hear it through the pillow at night. But I know that there is a place where you can hear it even better than that.

Here is what you do. You ease yourself into a tub of water, you ease yourself down. You lie back and wait for the ripples to smooth away. Then you take a deep breath, and slide your head under, and listen for the playfulness of your heart.

TONIGHT IS A FAVOR TO HOLLY

A blind date is coming to pick me up, and unless my hair grows an inch by seven o'clock, I am not going to answer the door. The problem is the front. I cut the bangs myself; now I look like Mamie Eisenhower.

Holly says no, I look like Claudette Colbert. But I know why she says that is so I will meet this guy. Tonight is a favor to Holly.

What I'd rather do is what we usually do—mix our rum and Cokes, and drink them on the sand while the sun goes down.

We live the beach life.

Not the one with sunscreen and resort wear. I mean, we just live at the beach. Out the front door is sand. There's the ocean, and we see it every day of the year.

The beach is near the airport—so this town doesn't even have the class L.A. lacks. What it has is airline personnel. For them, it's a twelve-minute shuttle from the concourse home—home meaning a complex of apartments done in fake Spanish Colonial.

It copies the Spanish missions in every direction. But show me the mission with wrought-iron handrails running up the side.

Also, there's a courtyard fountain that splashes onto mosaic tiles. What's irritating is that the tiles were chemically treated to "age" them from the start. What you want to say is, Look, relics are *leftovers,* you know?

The place is called Rancho La Brea, but what it's really called, because of the stewardesses, is Rancho Libido. Inside, the apartments have white sparkle ceilings.

Holly's no stewardess, and neither am I. We're renting month to month while our house is restored from the mud and water damage of the last slide.

Holly sings backup, and sometimes she records. The idea was she would tour, and I'd mostly have the place to myself. But she's not touring. The distribution on her last release was half what she expected. The record company said they had to reorganize their marginal talent, so while Holly looks for another label, she's home nights and my three days off.

Four days a week I drive to La Mirada, to the travel agency where I have a job. It takes me fifty-five minutes to drive one way, and I wish the commute were longer. I like radio personalities, and I like to change lanes. And losing yourself on the freeway is like living at the beach—you're not aware of lapsed time, and suddenly you're there, where it was you were going.

My job fits right in. I *do* nothing, it *pays* nothing, but— you guessed it—it's *better* than nothing.

A sense of humor helps.

The motto of this agency is We Never Knowingly Ruin Your Vacation.

We do two big tours a year, and neither of them now. If I

can hold on to it, it's the job I am going to have until my parents die.

I thought I would mind that Holly's always around, but it turns out it's okay. Mornings, we walk to the Casa de Fruta Fruit Stand and Bait Shop. Everything there is the size of something else: strawberries are the size of tomatoes, apples are the size of grapefruits, papayas are the size of watermelons. The one-day sale on cantaloupe is into its third week. We buy enough to fill a blender, plus eggs.

But, back up—because before we get to Casa de Fruta, we have to put on faded Danskins and her ex's boxer shorts, and then be out on the beach watching the lifeguard's jeep drag rakes like combs through the tangled sand.

I like my prints to be the first of the day. Holly's the one who scrapes her blackened feet and curses the tar.

Then the rest of the day happens. Maybe we drain a half tank cruising Holly's territory. Holly calls it research, this looking at men on the more northern sand.

"I'd sooner salt myself away and call it a life," Holly says. "But there's all this research."

Sometimes we check in on Suzy and Hard, the squatters who live at the end of the block. Their aluminum shack has been there for years. The story is he found her at the harbor. She lived from boat to boat, staying with the owner till a fight sent her one berth over.

Suzy has massive sunburned arms and wide hips that jerk unevenly when she walks.

Hard is tall and thin.

His real name is Howard. But Suzy is a slurrer, so it comes out Hard. It seems to fit. Hard has shoulder-length black hair and a mouth as round and mean as a lamprey.

If things are quiet down the block, if the air is thick and still, we float ourselves in the surf. Sometimes a rain begins while we are underwater.

I don't get used to living at the beach, to seeing that wet horizon. It's the edge, the country's aisle seat. But if you made me tell the truth, I'd have to say it's not a good thing. The people who live here, what you hear them say is *I'm supposed to, I'll try, I would have.*

There is no friction here.

It's a kind and buoyant place.

What you forget, living here, is that just because you have stopped sinking doesn't mean you're not still underwater.

Earlier today, Holly answered the phone and took a dinner reservation. Our number is one digit off from Trader Don's, and Holly takes names when she's in a bad mood.

"How many in your party, sir?" she says.

She's afraid I won't go through with what was not my idea. In fact, I am not a person who goes on a date. I don't want to meet men.

I know some already.

We talk about those a lot, and about the ones that Holly knows, too. It's the other thing we do together on my days off.

"You dish, I'll dry," Holly says.

I'll kick things off by calling one a scale model of a man. Holly will say again how if her ex saw a film of the way he had treated her, he would crawl off into the bushes, touch blade, and say good-bye.

Her ex still sends snapshots—pictures of himself on camping trips at the foot of El Capitan or on the shore of Mono Lake. He mounts the pictures on cardboard, which just makes them harder to tear up.

He even stops by when he's in town, and we pretend he's welcome. The two of them, Holly and this ex of hers, sit around and depress each other. They know all of each other's weak points and failings, so they can bring each other down in two-tenths of a second.

When she sees him, Holly says, it's like the sunsets at the beach—once the sun drops, the sand chills quickly. Then it's like a lot of times that were good ten minutes ago and don't count now.

These men, it's not like we don't see them coming. Our intuition is good; the problem is we ignore it.

We keep wanting people to be different.

But who are the people you meet down here?

There are two kinds to choose from: those who are going under and those who aren't moving ahead.

I think Suzy and Hard have more energy than us all. Last night I heard them in the alley. Suzy was screaming. She yelled, "Hard! Look out! You wanna give someone an accident?"

I could see all this from the kitchen. I could see Hard pick up a hubcap and pitch it at Suzy. Suzy squealed and limped away, even though it was her arm he had clipped her on. But then she whirled around and rushed at him. She grabbed his throwing hand and brought it to her mouth. She opened wide to bite. But the scream that followed was hers.

The alley is lighted, so I could actually see the white teeth in his hand. Hard stood with his feet apart, and turned sideways. Like a discus-thrower going for the record, he hurled Suzy's dentures onto the roof of Rancho Libido.

I'm hoping this story will break the ice tonight.

Oh, I'll go out with this guy for Holly.

My hair is too short, but I've got teeth in my mouth. I'll be Claudette or Mamie, and he'll be a pretty strange customer himself. He'll be a pimp who's gone through est.

He'll be Hard's brother.

He'll be so dumb there aren't any examples.

All right, I'm smiling when I say this. But the favor I'll expect in return is to not have to do it again.

At least I can look forward to getting home. Holly will be waiting up. She'll make us a Cobra Kiss—that's putting the rum in pomegranate juice. We'll have seconds. Then she'll carry herself to the bedroom like a completed jigsaw puzzle.

I'll get the lights and come after.

The one light I leave on makes the ceiling dance like galaxies. We're hoping next month we can say good-bye to the sparkle ceilings of Rancho Libido. Our old place is cleaning up nicely. Tighter-fitting seals are on the windows, and plywood reinforcements flank the walls. When the next big rain sets off slides, it won't be us at the bottom of the hill, trapped beneath collapsed architecture.

For now, we have our angled beds. Holly's faces east because she claims that facing east wakes you calm and alert. My own goes north to south; unless I'm mistaken, east to west is how they sleep you in your grave.

*   *   *

Sometimes we talk about trips. The joke is, the places we think of are beaches, the ones on the folders in my travel office.

What we need to do is move—find some landlocked place where at least half the year the air is cool and dry. It's likely we'll do it, too.

"Sure thing," Holly says. "From the people who brought you Fat Chance."

The truth is, the beach is like excess weight. If we lost it, what would the excuse be then?

A couple of years ago, I *did* go away.

I went east.

A mistake. A few months later the movers packed me up.

There's a thing that happens here, and I thought about it then. Highway One, the coast route, has many scenic lookout points. What happens is that people fall over these cliffs, craning to see to the bottom of them. Sometimes the floor is brush, and sometimes it is rock. It's called going west on Highway One. There is even a club for the people who fall, membership being awarded posthumously.

That's what I thought of when the moving van crashed. It spilled my whole life down a mud ravine, where for two weeks rain kept a crew from hauling it out. Mold embroidered the tablecloths, and newts danced in my shoes.

The message was heavy-handed, but I changed lanes and continued west toward home.

I say an omen that big can be ignored.

CELIA IS BACK

"Luck isn't luck," the father told his kids. "Luck is where preparation meets opportunity."

The boy backed up his father's statement. "That's what the *big* winners say," he agreed.

The boy and his sister were entering contests. The kitchen table was littered with forms and the entry blanks off cereal boxes. The boy held a picture of a blue Rolls-Royce, the grand prize in a sweepstakes he was too young to enter.

"Do you think it has to be blue?" he asked. "Do you think I can get it in a different color?"

"You can't drive," the girl said. "So it's a moot point."

She tore a sheet of paper from a legal pad and drew up an affidavit. It promised her the Rolls when her father won it in the sweepstakes next fall. She penciled in a line on the paper for his signature, and a line below that, and titled the second one *Witnessed By.*

The father had time before his weekly appointment, so he poured himself coffee and filled in some of the blanks. In spite of what he said, the father knew he had luck. In the time that he had been home, he had won two prizes. He had won a week for two in Hawaii, airfare included, and a ride in a hot-air balloon.

Sweepstakes were easy, the father explained. There was nothing to guess, no jingle to compose, no skill required at all. You wrote your name and address, then you soaked the paper in water so that it dried stiff and crackly, and was therefore easy for the judge to get a grip on in the bin. You could enter a sweepstakes as often as you liked—you could flood it if the prize or the winning was worth the bother.

The father held his hand up like an Indian saying How. "Remember the Three *P*'s," he told his kids. "Patience, Perseverance, and Postage. The people who win these things know the Three *P*'s."

Contests were different from sweepstakes, he said. You needed talent to win a contest, or at least you needed the knack.

"S-O-S," the father informed. "What you want to remember is: Be Simple, be Original, be Sincere. That's the winning system."

When the sweepstakes entries were completed and stamped, the kids detained their father for the Jell-O pudding contest.

They said, *"Daddy* will help us—Daddy *always* wins!"

"All right," the father said. "But don't make me late for my appointment."

You had to tell the judges why you liked Jell-O pudding. You had to complete the sentence, "I like Jell-O pudding because————."

First, the father looked at what his kids had written down. "It's sincere," he said. "But what about original?" He said that the first thing that popped into their heads would have popped into the heads of other people, too.

The father said, "Think. What is the thing about Jell-O pudding? What is really the thing?"

He paused for so long that the kids looked at each other. "What?" the girl said.

The father closed his eyes, and leaned back in his chair. He said, "I like Jell-O pudding because I like a good hearty meal after a brisk walk on a winter's day—something to really warm me up."

The boy giggled and the girl giggled.

The father looked confused. "This is the Jell-O pudding contest, isn't that what you said?" he said. "Well, okay then," he said. "I like Jell-O pudding because it has a tough satin finish that resists chipping and peeling. No, no," he said, "I mean, I like Jell-O pudding because it has a fruitier taste. Because it's garden fresh," he said. "Because it goes on dry to protect me from wetness longer. Oh, Jell-O pudding," the father said. "I like it because it's more absorbent than those other brands. Won't chafe or ride up."

He opened his eyes and saw his son leave the room. The sound that had made the father open his eyes was the pen that the boy had thrown to the floor.

"You may already be a winner," the father said.

He closed his eyes again. "You know," he continued, "most pudding makes me edgy. But not *Jell-O* pudding. That's because it has no caffeine. Tastes right—and is built to stay that way.

"Yes, I like Jell-O pudding because it's the one thing to take when you really want to buffacate a headache. Or when you need to mirtilize bad breath, unless you want your bad breath to mirtilize you."

This time the sound that brought him around was the sound of his car keys swinging on their chain. His daughter held the keys. She said, "Daddy, come on. You'll be late."

"That's what I told you, didn't I?" the father said. "I said, 'Don't make me late for my appointment.'"

He followed his daughter out to the car. "Did I tell you the thing about Jell-O?" he said.

His motor skills were not impaired.

He drove slowly, carefully, the girl on the seat beside him. He turned off the freeway onto a wide commercial drive of franchised food and failing business. The place he was going to was blocks away.

A red light stopped him opposite the House of Marlene. There was a handwritten sign in a grimy window. The sign said, CELIA, FORMERLY OF MR. EDWARD, HAS REJOINED OUR STAFF.

The father's hands relaxed on the wheel.

Celia, he thought.

Celia has come back to make everything okay. The wondrous Celia brings her powers to bear.

The traffic light turned green. Is she really back? he wondered. Is Celia back to stay?

Through the horns going off behind him, through the fists of his daughter beside him, the father stayed stopped.

Everything will be fine, he thought, now that Celia's here.

NASHVILLE GONE TO ASHES

After the dog's cremation, I lie in my husband's bed and watch the Academy Awards for animals. That is not the name of the show, but they give prizes to animals for Outstanding Performance in a movie, on television, or in a commercial. Last year the Schlitz Malt Liquor bull won. The time before that, it was Fred the Cockatoo. Fred won for draining a tinky bottle of "liquor" and then reeling and falling over drunk. It is the best thing on television is what my husband, Flea, said.

With Flea gone, I watch out of habit.

On top of the warm set is big white Chuck, catching a portion of his four million winks. His tail hangs down and bisects the screen. On top of the dresser, and next to the phone, is the miniature pine crate that holds Nashville's gritty ashes.

Neil the Lion cops the year's top honors. The host says Neil is on location in Africa, but accepting for Neil is his grandson Winston. A woman approaches the stage with a ten-week cub in her arms, and the audience all goes *Awwww*. The home audience, too, I bet. After the cub, they bring the winners on stage together. I figure they must have been sedated—because none of them are biting each other.

*   *   *

I have my own to tend to. Chuck needs tomato juice for his urological problem. Boris and Kirby need brewer's yeast for their nits. Also, I left the vacuum out and the mynah bird is shrieking. Birds think a vacuum-cleaner hose is a snake.

Flea sold his practice after the stroke, so these are the only ones I look after now. These are the ones that always shared the house.

My husband, by the way, was F. Lee Forest, D.V.M.

The hospital is right next door to the house.

It was my side that originally bought him the practice. I bought it for him with the applesauce money. My father made an applesauce fortune because *his* way did not use lye to take off the skins. Enough of it was left to me that I had the things I wanted. I bought Flea the practice because I could.

Will Rogers called vets the noblest of doctors because their patients can't tell them what's wrong. The doctor has to reach, and he reaches with his heart.

I think it was that love that I loved. That kind of involvement was reassuring; I felt it would extend to me, as well. That it did not or that it did, but only as much and no more, was confusing at first. I thought, My love is so good, why isn't it calling the same thing back?

Things might have collapsed right there. But the furious care he gave the animals gave me hope and kept me waiting.

I did not take naturally to my husband's work. For instance, I am allergic to cats. For the past twenty years, I have had to receive immunotherapy. These are not pills; they are injections.

Until I was seventeen, I thought a ham was an animal. But I was not above testing a stool sample next door.

I go to the mynah first and put the vacuum cleaner away.

This bird, when it isn't shrieking, says only one thing. Flea taught it what to say. He put a sign on its cage that reads TELL ME I'M STUPID. So you say to the bird, "Okay, you're stupid," and the bird says, real sarcastic, "I can talk—can *you fly?*"

Flea could have opened in Vegas with that. But there is no cozying up to a bird.

It will be the first to go, the mynah. The second if you count Nashville.

I promised Flea I would take care of them, and I am. I screened the new owners myself.

Nashville was his favorite. She was a grizzle-colored saluki with lightly feathered legs and Nile-green eyes. You know those skinny dogs on Egyptian pots? Those are salukis, and people worshiped them back then.

Flea acted like he did, too.

He fed that dog dates.

I used to watch her carefully spit out the pit before eating the next one. She sat like a sphinx while he reached inside her mouth to massage her licorice gums. She let him nick tartar from her teeth with his nail.

This is the last time I will have to explain that name. The pick of the litter was named Memphis. They are supposed to have Egyptian names. Flea misunderstood and named his Nashville. A woman back East owns Boston.

At the end of every summer, Flea took Nashville to the Central Valley. They hunted some of the rabbits out of the vineyards. It's called coursing when you use a sight hound. With her keen vision, Nashville would spot a rabbit and point it for Flea to come after. One time she sighted straight up at the sky—and he said he followed her gaze to a plane crossing the sun.

Sometimes I went along, and one time we let Boris hunt, too.

Boris is a Russian wolfhound. He is the size of a float in the Rose Bowl Parade.

He's a real teenager of a dog—if Boris didn't have whiskers, he'd have pimples. He goes through two nylabones a week, and once he ate a box of nails.

That's right, a box.

The day we loosed Boris on the rabbits he had drunk a cup of coffee. Flea let him have it, with Half-and-Half, because caffeine improves a dog's trailing. But Boris was so excited, he didn't distinguish his prey from anyone else. He even charged *me*—him, a whole hundred pounds of wolfhound, cranked up on Maxwell House. A sight like that will put a hem in your dress. Now I confine his hunting to the park, let him chase park squab and bald-tailed squirrel.

The first thing F. Lee said after his stroke, and it was three weeks after, was "hanky panky." I believe these words were intended for Boris. Yet Boris was the one who pushed the wheelchair for him. On a flat pave of sidewalk, he took a running start. When he jumped, his front paws pushed at the back of the chair, rolling Flea yards ahead with surprising grace.

I asked how he'd trained Boris to do that, and Flea's answer was, "I didn't."

I could love a dog like that, if he hadn't loved him first.

Here's a trick I found for how to finally get some sleep. I sleep in my husband's bed. That way the empty bed I look at is my own.

Cold nights I pull his socks on over my hands. I read in his bed. People still write from when Flea had the column. He did a pet Q and A for the newspaper. The new doctor sends along letters for my amusement. Here's one I liked—a man thinks his cat is homosexual.

The letter begins, "My cat Frank (not his real name) . . ."

In addition to Flea's socks, I also wear his watch.

A lot of us wear our late-husband's watch.

It's the way we tell each other.

At bedtime, I think how Nashville slept with Flea. She must have felt to him like a sack of antlers. I read about a marriage breaking up because the man let his Afghan sleep in the marriage bed.

I had my own bed. I slept in it alone, except for those times when we needed—not sex—but sex was how we got there.

In the mornings, I am not alone. With Nashville gone, Chuck comes around.

Chuck is a white-haired, blue-eyed cat, one of the few that aren't deaf—not that he comes when he hears you call. His fur is thick as a beaver's; it will hold the tracing of your finger.

Chuck, behaving, is the Nashville of cats. But the most fun he knows is pulling every tissue from a pop-up box of Kleenex. When he gets too rowdy, I slow him down with a comb. Flea showed me how. Scratching the teeth of a comb will make a cat yawn. Then you have him where you want him—any cat, however cool.

Animals are pure, Flea used to say. There is nothing deceptive about them. I would argue: Think about cats. They stumble and fall, then quickly begin to wash—I *meant* to do that. Pretense is deception, and cats pretend: Who, me? They move in next door where the food is better and meet you in the street and don't know your name, or *their* name.

But in the morning Chuck purrs against my throat, and it feels like prayer.

In the morning is when I pray.

The mailman changed his mind about the bird, and when Mrs. Kaiser came for Kirby and Chuck, I could not find either one. I had packed their supplies in a bag by the door—Chuck's tomato juice and catnip mouse, Kirby's milk of magnesia tablets to clean her teeth.

You would expect this from Chuck. But Kirby is responsible. She's been around the longest, a delicate smallish golden retriever trained by professionals for television work. She was going to get a series, but she didn't grow to size. Still, she can do a number of useless tricks. The one that wowed them in the waiting room next door was Flea putting Kirby under arrest.

"Kirby," he'd say, "I'm afraid you are under arrest." And the dog would back up flush to the wall. "I am going to have to frisk you, Kirb," and she'd slap her paws against the wall, standing still while Flea patted her sides.

Mrs. Kaiser came to visit after her own dog died.

When Kirby laid a paw in her lap, Mrs. Kaiser burst into tears.

I thought, God love a dog that hustles.

It is really just that Kirby is head-shy and offers a paw instead of her head to pat. But Mrs. Kaiser remembered the gesture. She agreed to take Chuck, too, when I said he needed a childless home. He gets jealous of kids and has asthma attacks. Myself, I was thinking, with Chuck gone I could have poinsettias and mistletoe in the house at Christmas.

When they weren't out back, I told Mrs. Kaiser I would bring them myself as soon as they showed. She was standing in the front hall talking to Boris. Rather, she was talking *for* Boris.

" 'Oh,' he says, he says, 'what a nice bone,' he says, he says, 'can *I* have a nice bone?' "

Boris walked away and collapsed on a braided rug.

" 'Boy,' he says, he says, 'boy, am I bushed.' "

Mrs. Kaiser has worn her husband's watch for years.

When she was good and gone, the animals wandered in. Chuck carried a half-eaten chipmunk in his mouth. He dropped it on the kitchen floor, a reminder of the cruelty of a world that lives by food.

After F. Lee's death, someone asked me how I was. I said that I finally had enough hangers in the closet. I don't think that that is what I meant to say. Or maybe it is.

Nashville *died* of *her* broken heart. She refused her food and simply called it quits.

An infection set in.

At the end, I myself injected the sodium pentobarbital.

I felt upstaged by the dog, will you just listen to me!

But the fact is, I think all of us were loved just the same. The love Flea gave to me was the same love he gave them. He did not say to the dogs, I will love you if you keep off the rug. He would love them no matter what they did.

It's what I got, too.

I wanted conditions.

God, how's that for an admission!

*   *   *

My husband said an animal can't disappoint you. I argued this, too. I said, Of course it can. What about the dog who goes on the rug? How does it feel when your efforts to alter behavior come to nothing?

I *know* how it feels.

I would like to think bigger thoughts. But it looks like I don't have a memory of our life that does not include one of the animals.

Kirby still carries in his paper Sunday mornings.

She used to watch while Flea did the crossword puzzle. He pretended to consult her: "I can see why you'd say *dog,* but don't you see—*cat* fits just as well?"

Boris and Kirby still scrap over his slippers. But as Flea used to say, the trouble seldom exceeds their lifespan.

Here we all still are. Boris, Kirby, Chuck—Nashville gone to ashes. Before going to bed I tell the mynah bird she may not be dumb but she's stupid.

Flowers were delivered on our anniversary. The card said the roses were sent by F. Lee. When I called the florist, he said Flea had "love insurance." It's a service they provide for people who forget. You tell the florist the date, and automatically he sends flowers.

Getting the flowers that way had me spooked. I thought I would walk it off, the long way, into town.

Before I left the house, I gave Laxatone to Chuck. With the weather warming up, he needs to get the jump on fur balls. Then I set his bowl of kibbles in a shallow dish of water. I added to the water a spoonful of liquid dish soap. Chuck eats throughout the day; the soapy moat keeps bugs off his plate.

On the walk into town I snapped back into myself.

Two things happened that I give the credit to.

The first thing was the beggar. He squatted on the walk with a dog at his side. He had with him an aged sleeping collie with granular runny eyes. Under its nose was a red plastic dish with a sign that said FOOD FOR DOG—DONATION, PLEASE.

The dog was as quiet as any Flea had healed and then rocked in his arms while the anesthesia wore off.

Blocks later, I bought a pound of ground beef.

I nearly ran the distance back.

The two were still there, and a couple of quarters were in the dish. I felt pretty good about handing over the food. I felt good until I turned around and saw the man who was watching me. He leaned against the grate of a closed shoe-repair with an empty tin cup at his feet. He had seen. And I was giving *him—nothing*.

How far do you take a thing like this? I think you take it all the way to heart. We give what we can—that's as far as the heart can go.

This was the first thing that turned me back around to home. The second was just plain rain.

SAN FRANCISCO

Do you know what I think?

I think it was the tremors. That's what must have done it. The way the floor rolled like bongo boards under our feet? Remember it was you and Daddy and me having lunch? "I guess that's not an earthquake," you said. "I guess you're shaking the table?"

That's when it must have happened. A watch on a dresser, a small thing like that—it must have been shaken right off, onto the floor.

And how would Maidy know? Maidy at the doctor's office? All those years on a psychiatrist's couch and suddenly the couch is *moving*.

Good God, she is on that couch when the big one hits.

Maidy didn't tell you, but you know what her doctor said? When she sprang from the couch and said, "My God, was that an earthquake?"

The doctor said this: "Did it *feel* like an earthquake to you?"

I think we are agreed, you have to look on the light side.

*   *   *

So that's when I think it must have happened. Not that it matters to me. Maidy is the one who wants to know. She thinks she has it coming, being the older daughter. Although where was the older daughter when it happened? Which daughter was it that found you?

When Maidy started asking about your watch, I felt I had to say it. I said, "With the body barely cold?"

Maidy said the body is not the person, that the *essence* is the person, and that the essence leaves the body behind it, along with the body's possessions—for example, its watch?

"Time flies," I said. "Like an arrow.

"Fruit flies," I said, and Maidy said, "What?"

"Fruit flies," I said again. "Fruit flies like a banana."

That's how easy it is to play a joke on Maidy.

Remember how easy?

Now Maidy thinks I took your watch. She thinks because I got there first, my first thought was to take it. Maidy keeps asking, "Who took Mama's watch?" She says, "Did *you* take Mama's watch?"

IN THE CEMETERY
WHERE AL JOLSON IS BURIED

"Tell me things I won't mind forgetting," she said. "Make it useless stuff or skip it."

I began. I told her insects fly through rain, missing every drop, never getting wet. I told her no one in America owned a tape recorder before Bing Crosby did. I told her the shape of the moon is like a banana—you see it looking full, you're seeing it end-on.

The camera made me self-conscious and I stopped. It was trained on us from a ceiling mount—the kind of camera banks use to photograph robbers. It played us to the nurses down the hall in Intensive Care.

"Go on, girl," she said. "You get used to it."

I had my audience. I went on. Did she know that Tammy Wynette had changed her tune? Really. That now she sings "Stand by Your *Friends*"? That Paul Anka did it, too, I said. Does "You're Having *Our* Baby." That he got sick of all that feminist bitching.

"What else?" she said. "Have you got something else?"

Oh, yes.

For her I would always have something else.

"Did you know that when they taught the first chimp to talk, it lied? That when they asked her who did it on the desk, she signed back the name of the janitor. And that when they pressed her, she said she was sorry, that it was really the project director. But she was a mother, so I guess she had her reasons."

"Oh, that's good," she said. "A parable."

"There's more about the chimp," I said. "But it will break your heart."

"No, thanks," she says, and scratches at her mask.

We look like good-guy outlaws. Good or bad, I am not used to the mask yet. I keep touching the warm spot where my breath, thank God, comes out. She is used to hers. She only ties the strings on top. The other ones—a pro by now—she lets hang loose.

We call this place the Marcus Welby Hospital. It's the white one with the palm trees under the opening credits of all those shows. A Hollywood hospital, though in fact it is several miles west. Off camera, there is a beach across the street.

She introduces me to a nurse as the Best Friend. The impersonal article is more intimate. It tells me that *they* are intimate, the nurse and my friend.

"I was telling her we used to drink Canada Dry ginger ale and pretend we were in Canada."

"That's how dumb we were," I say.

"You could be sisters," the nurse says.

So how come, I'll bet they are wondering, it took me so long to get to such a glamorous place? But do they ask?

They do not ask.

Two months, and how long is the drive?

The best I can explain it is this—I have a friend who worked one summer in a mortuary. He used to tell me stories. The one that really got to me was not the grisliest, but it's the one that did. A man wrecked his car on 101 going south. He did not lose consciousness. But his arm was taken down to the wet bone—and when he looked at it—it scared him to death.

I mean, he died.

So I hadn't dared to look any closer. But now I'm doing it—and hoping that I will live through it.

She shakes out a summer-weight blanket, showing a leg you did not want to see. Except for that, you look at her and understand the law that requires *two* people to be with the body at all times.

"I thought of something," she says. "I thought of it last night. I think there is a real and present need here. You know," she says, "like for someone to do it for you when you can't do it yourself. You call them up whenever you want—like when·push comes to shove."

She grabs the bedside phone and loops the cord around her neck.

"Hey," she says, "the end o' the line."

She keeps on, giddy with something. But I don't know with what.

"I can't remember," she says. "What does Kübler-Ross say comes after Denial?"

It seems to me Anger must be next. Then Bargaining, Depression, and so on and so forth. But I keep my guesses to myself.

"The only thing is," she says, "is where's Resurrection?

God knows, I want to do it by the book. But she left out Resurrection."

She laughs, and I cling to the sound the way someone dangling above a ravine holds fast to the thrown rope.

"Tell me," she says, "about that chimp with the talking hands. What do they do when the thing ends and the chimp says, 'I don't want to go back to the zoo'?"

When I don't say anything, she says, "Okay—then tell me another animal story. I like animal stories. But not a sick one—I don't want to know about all the seeing-eye dogs going blind."

No, I would not tell her a sick one.

"How about the hearing-ear dogs?" I say. "They're not going deaf, but they are getting very judgmental. For instance, there's this golden retriever in New Jersey, he wakes up the deaf mother and drags her into the daughter's room because the kid has got a flashlight and is reading under the covers."

"Oh, you're killing me," she says. "Yes, you're definitely killing me."

"They say the smart dog obeys, but the smarter dog knows when to disobey."

"Yes," she says, "the smarter anything knows when to disobey. Now, for example."

She is flirting with the Good Doctor, who has just appeared. Unlike the Bad Doctor, who checks the IV drip before saying good morning, the Good Doctor says things like "God didn't give epileptics a fair shake." The Good Doctor awards himself points for the cripples he could have hit in the parking lot.

Because the Good Doctor is a little in love with her, he says maybe a year. He pulls a chair up to her bed and suggests I might like to spend an hour on the beach.

"Bring me something back," she says. "Anything from the beach. Or the gift shop. Taste is no object."

He draws the curtain around her bed.

"Wait!" she cries.

I look in at her.

"Anything," she says, "except a magazine subscription."

The doctor turns away.

I watch her mouth laugh.

What seems dangerous often is not—black snakes, for example, or clear-air turbulence. While things that just lie there, like this beach, are loaded with jeopardy. A yellow dust rising from the ground, the heat that ripens melons overnight—this is earthquake weather. You can sit here braiding the fringe on your towel and the sand will all of a sudden suck down like an hourglass. The air roars. In the cheap apartments on-shore, bathtubs fill themselves and gardens roll up and over like green waves. If nothing happens, the dust will drift and the heat deepen till fear turns to desire. Nerves like that are only bought off by catastrophe.

"It never happens when you're thinking about it," she once observed. "Earthquake, earthquake, earthquake," she said.

"Earthquake, earthquake, earthquake," I said.

Like the aviaphobe who keeps the plane aloft with prayer, we kept it up until an aftershock cracked the ceiling.

That was after the big one in '72. We were in college; our dormitory was five miles from the epicenter. When the ride was over and my jabbering pulse began to slow, she served five parts champagne to one part orange juice, and joked about living in Ocean View, Kansas. I offered to drive her to Hawaii on the new world psychics predicted would surface the next time, or the next.

I could not say that now—next.

Whose next? she could ask.

Was I the only one who noticed that the experts had stopped saying *if* and now spoke of *when*? Of course not; the fearful ran to thousands. We watched the traffic of Japanese beetles for deviation. Deviation might mean more natural violence.

I wanted her to be afraid with me. But she said, "I don't know. I'm just not."

She was afraid of nothing, not even of flying.

I have this dream before a flight where we buckle in and the plane moves down the runway. It takes off at thirty-five miles an hour, and then we're airborne, skimming the tree tops. Still, we arrive in New York on time.

It is so pleasant.

One night I flew to Moscow this way.

She flew with me once. That time she flew with me she ate macadamia nuts while the wings bounced. She knows the wing tips can bend thirty feet up and thirty feet down without coming off. She believes it. She trusts the laws of aerodynamics. My mind stampedes. I can almost accept that a battleship floats when everybody knows steel sinks.

I see fear in her now, and am not going to try to talk her out of it. She is right to be afraid.

After a quake, the six o'clock news airs a film clip of first-graders yelling at the broken playground per their teacher's instructions.

"*Bad* earth!" they shout, because anger is stronger than fear.

But the beach is standing still today. Everyone on it is tranquilized, numb, or asleep. Teenaged girls rub coconut oil on each other's hard-to-reach places. They smell like macaroons. They pry open compacts like clamshells; mirrors catch the sun and throw a spray of white rays across glazed shoulders. The girls arrange their wet hair with silk flowers the way they learned in *Seventeen*. They pose.

A formation of low-riders pulls over to watch with a six-pack. They get vocal when the girls check their tan lines. When the beer is gone, so are they—flexing their cars on up the boulevard.

Above this aggressive health are the twin wrought-iron terraces, painted flamingo pink, of the Palm Royale. Someone dies there every time the sheets are changed. There's an ambulance in the driveway, so the remaining residents line the balconies, rocking and not talking, one-upped.

The ocean they stare at is dangerous, and not just the undertow. You can almost see the slapping tails of sand sharks keeping cruising bodies alive.

If she looked, she could see this, some of it, from her window. She would be the first to say how little it takes to make a thing all wrong.

There was a second bed in the room when I got back to it!

For two beats I didn't get it. Then it hit me like an open coffin.

She wants every minute, I thought. She wants my life.

"You missed Gussie," she said.

Gussie is her parents' three-hundred-pound narcoleptic maid. Her attacks often come at the ironing board. The pillowcases in that family are all bordered with scorch.

"It's a hard trip for her," I said. "How is she?"

"Well, she didn't fall asleep, if that's what you mean. Gussie's great—you know what she said? She said, 'Darlin', stop this worriation. Just keep prayin', down on your knees'—me, who can't even get out of bed."

She shrugged. "What am I missing?"

"It's earthquake weather," I told her.

"The best thing to do about earthquakes," she said, "is not to live in California."

"That's useful," I said. "You sound like Reverend Ike—'The best thing to do for the poor is not to be one of them.'"

We're crazy about Reverend Ike.

I noticed her face was bloated.

"You know," she said, "I feel like hell. I'm about to stop having fun."

"The ancients have a saying," I said. "'There are times when the wolves are silent; there are times when the moon howls.'"

"What's that, Navaho?"

"Palm Royale lobby graffiti," I said. "I bought a paper there. I'll read you something."

"Even though I care about nothing?"

I turned to the page with the trivia column. I said, "Did you know the more shrimp flamingo birds eat, the pinker their feathers get?" I said, "Did you know that Eskimos need refrigerators? Do you know *why* Eskimos need refrigerators? Did you know that Eskimos need refrigerators because how else would they keep their food from freezing?"

I turned to page three, to a UPI filler datelined Mexico City. I read her MAN ROBS BANK WITH CHICKEN, about a man who bought a barbecued chicken at a stand down the block from a bank. Passing the bank, he got the idea. He walked in and approached a teller. He pointed the brown paper bag at her and she handed over the day's receipts. It was the smell of barbecue sauce that eventually led to his capture.

The story had made her hungry, she said—so I took the elevator down six floors to the cafeteria, and brought back all the ice cream she wanted. We lay side by side, adjustable beds cranked up for optimal TV-viewing, littering the sheets with Good Humor wrappers, picking toasted almonds out of the gauze. We were Lucy and Ethel, Mary and Rhoda in extremis. The blinds were closed to keep light off the screen.

We watched a movie starring men we used to think we wanted to sleep with. Hers was a tough cop out to stop mine, a vicious rapist who went after cocktail waitresses.

"This is a good movie," she said when snipers felled them both.

I missed her already.

A Filipino nurse tiptoed in and gave her an injection. The nurse removed the pile of Popsicle sticks from the nightstand—enough to splint a small animal.

The injection made us both sleepy. We slept.

I dreamed she was a decorator, come to furnish my house. She worked in secret, singing to herself. When she finished, she guided me proudly to the door. "How do you like it?" she asked, easing me inside.

Every beam and sill and shelf and knob was draped in gay bunting, with streamers of pastel crepe looped around bright mirrors.

"I have to go home," I said when she woke up.

She thought I meant home to her house in the canyon, and I had to say No, *home* home. I twisted my hands in the time-honored fashion of people in pain. I was supposed to offer something. The Best Friend. I could not even offer to come back.

I felt weak and small and failed.

Also exhilarated.

I had a convertible in the parking lot. Once out of that room, I would drive it too fast down the Coast highway through the crab-smelling air. A stop in Malibu for sangria. The music in the place would be sexy and loud. They'd serve papaya and shrimp and watermelon ice. After dinner I would shimmer with lust, buzz with heat, vibrate with life, and stay up all night.

Without a word, she yanked off her mask and threw it on the floor. She kicked at the blankets and moved to the door. She must have hated having to pause for breath and balance before slamming out of Isolation, and out of the second room, the one where you scrub and tie on the white masks.

A voice shouted her name in alarm, and people ran down the corridor. The Good Doctor was paged over the intercom. I opened the door and the nurses at the station stared hard, as if this flight had been my idea.

"Where is she?" I asked, and they nodded to the supply closet.

I looked in. Two nurses were kneeling beside her on the floor, talking to her in low voices. One held a mask over her nose and mouth, the other rubbed her back in slow circles. The nurses glanced up to see if I was the doctor—and when I wasn't, they went back to what they were doing.

"There, there, honey," they cooed.

On the morning she was moved to the cemetery, the one where Al Jolson is buried, I enrolled in a "Fear of Flying" class. "What is your worst fear?" the instructor asked, and I answered, "That I will finish this course and still be afraid."

I sleep with a glass of water on the nightstand so I can see by its level if the coastal earth is trembling or if the shaking is still me.

What do I remember?

I remember only the useless things I hear—that Bob Dylan's mother invented Wite-Out, that twenty-three people must be in a room before there is a fifty-fifty chance two will have the same birthday. Who cares whether or not it's true? In my head there are bath towels swaddling this stuff. Nothing else seeps through.

I review those things that will figure in the retelling: a kiss through surgical gauze, the pale hand correcting the position of the wig. I noted these gestures as they happened, not in any retrospect—though I don't know why looking back should show us more than looking *at*.

It is just possible I will say I stayed the night.

And who is there that can say that I did not?

*　　*　　*

I think of the chimp, the one with the talking hands.

In the course of the experiment, that chimp had a baby. Imagine how her trainers must have thrilled when the mother, without prompting, began to sign to her newborn.

Baby, drink milk.

Baby, play ball.

And when the baby died, the mother stood over the body, her wrinkled hands moving with animal grace, forming again and again the words: Baby, come hug, Baby, come hug, fluent now in the language of grief.

for Jessica Wolfson

BEG, SL TOG, INC, CONT, REP

The mohair was scratchy, the stria too bulky, but the homespun tweed was right for a small frame. I bought slate-blue skeins softened with flecks of pink, and size-10 needles for a sweater that was warm but light. The pattern I chose was a two-tone *V*-neck with an optional six-stitch cable up the front. Pullovers mess the hair, but I did not want to buttonhole the first time out.

From a needlework book, I learned to cast on. In the test piece, I got the gauge and correct tension. Knit and purl came naturally, as though my fingers had been rubbed in spiderwebs at birth. The sliding of the needles was as rhythmic as water.

Learning to knit was the obvious thing. The separation of tangled threads, the working-together of raveled ends into something tangible and whole—this *mending* was as confounding as the groom who drives into a stop sign on the way to his wedding. Because symptoms mean just what they are. What about the woman whose empty hand won't close because she cannot grasp that her child is gone?

* * *

"Would you get me a Dr Pep, gal, and would you turn up the a-c?"

I put down my knitting. In the kitchen I found some sugar-free, and took it, with ice, to Dale Anne. It was August. Air-conditioning lifted her hair as she pressed the button on the Niagara bed. Dr. Diamond insisted she have it the last month. She was also renting a swivel TV table and a vibrating chaise—the Niagara adjustable home.

When the angle was right, she popped a Vitamin E and rubbed the oil where the stretch marks would be.

I could be doing this, too. But I had had the procedure instead. That was after the father had asked me, Was I sure? To his credit, he meant—sure that I *was,* not sure was it he. He said he had never made a girl pregnant before. He said that he had never even made a girl late.

I moved in with Dale Anne to help her near the end. Her husband is often away—in a clinic or in a lab. He studies the mind. He is not a doctor yet, but we call him one by way of encouragement.

I had picked up a hank of yarn and was winding it into a ball when the air conditioner choked to a stop.

Dale Anne sighed. "I will *cook* in this robe. Would you get me that flowered top in the second drawer?"

While I looked for the top, Dale Anne twisted her hair and held it tight against her head. She took one of my double-pointed six-inch needles and wove it in and out of her hair, securing the twist against her scalp. With the hair off her face, she looked wholesome and very young—"the person you would most like to go camping with if you couldn't have sex," is how she put it.

I turned my back while Dale Anne changed. She was as

modest as I was. If the house caught fire one night, we would both die struggling to hook brassieres beneath our gowns.

I went back to my chair, and as I did, a sensational cramp snapped me over until I was nearly on the floor.

"Easy, gal—what's the trouble?" Dale Anne started out of bed to come see.

I said it sometimes happens since the procedure, and Dale Anne said, "Let's not talk about that for at *least* ten years."

I could not think of what to say to that. But I didn't have to. The front door opened, earlier than it usually did. It was Dr. Diamond, home from the world of spooks and ghosts and loony bins and Ouija boards. I knew that a lack of concern for others was a hallmark of mental illness, so I straightened up and said, after he'd kissed his pregnant wife, "You look hot, Dr. Diamond. Can I get you a drink?"

I buy my materials at a place in the residential section. The owner's name is Ingrid. She is a large Norwegian woman who spells needles "kneedles." She wears sample knits she makes up for the class demonstrations. The vest she wore the day before will be hanging in the window.

There are always four or five women at Ingrid's round oak table, knitting through a stretch they would not risk alone.

Often I go there when I don't need a thing. In the small back room that is stacked high with pattern books, I can sift for hours. I scan the instructions abbreviated like musical notation: *K10, sl 1, K2 tog, psso, sl I, K10 to end.* I feel I could *sing* these instructions. It is compression of language into code; your ability to decipher it makes you privy to the secrets shared by Ingrid and the women at the round oak table.

In the other room, Ingrid tells a customer she used to knit two hundred stitches a minute.

I scan the French and English catalogs, noting the longer length of coat. There is so much to absorb on each visit.

Mary had a little lamb, I am humming when I leave the shop. *Its feet were—its fleece was white as wool.*

Dale Anne wanted a nap, so Dr. Diamond and I went out for margaritas. At La Rondalla, the colored lights on the Virgin tell you every day is Christmas. The food arrives on manhole covers and mariachis fill the bar. Dr. Diamond said that in Guadalajara there is a mariachi college that turns out mariachis by the classful. But I could tell that these were not graduates of even mariachi high school.

I shooed the serenaders away, but Dr. Diamond said they meant well.

Dr. Diamond likes for people to mean well. He could be president of the Well-Meaning Club. He has had a buoyant feeling of fate since he learned Freud died the day he was born.

He was the person to talk to, all right, so I brought up the stomach pains I was having for no bodily reason that I could think of.

"You know how I think," he said. "What is it you can't stomach?"

I knew what he was asking.

"Have you thought about how you will feel when Dale Anne has the baby?" he asked.

With my eyes, I wove strands of tinsel over the Blessed Virgin. That was the great thing about knitting, I thought—everything was fiber, the world a world of natural resource.

"I thought I would burn that bridge when I come to it,"

I said, and when he didn't say anything to that, I said, "I guess I will think that there is a mother who *kept* hers."

"*One* of hers might be more accurate," Dr. Diamond said.

I arrived at the yarn shop as Ingrid turned over the CLOSED sign to OPEN. I had come to buy Shetland wool for a Fair Isle sweater. I felt nothing would engage my full attention more than a pattern of ancient Scottish symbols and alternate bands of delicate design. Every stitch in every color is related to the one above, below, and to either side.

I chose the natural colors of Shetland sheep—the chalky brown of the Moorit, the blackish brown of the black sheep, fawn, gray, and pinky beige from a mixture of Moorit and white. I held the wool to my nose, but Ingrid said it was fifty years since the women of Fair Isle dressed the yarn with fish oil.

She said the yarn came from Sheep Rock, the best pasture on Fair Isle. It is a ten-acre plot that is four hundred feet up a cliff, Ingrid said. "Think what a man has to go through to harvest the wool."

I was willing to feel an obligation to the yarn, and to the hardy Scots who supplied it. There was heritage there, and I could keep it alive with my hands.

Dale Anne patted capers into a mound of raw beef, and spread some onto toast. It was not a pretty sight. She offered some to me, and I said not a chance. I told her Johnny Carson is someone else who won't go near that. I said, "Johnny says he won't eat steak tartare because he has seen things hurt worse than that get better."

"Johnny was never pregnant," Dale Anne said.

*　　*　　*

When the contractions began, I left a message with the hospital and with Dr. Diamond's lab. I turned off the air conditioner and called for a cab.

"Look at you," Dale Anne said.

I told her I couldn't help it. I get rational when I panic.

The taxi came in minutes.

"Hold on," the driver said. "I know every bump in these roads, and I've never been able to miss one of them."

Dale Anne tried to squeeze my wrist, but her touch was weightless, as porous as wet silk.

"When this is over . . ." Dale Anne said.

When the baby was born, I did not go far. I sublet a place on the other side of town. I filled it with patterns and needles and yarn. It was what I did in the day. On a good day, I made a front and two sleeves. On a bad day, I ripped out stitches from neck to hem. For variety, I made socks. The best ones I made had beer steins on the sides, and the tops spilled over with white angora foam.

I did not like to work with sound in the room, not even the sound of a fan. Music slowed me down, and there was a great deal to do. I planned to knit myself a mailbox and a car, perhaps even a dog and a lead to walk him.

I blocked the finished pieces and folded them in drawers.

Dr. Diamond urged me to exercise. He called from time to time, looking in. He said exercise would set me straight, and why not have some fun with it? Why not, for example, tap-dancing lessons?

I told him it would be embarrassing because the rest of the class would be doing it right. And with all the knitting, there wasn't time to dance.

Dale Anne did not look in. She had a pretty good reason not to.

The day I went to see her in the hospital, I stopped at the nursery first. I saw the baby lying facedown. He wore yellow duck-print flannels. I saw that he was there—and then I went straight home.

That night the dreams began. A giant lizard ate people from the feet upward, swallowing the argyles on the first bite, then drifting into obscurity like a ranger of forgotten death. I woke up remembering and, like a chameleon, assumed every shade of blame.

Asleep at night, I went to an elegant ball. In the center of the dance floor was a giant aquarium. Hundreds of goldfish swam inside. At a sign from the bandleader, the tank was overturned. Until someone tried to dance on the fish, the floor was aswirl with gold glory.

Dr. Diamond told a story about the young daughter of a friend. The little girl had found a frog in the yard. The frog appeared to be dead, so her parents let her prepare a burial site—a little hole surrounded by pebbles. But at the moment of the lowering, the frog, which had only been stunned, kicked its legs and came to.

"Kill him!" the girl had shrieked.

*   *   *

I began to take walks in the park. In the park, I saw a dog try to eat his own shadow, and another dog—I am sure of it—was herding a stand of elms. I stopped telling people how handsome their dogs were; too many times what they said was, "You want him?"

When the weather got nicer, I stayed home to sit for hours.

I had accidents. Then I had bigger ones. But the part that hurt was never the part that got hurt.

The dreams came back and back until they were just—again. I wished that things would stay out of sight the way they did in mountain lakes. In one that I know, the water is so cold, gas can't form to bring a corpse to the surface. Although you would not want to think about the bottom of the lake, what you can say about it is—the dead stay down.

Around that time I talked to Dr. Diamond.

The point that he wanted to make was this: that conception was not like walking in front of traffic. No matter how badly timed, it was, he said, an affirmation of life.

"You have to believe me here," he said. "Do you see that this is true? Do you know this about yourself?"

"I do and I don't," I said.

"You do and you *do*," he said.

I remembered when another doctor made the news. A young retarded boy had found his father's gun, and while the family slept, he shot them all in bed. The police asked the boy what he had done. But the boy went mute. He told them nothing. Then they called in the doctor.

"We know *you* didn't do it," the doctor said to the boy, "but tell me, did the *gun* do it?"

And yes, the boy was eager to tell him just what that gun had done.

I wanted the same out, and Dr. Diamond wouldn't let me have it.

"Dr. Diamond," I said, "I am giving up."

"Now you are ready to begin," he said.

I thought of Andean alpaca because that was what I planned to work up next. The feel of that yarn was not the only wonder—there was also the name of it: Alpaquita Superfina.

Dr. Diamond was right.

I was ready to begin.

Beg, sl tog, inc, cont, rep.

Begin, slip together, increase, continue, repeat.

Dr. Diamond answered the door. He said Dale Anne had run to the store. He was leaving, too, flying to a conference back East. The baby was asleep, he said, I should make myself at home.

I left my bag of knitting in the hall and went into Dale Anne's kitchen. It had been a year. I could have looked in on the baby. Instead, I washed the dishes that were soaking in the sink. The scouring pad was steel wool waiting for knitting needles.

The kitchen was filled with specialized utensils. When Dale Anne couldn't sleep she watched TV, and that's where the stuff was advertised. She had a thing to core tomatoes—it was called a Tomato Shark—and a metal spaghetti wheel for measuring out spaghetti. She had plastic melon-ballers and a push-in device that turned ordinary cake into ladyfingers.

I found pasta primavera in the refrigerator. My fingers wanted to knit the cold linguini, laying precisely cabled strands across the oily red peppers and beans.

Dale Anne opened the door.

"*Look* out, gal," she said, and dropped a shopping bag on the counter.

I watched her unload ice cream, potato chips, carbonated drinks, and cake.

"It's been a long time since I walked into a market and expressed myself," she said.

She turned to toss me a carton of cigarettes.

"Wait for me in the bedroom," she said. "*West Side Story* is on."

I went in and looked at the color set. I heard the blender crushing ice in the kitchen. I adjusted the contrast, then Dale Anne handed me an enormous peach daiquiri. The goddamn thing had a tide factor.

Dale Anne left the room long enough to bring in the take-out chicken. She upended the bag on a plate and picked out a leg and a wing.

"I like my dinner in a bag and my life in a box," she said, nodding toward the TV.

We watched the end of the movie, then part of a lame detective program. Dale Anne said the show *owed* Nielsen four points, and reached for the *TV Guide*.

"Eleven-thirty," she read. "*The Texas Whiplash Massacre*: Unexpected stop signs were their weapon."

"Give me that," I said.

Dale Anne said there was supposed to be a comet. She said we could probably see it if we watched from the living room. Just to be sure, we pushed the couch up close to the window. With the lights off, we could see everything without it seeing us. Although both of us had quit, we smoked at either end of the couch.

"Save my place," Dale Anne said.

She had the baby in her arms when she came back in. I looked at the sleeping child and thought, Mercy, Land Sakes, Lordy Me. As though I had aged fifty years. For just a moment then I wanted nothing that I had and everything I did not.

"He told his first joke today," Dale Anne said.

"What do you mean he told a joke?" I said. "I didn't think they could talk."

"Well, he didn't really *tell* a joke—he poured his orange juice over his head, and when I started after him, he said, 'Raining?'"

"'Raining?' That's what he said? The kid is a genius," I told Dale Anne. "What Art Linkletter could do with this kid."

Dale Anne laid him down in the middle of the couch, and we watched him or watched the sky.

"What a gyp," Dale Anne said at dawn.

There had not been a comet. But I did not feel cheated, or even tired. She walked me to the door.

The knitting bag was still in the hall.

"Open it later," I said. "It's a sweater for him."

But Dale Anne had to see it then.

She said the blue one matched his eyes and the camel one matched his hair. The red would make him glow, she said, and then she said, "Help me out."

Cables had become too easy; three more sweaters had pictures knitted in. They buttoned up the front. Dale Anne held up a parade of yellow ducks.

There were the Fair Isles, too—one in the pattern called Tree of Life, another in the pattern called Hearts.

It was an excess of sweaters—a kind of precaution, a rehearsal against disaster.

Dale Anne looked at the two sweaters still in the bag. "Are you really okay?" she said.

The worst of it is over now, and I can't say that I am glad. Lose that sense of loss—you have gone and lost something else. But the body moves toward health. The mind, too, in steps. One step at a time. Ask a mother who has just lost a child, How many children do you have? "Four," she will say, "—three," and years later, "Three," she will say, "—four."

It's the little steps that help. Weather, breakfast, crossing with the light—sometimes it is all the pleasure I can bear to sleep, and know that on a rack in the bath, damp wool is pinned to dry.

Dale Anne thinks she would like to learn to knit. She measures the baby's crib and I take her over to Ingrid's. Ingrid steers her away from the baby pastels, even though they are machine-washable. Use a pure wool, Ingrid says. Use wool in a grown-up shade. And don't boast of your achievements or you'll be making things for the neighborhood.

On Fair Isle there are only five women left who knit. There is not enough lichen left growing on the island for them to dye their yarn. But knitting machines can't produce their designs, and they keep on, these women, working the undyed colors of the sheep.

I wait for Dale Anne in the room with the patterns. The songs in these books are like lullabies to me.

K tog rem st. Knit together remaining stitches.

Cast off loosely.

GOING

There is a typo on the hospital menu this morning. They mean, I think, that the pot roast tonight will be served with buttered noodles. But what it says here on my breakfast tray is that the pot roast will be *severed* with buttered noodles.

This is not a word you want to see after flipping your car twice at sixty per and then landing side-up in a ditch.

I did not spin out on a stretch of highway called Blood Alley or Hospital Curve. I lost it on flat dry road—with no other car in sight. Here's why: In the desert I like to drive through binoculars. What I like about it is that things are two ways at once. Things are far away and close with you still in the same place.

In the ditch, things were also two ways at once. The air was unbelievably hot and my skin was unbelievably cold.

"Son," the doctor said, "you shouldn't be alive."

The impact knocked two days out of my head, but all you can see is the cut on my chin. I total a car and get twenty stitches that keep me from shaving.

It's a good thing, too, that that is all it was. This hospital place, this clinic—it is not your City of Hope. The instruments don't come from a first-aid kit, they come from a tool-box. It's the desert. The walls of this room are not rose-beige or sanitation-plant green. The walls are the color of old chocolate going chalky at the edges.

And there's a worm smell.

Though I could be mistaken about the smell.

I'm given to olfactory hallucinations. When my parents' house was burning to the ground, I smelled smoke three states away.

Now I smell worms.

The doctor wants to watch me because I knocked my head. So I get to miss a few days of school. It's okay with me. I believe that 99 percent of what anyone does can effectively be postponed. Anyway, the accident was a learning experience.

You know—pain teaches?

One of the nurses picked it up from there. She was bending over my bed, snatching pebbles of safety glass out of my hair. "What do we learn from this?" she asked.

It was like that class at school where the teacher talks about Realization, about how you could realize something big in a commonplace thing. The example he gave—and the liar said it really happened—was that once while drinking orange juice, he'd realized he would be dead someday. He wondered if we, his students, had had similar "realizations."

Is he kidding? I thought.

Once I cashed a paycheck and I realized it wasn't enough.

Once I had food poisoning and realized I was trapped inside my body.

What interests me now is this memory thing. Why two *days*? Why *two* days? The last I know is not getting carded in a two-shark bar near the Bonneville flats. The bartender served me tequila and he left the bottle out. He asked me where I was going, and I said I was just going. Then he brought out a jar with a scorpion in it. He showed me how a drop of tequila on its tail makes a scorpion sting itself to death.

What happened after that?

Maybe those days will come back and maybe they will not. In the meantime, how's this: I can't even remember all I've forgotten.

I do remember the accident, though. I remember it was like the binoculars. You know—two ways? It was fast and it was slow. It was both.

The pot roast wasn't bad. I ate every bit of it. I finished the green vegetables and the citrus vegetables too.

Now I'm waiting for the night nurse. She takes a blood pressure about this time. You could call this the high point of my day. That's because this nurse makes every other woman look like a sex-change. Unfortunately, she's in love with the Lord.

But she's a sport, this nurse. When I can't sleep she brings in the telephone book. She sits by my bed and we look up funny names. Calliope Ziss and Maurice Pancake live in this very community.

I like a woman in my room at night.

The night nurse smells like a Christmas candle.

After she leaves the room, for a short time the room is like when she was here. She is not here, but the idea of her is.

It's not the same—but it makes me think of the night my mother died. Three states away, the smell in my room was the smell of the powder on her face when she kissed me good night—the night she wasn't there.

POOL NIGHT

This time it happened with fire. Just the way it happened before, the time it happened with water. Someone was losing everything—to water, to fire—and not trying not to.

Maybe I wasn't losing everything. But I didn't try to save it. That is what makes it like the first time. They had to lead me out of the house, and not because I didn't know my way out in the smoke.

The first time, no one said anything. Or we talked about everything but. It was twenty-eight years since the river topped its banks, all that time since a flood skunked the reservoir and washed out people's homes.

We watched the water come, when it did. From patios late at night, the neighborhood watched the water move. A flash of light like strobe light would go off on the ground as the watery debris snapped a high-tension tower. When the wires touched the water, that part of town went black. This was the thing we watched—the city going dark along the path of the flood.

It was not supposed to reach us.
And then it did.

*   *   *

Evacuation was calm and quick, except for Dr. Winton. Dr. Winton drank down most of his liquor cabinet and stared at the Red Cross volunteers who put their van in park and went in and hauled him out.

Most of us saw that happen. But during the days of cleanup it was not what anyone mentioned. We talked about the racehorses loose from Centennial Track, how they had cantered over lawns and stumbled on buried sprinkler heads. Indoors were rolls of wet toilet paper swelling on bathroom rods. We found letters, and water had washed off the ink.

We talked about Bunny Winton, who ordered a new living room the first morning after. She said she was happy to see her armchairs go, the padded arms cat-scratched down to cotton batting.

"You open up or you shut down," Bunny said, and went out and got her hair styled new.

Film crews photographed the swim team at the club. They were lined up by the snack bar, waiting to get a tetanus shot so they could shovel mud. Bunny made the nightly news; the Vidifont spelled out VICTIM on her chest.

They showed her in a tree wrapping washcloths around a branch so that the wet bent wood would not squeak against the roof.

The first time was fifteen years ago, on what was, or on what would have been, Pool Night.

"It's all in the mouth," he said, and showed me again and again. Grey said, "If the mouth is relaxed, the person looks good."

We were looking at pictures of ourselves and family. The looking was my mother's idea—my mother, who was the thoughtful one. Here's what my mother thought of when she heard that Bunny Winton had lost her photograph album: She put me to work on ours. Grey came over to help me—at her invitation, of course.

Grey was Bunny and the doctor's son, the child they could not now watch grow up in snapshots, page after page. Until my mother remembered that he grew up in ours. We would pull every picture that included Grey Winton, print up another, and present a new album to his grateful parents.

Grey was a junior lifeguard at the pool. He tanned to the color of the corn flakes he ate each morning, and I knew girls who saved his chewed gum.

Grey was the only boy excused from working cleanup. That was the week he was under observation.

He and my brother were Aquazaniacs.

They trained with a coach to do slapstick acrobatics off the high dive at the pool. There were six Aquazaniacs in 1890s stripes who hurled themselves into the water in syncopated ways. Grey would stand on my brother's shoulders and together they dove as the Twelve-Foot Man.

In the pratfall sport of Clown Diving, the Walk-Around Gainer is a popular stunt. This is where you run to the end of the board and then keep on running, out in the air, a cartoon, so fast you flip over backward.

"Put gravity at your service" is how they said they did it.

But during rehearsal, Grey candied out. He hit his head on the board coming down. It would have kept him from diving on Pool Night, if we had had Pool Night. But the rain date gave him time to try to perfect the Fire Dive.

*   *   *

In the album there were pictures of Grey in water. The first one was in our bathtub, playing Stormy Ocean with my brother as a baby. Later, they pole a raft across a lake, poking an oar at snapping turtles. There's a picture of the three of us on skates, on ice. Around my neck I wear snowballs of rabbit fur on black velvet cord. The pictures that follow show the boys pulling the snowballs off, then coming from behind, the velvet rope stretched out tight—a garrote.

Some of the photographs were Polaroid ones. They were faded, but the fugitive images remained. Emulsion on others had turned metallic bronze; the snapshots held deep tarnish, like a mirror.

There were quite a few pictures of Bunny, too. With the unphotogenic's eagerness to pose, she increased her chances of the one good shot that would let her relax, having proof at last that she had once looked good, just once.

The doctor couldn't make it to the picnics or to the skating—so he didn't show up in the pictures, either. The effect was of him saying after the flood: What I lose will always be lost.

"His problem is the past," Grey said about his father. "He says only do things you have done before and liked. Whereas me, what's *coming* is the thing I'm looking out for."

I thought the present was the safer bet. We can only die in the future, I thought; right now we are always alive.

Grey trusted water. He continued to trust it after the flood. He believed it would save him, and he counted on this for the Fire Dive.

I saw him do it once, which is all the times he did it.

When the swimming pool was filtered and rechlorinated, he carried a can of gasoline to the high board. He wore a sweatshirt with a hood and matching drawstring pants. He dove into the water with the top and bottoms on, then pulled himself out by the ladder on the side. It was night, and I had my camera ready.

He sprinkled his wet clothes with gasoline as though he were watering plants. He said wet cloth would pull the fuel away from his skin.

He said to imagine this: that the moment he hit the water aflame, when he made this dive on the next Pool Night, that's when he would have a cannon go off!

Then he struck a lighter and he lit himself up good.

I got it all on film—the human torch, the flaming spiral twists that he scripted in the air, the hiss of reclaimed life when the water took him in.

It only lasted seconds. It seemed an extravagant risk, and that is how I put it.

He said, "I made those seconds live."

I took one more picture that night. It was after Grey had walked me home. He found a box of photograph corners, the black stick-on kind that frame the picture on the page. He opened up our album, pasted four of them in place.

It was *Grey* who took the picture; the picture he took was of me. It was candid—I wasn't posed—and the instant, the Polaroid, is what he used. When the blank square of film emerged from the camera, he tore it off and slipped it in the corners on the page, and then he closed the album cover before the image could develop.

That picture is something I lost in the fire.

*   *   *

One thing smoke does is lower your voice. It did not sound like me, thanking the firefighters. I said thanks, but I did not feel grateful. I stood aside and watched, breathing the tarry air. I watched myself lose all that I was losing, and I knew why Dr. Winton had stayed inside his house.

I know about this now.

I know that homes burn and that you should think what to save before they start to. Not because, in the heat of it, everything looks as valuable as everything else. But because nothing looks worth the bother, not even your life.

THREE POPES WALK INTO A BAR

Sydney Lawton Square is a park for a transient population; there are no benches. You can walk it end to end in minutes. The architect for the Gateway Condominiums squeezed it in between the barbecue place and the parking garage. You would put quotes around this "park" the way you might send traffic fines to the Hall of "Justice." But this feeble attempt at nature is walking distance from the club—so that's where I meet Wesley, at the Fountain of Four Seasons.

The fountain yields dead earthworms, not coins; the worms outnumber pull-tabs, cigarettes, and leaves. At the nearby north entrance to the square there is a faded brick arch with a bronzelike plaque that says HISTORICAL SITE. All of it is contrived to suggest that something was once there, but none of it tells you what.

Wesley calls out "Ahoy," so I know he has made up his mind.

"You think it's a crime to change your mind?" he says. "Just because you are able to do a thing doesn't mean that's what you have to do, does it? Because I could but I don't want to," he says as we walk the tarmac path.

He is talking about performing. He's still funny, and he wants to stop.

"I could keep on," he says, "and you know what I'd have to show for it? Ten percent liver function and a felony in my bed."

"I think what counts is timing," I say. "As long as you try your first choice first."

Three popes walk into a bar.

A guy in the airport Clipper Club recognized Wesley and bet him he couldn't get a punchline out of it. They boarded a plane in Honolulu; Wesley had the five hours to San Francisco to make it a joke. *Three popes walk into a bar.* He lost money on this, but I didn't ask how much. Coming off a tour he is sick with foreign germs. I met him at the gate and drove him straight to the club. It's what Eve usually did, but she delegated to me. Eve Grant is Wesley Grant's future former wife.

"Eve cabled the hotel that she's coming tonight," Wesley said. "But she won't laugh."

"You won't hear her not laughing over the six hundred other people," I said. "You're sold out."

"But I always know. You *know.* She wants me to buy a boat, is all. After, of course, I have stopped performing."

"What's it to her?" I said. "She's leaving you."

"Or not," Wesley said. "Maybe she's not leaving if I buy the boat."

"That doesn't put you on the spot or anything."

"You talk to her tonight," he said.

About Eve Grant, Wesley has said that he married the most beautiful woman he ever saw and learned the irrelevance of beauty.

He met her at a club where she danced topless. She told him that Wesley was the name of the first monkey in space. She told him how NASA used that Wesley up and then abandoned him to an animal shelter for destruction. Then a group of women kidnapped that Wesley and took him to a zoo, where he lived out his life in comfort.

Wesley knew the monkey's name was Steve, but thought it was sweet of her to say otherwise.

With Wesley's encouragement, Eve stopped dancing and pursued a career in journalism. She thought she would be a natural at it because people always wanted to talk to her. She wrote an article on spec for the Sunday paper and had it returned six weeks later. Wesley asked the editor what was wrong with it, wasn't it boring enough? Then he cashed a favor with a publicist and got Eve a job at a fanzine doing a monthly column on vanished TV actors. The column was called "Where Are They Now?" but we all called it "Why Aren't They Dead?"

Wesley signaled the waitress and placed a special order. In a moment, she returned with a bowl of canned peach halves. Wesley took a bottle of Romilar cough suppressant from his coat pocket and poured most of it into the bowl.

"I really admire you," I told him. "I couldn't go out there and make people laugh if *I* were sick."

"Don't be silly," he said. "You couldn't do it if you were well."

He forced down the reddened peaches.

"But I'll tell you what you *can* do. You can tickle me," he said.

Eve usually did that, too. His grandmother started it

when he was a boy. She used to tickle Wesley beyond fun, he said, until he felt trapped and helpless and would have cried except that he learned to give in to it, and at that moment felt relief and calm move in.

It is this tickling and giving in that makes him funny, he thinks. Like every kind of recovery, comedy demands surrender.

Wesley cleared away the chairs and squared off in front of me. At the signal I dove at his belt.

I get something out of this, too.

The club manager's office was open and empty, so we took a couple of drinks in and closed the door. Wesley scanned the shelves of videocassettes, pulled one out, and popped it into the deck. He joined me on the couch.

It was a tape of every low-budget commercial he had made for local affiliate stations. This, Wesley said, is comedy.

The tape kicked in and there he was in suit and tie for the Cherry Hills Shopping Mall over in the East Bay.

"Tell me when it's safe," he said, and covered his eyes with a hand.

On screen, he said, "That's Cherry Hills, between the MacArthur and the Nimitz. MacArthur and Nimitz—both fine men, both fine freeways."

"Oh, I hate myself," he moaned.

The machine sizzled with static.

"This next one is Eve's favorite."

The product was a deep-penetrating epoxy sealer that you pumped into cracked cement to bind it into one integral piece again. The homeowner in the background eyeing his cracked sidewalk was Wesley's former partner, Larry Banks.

They split up a couple of years ago when Banks ran for mayor on the campaign platform "Anything You Want."

The machine jammed on the tagline "Cement cracks, this we know."

Wesley turned off the machine and opened the door. He asked the waitress for vodka.

"I tell you about the night I met Banks?" he said. "My manager brought him to watch me work. Then after the show we all go to this Polynesian place to get stewed. Banks, he was just starting out, he orders this sissy drink for two, only he doesn't realize it's for two. So the waiter shows up with this washpan of rum, and Banks is all embarrassed and so on. I told him, comics can't *get* embarrassed."

Wesley sat back down beside me and said it was time to change his life. He wanted to. "But how does a person start?"

"Small," I said. "Start small and work up. The way you would clean a house. You start in one room. Maybe you give yourself more time than you need to finish that room, just so you finish it. Then you go on to the next one. You start small, and then everything you do gets bigger."

I myself have never done it this way.

"Of course, I could be different," Wesley said. "Maybe everything I do will get smaller. On the other hand, there's still the stage, you know—when it's good up there, when I stand up there and have nothing to say but it has to work! It's— being human on purpose, it's falling back on the language in your mouth. It's facing these people and saying, You think Jesus had it rough! Ah, when it's good," he said. "And when Evie's good, too. When Evie's there. In the night. Do you know what I'm saying?" he said. "Because she's the one who is there in the night. Before her I had what you'd call contacts. Like the last one, this one that was hanging around one of the clubs—so I asked her if she'd like to go out. And she said she did. She said she wanted to go all the way out."

Wesley swallowed vodka.

"Which is something I don't even understand," he said. "How about you? Did you ever want to die? I mean, try to *make* yourself die?"

"Only once," I said. "I drove my car real fast and I was going to have an accident but then I wasn't going to."

"Well, not me, not ever," Wesley said. "I sometimes think this is how depressed the people who commit suicide get. And then I thank God I'm a Leo."

An hour before the show, Eve met us in the bar. She looked good; Wesley said so, and everyone else noticed right along with him. Marzipan skin, white-blond hair that always looked backlit. Eve would look good in barbed wire.

"God, my jeans are full of me," Eve said, and undid a narrow snakeskin belt.

A waitress came to our table and asked what could she get us.

"I'm not drinking," Eve said. "Just a 7UP."

The waitress asked if Sprite was okay.

"No—then make it a Tab."

"Eve here used to live next door to the vice president of 7UP," Wesley explained, "so she's hip to lemon-lime drinks."

"So who's here?" Eve said. "L.A.?"

L.A. is any Hollywood agent who comes north to look at talent.

"Supposed to be, but not," Wesley said.

"It's just as well," Eve said. "They're such a tease. They fall all over you and then you never see them again." She sighed. "Just like everybody else."

She touched Wesley's shoulder, and he turned in his seat so that she could massage his neck with both hands.

"She's too good to me," Wesley said.

"Oh, I'm banking this," Eve said. "I'm not just throwing it off a cliff."

A voice broke in behind them. "Who said comedians don't have groupies."

It was the owner of the club, the man who would introduce Wesley onstage.

The owner told Wesley to join him backstage. Eve and I blew a kiss and carried our drinks upstairs. We passed people in line at the ticket window. To one side of the box office there was an eight-by-ten of Wesley. It was a publicity shot from years ago, the sincere-looking one. It was the same picture he had on his mantel at home, only there it carries a caption: "He aimed for the top. He started at the bottom. He ended up somewhere below in-between."

We found the small round table reserved for us up front. Eve offered me the first sip of her Tab so that it would be me who would get the one calorie.

"Look over there," she said, nodding far right. I looked, and saw four men, twentyish, crowded together, a pitcher of beer on their table. They were novices who played smaller clubs on open-mike nights.

"They're something," Eve said. "Watch them when Wesley's on. When he makes you laugh, look at them. One will say, 'That's funny,' and they'll all nod their heads madly and none of them will smile.

"A couple of months ago that little blond one opened for somebody here. He saw us in the bar after and asked Wesley what he thought of his act. Wesley said, 'Well, Bob Hope can't live forever.' The guy took it as a compliment."

Eve smiled her great rectangular smile.

I asked if she had changed her mind about Wesley, and she said, "Mmmm. Can we not talk about that?"

I worked at my drink. Eve stared at the empty stage. I said I was glad we weren't talking about *that*.

"I have a fondness for him," she said. "Sometimes it's weak . . . Did he seem nervous to you?"

"Always."

"That's what I mean," she said. "That's why the boat. That's why," the lights went down, "I'm always here."

The owner of the club bounded onto the stage. He grabbed the microphone off its stand and began to speak. Seconds later the sound came on.

He said, "Every night I come out here and tell you what a great show we have and you know, it's the God's honest truth. But tonight I really mean it."

Eve and I scooted together till our shoulders touched. We heard him say Wesley's name. A blue spotlight followed Wesley onstage. We heard Wesley tell the audience how great it was to be back in L.A.

In Sydney Lawton Square, the knolls roll carefully into each other, but the trees don't match, and there aren't enough of them. Wesley and I pass the doggy station—half a dozen segments of yellow-painted phone pole carved into hydrants, to *receive* water, not give it.

"I did what she wants," Wesley says. "I got a boat, and we're leaving the first of whatever comes after July. Hell, I did what *I* want. I've always been a seaman at heart—your Conrad, your Old Man and the Sea, your fish. It'll be good to get out on the waves and sort of expand my limitations. Sink in *water* for a change.

"As for Eve, she's not sure it will work. But it will. I told her, The trick is this—I do what I want, and you do what I want."

He laughs at himself. "And because, too, I love her to death. I watch that girl like a movie. 'Eve Grant Does Three Hours of Laundry.' I'm watching."

"Why don't you tell her these nice things?" I say.

"I could," Wesley says, doubtful. "But, hey—I guess I'm just a jerk."

"Can you just up and go?" I say.

"I get residuals, remember—Cement cracks, this we know. And Eve can always apply for Aid to the Totally Disabled. You'll want to tell her I said that."

A teenage boy hefting a tape deck matched his pace to ours and Stevie Wondered us to death.

"You know," Wesley says, as if he doesn't hear the music, "I meet a person, and in my mind I'm saying three minutes; I give you three minutes to show me the spark. It's always there with Eve, and it's been how long? So I keep thinking—can't we just be together all the time whether we're together or not?"

Ahead of us poplars wave against the sky, just as if they had grown here.

"Isn't it true that that's what people can do?" Wesley asks.

And I say, "Who's to live in a world where that isn't true?" But I think, *Three popes walk into a bar.*

THE MAN IN BOGOTÁ

The police and emergency service people fail to make a dent. The voice of the pleading spouse does not have the hoped-for effect. The woman remains on the ledge—though not, she threatens, for long.

I imagine that I am the one who must talk the woman down. I see it, and it happens like this.

I tell the woman about a man in Bogotá. He was a wealthy man, an industrialist who was kidnapped and held for ransom. It was not a TV drama; his wife could not call the bank and, in twenty-four hours, have one million dollars. It took months. The man had a heart condition, and the kidnappers had to keep the man alive.

Listen to this, I tell the woman on the ledge. His captors made him quit smoking. They changed his diet and made him exercise every day. They held him that way for three months.

When the ransom was paid and the man was released, his doctor looked him over. He found the man to be in excellent health. I tell the woman what the doctor said then—that the kidnap was the best thing to happen to that man.

*   *   *

Maybe this is not a come-down-from-the-ledge story. But I tell it with the thought that the woman on the ledge will ask herself a question, the question that occurred to that man in Bogotá. He wondered how we know that what happens to us isn't good.

WHEN IT'S HUMAN INSTEAD
OF WHEN IT'S DOG

It is just inside the front door. It is the first thing she sees when she stops to wipe her feet.

It has been raining for a week, and it won't be stopping soon. It's what the people were talking about on the bus ride in, and Mrs. Hatano guesses that's what they'll be talking about on the bus ride going home.

She wonders if the stain is from water leaking in. But the plaster isn't buckled on the ceiling above the spot. It's as big as a three-quart saucepan, though it is not a perfect circle.

It is two weeks since Mrs. Hatano cleaned this house. The Mr. gave her time off after the Mrs. died. Before, Mrs. Hatano left at five o'clock. Now the schedule is this: She will come every day at five o'clock to make dinner for the Mr. She will do some light cleaning—a load of laundry, an upstairs dusting—then she will wash the dinner dishes, collect her forty dollars, and let herself out.

No one seems to be at home. Mrs. Hatano at the kitchen counter tears a sheet of paper from the telephone message pad.

She draws a question mark at the top of the page. Under the question mark she writes in a column: lamb chop, pork chop, chicken, fish. She writes: bake or broil. Vegetables she will serve cut in strips and stir-fried. The rice can cook while she runs the vacuum.

Upstairs, there is one room she never cleaned. The door was always closed, the Mrs. never well. But the door is open now.

The room is dark—the shutters are closed—so Mrs. Hatano turns on a lamp.

The wastepaper basket is filled with cards. There is an open letter on the desk, and, although it is not in Mrs. Hatano's nature to pry, she begins to read. It is a sympathy note.

Mrs. Hatano hears the front door open. She puts down the letter and moves to the bed, which is stripped of its sheets. On a chair beside the bed is a stack of clean linen, and a queen-size folded blanket.

From the doorway the Mr. says hello. He smiles at Mrs. Hatano and offers to help her make up the bed.

Before she can tell him no, he should please read his paper, the man takes two corners of the blanket and flaps it over the mattress. He waits for Mrs. Hatano to smooth out her side. She is unable to tell him, until she does, that the sheet goes first.

"My God," the man says quietly. He stares a thousand miles into the bed.

At the smell of the dinner frying in sesame oil, the man's face changes. Mrs. Hatano reads the look as Other People's Food. In the freezer she saw dinners delivered by friends—shrimp casserole, curried chicken, lasagne; the recipes were included, taped to the foil.

After serving dinner, Mrs. Hatano opens the cabinet under the sink. She removes a plastic bucket and arranges inside it a sponge, a scrub brush, a bottle of white vinegar, water, and a can of spray-on carpet cleaner.

She leaves the kitchen by the door that opens into the hall.

Mrs. Hatano sings while she works, and the foreign sounds carry to the dining room. She waters down the vinegar—so that it will not take out the color. But scrubbing the stain with vinegar fails to bring up the nap. That place on the carpet, that darker surface like geography on a map, it can still be seen.

What would do it? Mrs. Hatano says to herself.

Maybe the spray cleaner, she thinks, and points the aerosol can. She presses the button and traces the spot with foam. It must be allowed to dry, so Mrs. Hatano returns to the kitchen. She opens the freezer and takes out what's inside. She empties the crusty white ice-cube trays, and fills them with clear cold water.

While the man has his dinner, Mrs. Hatano uses the phone. She calls her friend Ruthie, who cleans down the block.

Ruthie tells her vinegar, in the first fifteen minutes. She says, "A dog wets—you can pretty much forget it. Best idea, you cut a runner from one of those carpet squares, you just cover the whole thing up."

Then Ruthie tells her it wasn't a dog. "That's where the lady died," Ruthie says. "No dogs there."

And Ruthie tells Mrs. Hatano what she heard her people say, about the day the lady died and the man carried her down the stairs.

"It happened *then*—do you hear what I'm saying?" Ruthie says.

Mrs. Hatano tries Esther Fat next. It is Esther's day off so Mrs. Hatano phones her at home.

Esther Fat says lemon and soda water. She says lemon is acid, and a stain like that is the opposite.

"Unless I am confused and it is the other way around," Esther Fat says. "Is it different when it's human instead of when it's dog?"

Mrs. Hatano thinks, What the Chinese don't know about cleaning a house.

"Hell, *they* got money," Esther Fat says. "Let them get a new rug."

When the man finishes dinner, he helps Mrs. Hatano clear the table. Then he leaves her to the dishes. That is when Mrs. Hatano sees him see the carpet.

There is no question that they see the same thing. The thin line of foam has dried to white powder, calling attention to— a state on a map? No, Mrs. Hatano thinks it looks like something else now. The white traced shape is like a chalk-drawn victim on a sidewalk.

The man excuses himself after a pause, and Mrs. Hatano washes the dishes.

When the counters are clean and the pots are put away,

Mrs. Hatano gets her coat and boots. She takes the forty dollars from the table in the hall. In its place she leaves a five-dollar bill from her purse because she still could not get the spot out.

WHY I'M HERE

"Name a time when you are happy," is one of the questions. I am taking a test to find out what to do. The way to do this is to find out what you like. This is not obvious, the way it sounds. For example, the questions that say, "Would you prefer . . ." "Would you prefer to: (a) Answer questions about what you do, (b) Answer questions about what you know, (c) Answer questions about what you think?"

My answer is, "Depends." But it's not one of the choices. I am having to think in terms of Always, Sometimes, Never.

You cannot pass or fail this test; your grade is more of a profile.

After the written part of the test, I talk to the vocational-guidance counselor. She is fifty or so, a short, square woman in a dress like a blender cozy. Mrs. Deane is the one who asks me when I'm happy. She says, "Tell me the thing you do *anyway,* and let's find a way to get you paid for that."

I ask about a job throwing sticks for dogs to fetch, and she says, "Oh, now," and gives me the courtesy laugh.

I'm the wrong age to be doing this.

You take this test in college if you can't pick a major. Or you take it to help you change your life—later, after you've *had* a life. Somewhere in the middle is the reason why I'm here.

* * *

So—The Time When I Am Happy.

It starts with the sign that says OPEN HOUSE, and the colored cellophane flags on a string across the walk. Then the unlocked door into a furnished model home, or, even better, unfurnished rooms. Here you have to imagine the lives the way you see characters in a book as you read.

It doesn't stop here, with inspecting the rooms. The thing that I do anyway—I move into new apartments.

First, I get rid of most of what I have. My friends are loaded up with ironing boards and sofa beds. I hand out records and wicker and lamps. Never mind the plants.

The books alone!

When the place is pared down, I spell my new number. It works like this: You take your telephone prefix, say it's 7-7-6. That's P-r-o. Then you start dialing words until you reach a disconnect, an available number: Pro-mise, Pro-digy, Pro-verb, Pro-blem, Pro-voke, Pro-tect, Pro-sper . . .

I buy a few beers for the "Two Guys with Van" who will load up what is left. I hope for the best, though you can count on this for damage: Three moves equals a fire.

The new place brings a rush of settlement. Paper towels and spray cleaners, plastic bags to line plastic wastebaskets. There is glossy shelf paper to cut for the cabinets, and my name to put on the mailbox. It's the same thing again, three months later. Move enough times and you will never defrost a freezer.

I'm telling this to Mrs. Deane.

She says the key thing here is process—what she looks for on the Happiness Question. Does this happiness come from a person, place, or process?

I tell her I don't know, that sometimes I just have to move.

The place before this, this is what it was. I took a small apartment on the top floor of a house. It was a narrow gray Victorian with amber stained-glass windows on the landing.

The manager apologized for the faulty showerhead. He said he would fix it, and he did—the next day. He said that he used to live in the house. He said that he and his brother used to play in my apartment where they set up their HO trains.

On my way out one morning, I said hello to the manager. He was down on his knees on the carpeted stairs, suctioning lint with a special vacuum attachment. But something was different when I got home that night. It took me a minute. Nothing was moved. Then I noticed the rug. It covered the space between the fireplace and couch. Since I had been gone, that rug had been vacuumed.

That wasn't all.

There was something the manager said, the day he fixed the shower. He said now that the stream was strong, I could "really lather up."

"Lather up!" I repeat to Mrs. Deane.

Mrs. Deane scans the written portion of my test. She says I skipped a question, the one that says, "Would you prefer to: (a) Think about your plans for tomorrow, (b) Think about what you would do if you had a million dollars, (c) Think about how it would feel to be held up at gunpoint?"

I say, "I want the job for the person who picks (b)."

Mrs. Deane says, "What do you suppose would happen if

you just stayed put? If you just stayed still long enough to think a thing through?"

"I don't know," I say. "I won't feel like myself."

"Oh," she says, "but you will—you are."

BREATHING JESUS

Things turned around after I saw the Breathing Jesus. My lost diamond solitaire was recovered from under the couch. The orchestra noises in my head stopped warming up. My neighbor and I witnessed the Resurrection of Baby.

I had gone to the Civic Center to see the Breathing Jesus. This was an *outdoor* Jesus. He was featured in the carnival they put on every springtime near the City Hall dome. An artist made this Jesus. He sat large as life on a jeweled throne in the trailer-size room that was done up as a shrine.

Out in front of the shrine was a coin box for your quarter. I dropped one in the slot, and looked at the velvet-robed figure on the throne. I watched his chest rise with the intake of air, and then fall back in the instant after someone watching beside me said, "Jesus—he's *breathing*."

I matched my respiration to the rhythm of His, and drew breath with the Lord until my quarter ran out.

I have seen a lot of things I would not know how to explain. I've seen "sparkling rain" that crackled and struck up sparks when it hit the ground. I've seen a white rainbow over the full moon. I've seen Spooklights and will-o'-the-wisps—those cold flames and luminous bubbles of light that float over swamps. I've seen a meteor wiggle out of its arc before burning itself out. I have read by the light of the southern aurora at 3 a.m.

I saw these things because of the noises in my head. Because the sound—like that of a symphony tuning up—kept me awake at night. The noises only stopped when the breath left my body and, lying there, I couldn't move.

Things happen, or they stop happening, and who can tell you why?

Baby I can explain.

Baby was only lost, not dead. But I *thought* she was dead because that is what the Department of Highways told me she was. They said a dog of Baby's description had been found at the university off-ramp. They said that the body had already been disposed of.

This was worse than it was because Baby was my neighbor's dog, left in my care while my neighbor went away.

Baby was gone three days when my neighbor returned. It was raining that day, and there was thunder, too. I felt strangely calm, prepared to deliver the news. I felt lucky to have my wits about me, and worried that I might need them.

And then there was Baby before I had to say.

What brought her back from where she was could have been the tires on the gravel drive. Or maybe it was the thunderstorm, the first one of the season, with the low and rolling sounds that wake up those in hibernation.

If that wasn't it, then I don't know what was.

I don't know why the breathing stops. They don't know why you get it, and they can't make it go away. There's a name for when the breathing stops, and they think that it's the killer when those babies die in their cribs.

I'm careful going to sleep at night. Always there is the noise before I can't get air. What I do is put a sound there first, the sound of someone else's breathing, regular and deep. At night I am back in the carnival tent, breathing along with Jesus. It's—in with the good air, then out with the same good air, breathing with something that can't breathe by itself.

I breathe along with Jesus till my quarter runs out, until I run out of change and take up a dollar bill from my purse. In my mind I say to anyone, Give me change for a dollar? Can you get me another four quarters?

Because you have to believe that something will work. I don't, but you have got to.

The ticking of a clock is what does the trick for Baby.

The things I've seen I can't explain are nothing next to what I've heard—musical sand, whispering lakes, a shout whose echo came back as a song.

Oh, I've heard stranger things than that, but those were in my head.

TODAY WILL BE A QUIET DAY

"I think it's the other way around," the boy said. "I think if the quake hit now the *bridge* would collapse and the *ramps* would be left."

He looked at his sister with satisfaction.

"You are just trying to scare your sister," the father said. "You know that is not true."

"No, really," the boy insisted, "and I heard birds in the middle of the night. Isn't that a warning?"

The girl gave her brother a toxic look and ate a handful of Raisinets. The three of them were stalled in traffic on the Golden Gate Bridge.

That morning, before waking his children, the father had canceled their music lessons and decided to make a day of it. He wanted to know how they were, is all. Just—how were they. He thought his kids were as self-contained as one of those dogs you sometimes see carrying home its own leash. But you could read things wrong.

Could you ever.

The boy had a friend who jumped from a floor of Langley Porter. The friend had been there for two weeks, mostly playing Ping-Pong. All the friend said the day the boy visited and lost every game was never play Ping-Pong with a mental patient because it's all we do and we'll kill you. That night the friend had cut the red belt he wore in two and left the other half on his bed. That was this time last year when the boy was twelve years old.

You think you're safe, the father thought, but it's thinking you're invisible because you closed your eyes.

This day they were headed for Petaluma—the chicken, egg, and arm-wrestling capital of the nation—for lunch. The father had offered to take them to the men's arm-wrestling semifinals. But it was said that arm-wrestling wasn't so interesting since the new safety precautions, that hardly anyone broke an arm or a wrist anymore. The best anyone could hope to see would be dislocation, so they said they would rather go to Pete's. Pete's was a gas station turned into a place to eat. The hamburgers there were named after cars, and the gas pumps in front still pumped gas.

"Can I have one?" the boy asked, meaning the Raisinets.

"No," his sister said.

"Can I have two?"

"Neither of you should be eating candy before lunch," the father said. He said it with the good sport of a father who enjoys his kids and gets a kick out of saying Dad things.

"You mean dinner," said the girl. "It will be dinner before we get to Pete's."

Only the northbound lanes were stopped. Southbound traffic flashed past at the normal speed.

"Check it out," the boy said from the backseat. "Did you

see the bumper sticker on that Porsche? 'If you don't like way I drive, stay off the sidewalk.'"

He spoke directly to his sister. "I've just solved my Christmas shopping."

"I got the highest score in my class in Driver's Ed," she said.

"I thought I would let your sister drive home today," the father said.

From the backseat came sirens, screams for help, and then a dirge.

The girl spoke to her father in a voice rich with complicity. "Don't people make you want to give up?"

"Don't the two of you know any jokes? I haven't laughed all day," the father said.

"Did I tell you the guillotine joke?" the girl said.

"He hasn't laughed all day, so you must've," her brother said.

The girl gave her brother a look you could iron clothes with. Then her gaze dropped down. "Oh-oh," she said, "Johnny's out of jail."

Her brother zipped his pants back up. He said, "Tell the joke."

"Two Frenchmen and a Belgian were about to be beheaded," the girl began. "The first Frenchman was led to the block and blindfolded. The executioner let the blade go. But it stopped a quarter inch above the Frenchman's neck. So he was allowed to go free, and ran off shouting, 'C'est un miracle! C'est un miracle!'"

"What does that mean?" her brother asked.

"It's a miracle," the father said.

"Then the second Frenchman was led to the block, and

same thing—the blade stopped just before cutting off his head. So *he* got to go free, and ran off shouting *'C'est un miracle!'*

"Finally the Belgian was led to the block. But before they could blindfold him, he looked up, pointed to the guillotine, and cried, *'Voilà la difficulté!'*"

She doubled over.

"Maybe *I* would be wetting *my* pants if I knew what that meant," the boy said.

"You can't explain after the punchline," the girl said, "and have it still be funny."

"There's the problem," said the father.

The waitress handed out menus to the party of three seated in the corner booth of what used to be the lube bay. She told them the specialty of the day was Moroccan chicken.

"That's what I want," the boy said, "Morerotten chicken."

But he changed his order to a Studeburger and fries after his father and sister had ordered.

"So," the father said, "who misses music lessons?"

"I'm serious about what I asked you last week," the girl said. "About switching to piano? My teacher says a real flutist only breathes with the stomach, and I can't."

"The real reason she wants to change," said the boy, "is her waist will get two inches bigger when she learns to stomach-breathe. That's what *else* her teacher said."

The boy buttered a piece of sourdough bread and flipped a chunk of cold butter onto his sister's sleeve.

"Jeezo-beezo," the girl said, "why don't they skip the knife and fork and just set his place with a slingshot!"

"Who will ever adopt you if you don't mind your manners?" the father said. "Maybe we could try a little quiet today."

"You sound like your tombstone," the girl said. "Remember what you wanted it to say?"

Her brother joined in with his mouth full: "Today will be a quiet day."

"Because it never is with us around," the boy said.

"You guys," said the father.

The waitress brought plates. The father passed sugar to the boy and salt to the girl without being asked. He watched the girl shake out salt onto the fries.

"If I had a sore throat, I would gargle with those," he said.

"Looks like she's trying to melt a driveway," the boy offered.

The father watched his children eat. They ate fast. They called it Hoovering. He finished while they sucked at straws in empty drinks.

"Funny," he said thoughtfully, "I'm not hungry anymore."

Every meal ended this way. It was his benediction, one of the Dad things they expected him to say.

"That reminds me," the girl said. "Did you feed Rocky before we left?"

"Uh-uh," her brother said. "I fed him yesterday."

"*I* fed him yesterday!" the girl said.

"Okay, we'll compromise," the boy said. "We won't feed the cat today."

"I'd say you are out of bounds on that one," the father said.

He meant you could not tease her about animals. Once, during dinner, that cat ran into the dining room shot from guns. He ran around the table at top speed, then spun out on the parquet floor into a leg of the table. He fell onto his side and made short coughing sounds. "Isn't he smart?" the girl had crooned, kneeling beside him. "He knows he's hurt."

For years, her father had to say that the animals seen on shoulders of roads were napping.

"He never would have not fed Homer," she said to her father.

"Homer was a dog," the boy said. "If I forgot to feed him, he could just go into the hills and bite a deer."

"Or a Campfire Girl selling candy at the front door," their father reminded them.

"Homer," the girl sighed. "I hope he likes chasing sheep on that ranch in the mountains."

The boy looked at her, incredulous.

"You *believed* that? You actually *believed* that?"

In her head, a clumsy magician yanked the cloth and the dishes all crashed to the floor. She took air into her lungs until they filled, and then she filled her stomach, too.

"I thought she knew," the boy said.

The dog was five years ago.

"The girl's parents insisted," the father said. "It's the law in California."

"Then I hate California," she said. "I hate its guts."

The boy said he would wait for them in the car, and left the table.

"What would help?" the father asked.

"For Homer to be alive," she said.

"What would help?"

"Nothing."

"Help."

She pinched a trail of salt on her plate.

"A ride," she said. "I'll drive."

The girl started the car and screamed. "Goddammit!"

With the power off, the boy had tuned in the Spanish station. Mariachis exploded on ignition.

"'Dammit isn't God's last name,'" the boy said, quoting another bumper sticker.

"Don't people make you want to give up?" the father said.

"No talking," the girl said to the rearview mirror, and put the car in gear.

She drove for hours. Through groves of eucalyptus with their damp peeling bark, past acacia bushes with yellow flowers pulsing off their stems. She cut over to the coast route and the stony gray-green tones of Inverness.

"What you'd call scenic," the boy tried.

Otherwise, they were quiet.

No one said anything else until the sky started to close, and then it was the boy again, asking shouldn't they be going home.

"No, no," the father said, and made a show of looking out the window, up at the sky, and back at his watch. "No," he said, "keep driving—it's getting earlier."

But the sky spilled rain, and the girl headed south toward the bridge. She turned on the headlights and the dashboard lit up green. She read off the odometer on the way home: "Twenty-six thousand, three hundred eighty-three and eight-tenths miles."

"Today?" the boy said.

* * *

The boy got to Rocky first. "Let's play the cat," he said, and carried the Siamese to the upright piano. He sat on the bench holding the cat in his lap and pressed its paws to the keys. Rocky played "Born Free." He tried to twist away.

"Come on, Rocky, ten more minutes and we'll break."

"Give him to me," the girl said.

She puckered up and gave the cat a five-lipper.

"Bring the Rock upstairs," the father called. "Bring sleeping bags, too."

Pretty soon three sleeping bags formed a triangle in the master bedroom. The father was the hypotenuse. The girl asked him to brush out her hair, which he did while the boy ate a tangerine, peeling it up close to his face, inhaling the mist. Then he held each segment to the light to find seeds. In his lap, cat paws fluttered like dreaming eyes.

"What are you thinking?" the father asked.

"Me?" the girl said. "Fifty-seven T-bird, white with red interior, convertible. I drive it to Texas and wear skirts with rickrack. I'm changing my name to Ruby," she said, "or else Easy."

The father considered her dream of a checkered future.

"Early ripe, early rot," he warned.

A wet wind slammed the window in its warped sash, and the boy jumped.

"I hate rain," he said. "I hate its guts."

The father got up and closed the window tighter against the storm. "It's a real frog-choker," he said.

In darkness, lying still, it was no less camplike than if they had been under the stars singing to a stone-ringed fire burned down to embers.

They had already said good night some minutes earlier when the boy and girl heard their father's voice in the dark.

"Kids, I just remembered—I have some good news and some bad news. Which do you want first?"

It was his daughter who spoke. "Let's get it over with," she said. "Let's get the bad news over with."

The father smiled. They are all right, he decided. My kids are as right as this rain. He smiled at the exact spots he knew their heads were turned to his, and doubted he would ever feel—not better, but *more* than he did now.

"I lied," he said. "There is no bad news."

AT THE GATES OF
THE ANIMAL KINGDOM

DAYLIGHT COME

Belle developed a craving *after* she was pregnant. After she delivered herself of seven healthy pups, Belle went mad for lizards, catching and eating the island chameleons—who knew how many?—till we came to expect the dog to affect protective color, to rise white from the sand and swim—a blue-pawed dog—in the sea.

The lizards made Belle jumpy after dark, made her bark at the stars until one of the guests would yell, "Belle, take the rest of the night off!"

There were four guests on the island. The other couple were newlyweds, seventy years old, whose wedding rings slipped from their fingers underwater where, behind borrowed masks, they watched angelfish and a spotted ray, and correctly identified a lone barracuda.

The Wellers, Bing and Ruth, developed something of a craving of their own. They found they liked the fried flying fish; when the Wellers announced their choice for dinner, it sounded like they were making fun of Japanese people.

At the Wellers' feet during these dinners of flying fish, Belle nursed her puppies and a Siamese cat bleated like a lamb.

"Here's to you, Bingo," Ruth would say, lifting her glass.

We watched them from our table, on which red hibiscus

blossoms filled the opening of a conch. Ruth was the one who told us that the flowers lived only one day.

One day I stayed on shore and watched the orange tips of breathing tubes move the length of a distant reef. I followed the one that mattered to me, followed it to an anchored raft, watched the woman in the raft drop over the side to join him. Then I saw him walking toward me from a shelter of palms and knew my mistake.

That evening after dinner, sitting inside a circle of smoking coconut husks, I watched Ruth's face as Bing recalled earlier trips to the island, trips he had made with his first—I want to say "life." Ruth didn't mind, I didn't think, when Bing said "we" and meant them.

The Wellers with their message of affirmation were meant to warm the hearts of strangers. But I could not wait to get away from them. The Wellers had been widow and widower first.

Of course, the Wellers offered to take our picture. It was kind of them; it was expected. We gave them our camera, and while Bing got the feel of it, we ran into the water. We surfaced, arms around each other, and turned to face the Wellers.

In the picture it appears that I am being helped to stand. I am not looking at the Wellers. I am looking down, where the lost wedding rings are invisible, now the color of the sand or of the sea or of the flesh.

THE HARVEST

The year I began to say *vahz* instead of *vase,* a man I barely knew nearly accidentally killed me.

The man was not hurt when the other car hit ours. The man I had known for one week held me in the street in a way that meant I couldn't see my legs. I remember knowing that I shouldn't look, and knowing that I *would* look if it wasn't that I couldn't.

My blood was on the front of this man's clothes.

He said, "You'll be okay, but this sweater is ruined."

I screamed from the fear of pain. But I did not feel any pain. In the hospital, after injections, I knew there was pain in the room—I just didn't know whose pain it was.

What happened to one of my legs required four hundred stitches, which, when I told it, became five hundred stitches, because nothing is ever quite as bad as it *could* be.

The five days they didn't know if they could save my leg or not I stretched to ten.

The lawyer was the one who used the word. But I won't get around to that until a couple of paragraphs.

We were having the looks discussion—how important *are* they. Crucial, is what I had said.

I think looks are crucial.

But this guy was a lawyer. He sat in an aqua vinyl chair drawn up to my bed. What he meant by looks was how much my loss of them was worth in a court of law.

I could tell that the lawyer liked to say *court of law.* He told me he had taken the bar three times before he had passed. He said that his friends had given him handsomely embossed business cards, but where these lovely cards were supposed to say *Attorney-at-Law,* his cards said *Attorney-at-Last.*

He had already covered loss of earnings, that I could not now become an airline stewardess. That I had never considered becoming one was immaterial, he said, legally.

"There's another thing," he said. "We have to talk here about marriageability."

The tendency was to say marriage-a-*what?* although I knew what he meant the first time I heard it.

I was eighteen years old. I said, "First, don't we talk about *date*ability?"

The man of a week was already gone, the accident driving him back to his wife.

"Do you think looks are important?" I asked the man before he left.

"Not at first," he said.

In my neighborhood there is a fellow who was a chemistry teacher until an explosion took his face and left what was left behind. The rest of him is neatly dressed in dark suits and shined shoes. He carries a briefcase to the college campus.

What a comfort—his family, people said—until his wife took the kids and moved out.

In the solarium, a woman showed me a snapshot. She said, "This is what my son used to look like."

I spent my evenings in Dialysis. They didn't mind when a lounger was free. They had wide-screen color TV, better than they had in Rehab. Wednesday nights we watched a show where women in expensive clothes appeared on lavish sets and promised to ruin one another.

On one side of me was a man who spoke only in phone numbers. You would ask him how he felt, he would say, "924-3130." Or he would say, "757-1366." We guessed what these numbers might be, but nobody spent the dime.

There was sometimes, on the other side of me, a twelve-year-old boy. His lashes were thick and dark from blood-pressure medication. He was next on the transplant list, as soon as—the word they used was *harvest*—as soon as a kidney was harvested.

The boy's mother prayed for drunk drivers.

I prayed for men who were not discriminating.

Aren't we all, I thought, somebody's harvest?

The hour would end, and a floor nurse would wheel me back to my room. She would say, "Why watch that trash? Why not just ask me how my day went?"

I spent fifteen minutes before going to bed squeezing rubber grips. One of the medications was making my fingers stiffen. The doctor said he'd give it to me till I couldn't button my blouse—a figure of speech to someone in a cotton gown.

The lawyer said, "Charitable works."

He opened his shirt and showed me where an acupuncture

person had dabbed at his chest with cola syrup, sunk four needles, and told him that the real cure was charitable works.

I said, "Cure for what?"

The lawyer said, "Immaterial."

As soon as I knew that I would be all right, I was sure that I was dead and didn't know it. I moved through the days like a severed head that finishes a sentence. I waited for the moment that would snap me out of my seeming life.

The accident happened at sunset, so that is when I felt this way the most. The man I had met the week before was driving me to dinner when it happened. The place was at the beach, a beach on a bay that you can look across and see the city lights, a place where you can see everything without having to listen to any of it.

A long time later I went to that beach myself. *I* drove the car. It was the first good beach day; I wore shorts.

At the edge of the sand I unwound the elastic bandage and waded into the surf. A boy in a wet suit looked at my leg. He asked me if a shark had done it; there were sightings of great whites along that part of the coast.

I said that, yes, a shark had done it.

"And you're going back in?" the boy asked.

I said, "And I'm going back in."

I leave a lot out when I tell the truth. The same when I write a story. I'm going to start now to tell you what I left out of "The Harvest," and maybe begin to wonder why I had to leave it out.

There was no other car. There was only the one car, the one that hit me when I was on the back of the man's motorcycle. But think of the awkward syllables when you have to say *motorcycle*.

The driver of the car was a newspaper reporter. He worked for a local paper. He was young, a recent graduate, and he was on his way to a labor meeting to cover a threatened strike. When I say I was then a journalism student, it is something you might not have accepted in "The Harvest."

In the years that followed, I watched for the reporter's byline. He broke the People's Temple story that resulted in Jim Jones's flight to Guyana. Then he covered Jonestown. In the city room of the *San Francisco Chronicle*, as the death toll climbed to nine hundred, the numbers were posted like donations on pledge night. Somewhere in the hundreds, a sign was fixed to the wall that said JUAN CORONA, EAT YOUR HEART OUT.

In the emergency room, what happened to one of my legs required not four hundred stitches but just over three hundred stitches. I exaggerated even before I began to exaggerate, because it's true—nothing *is* ever quite as bad as it could be.

My lawyer was no attorney-at-last. He was a partner in one of the city's oldest law firms. He would never have opened his shirt to reveal the site of acupuncture, which is something that he never would have had.

"Marriageability" was the original title of "The Harvest."

The damage to my leg was considered cosmetic although I am still, fifteen years later, unable to kneel. In an out-of-court settlement the night before the trial, I was awarded nearly $100,000. The reporter's car insurance went up $12.43 per month.

It had been suggested that I rub my leg with ice, to bring

up the scars, before I hiked my skirt three years later for the court. But there was no ice in the judge's chambers, so I did not get a chance to pass or fail that moral test.

The man of a week, whose motorcycle it was, was not a married man. But when you thought he had a wife, wasn't I liable to do anything? And didn't I have it coming?

After the accident, the man got married. The girl he married was a fashion model. ("Do you think looks are important?" I asked the man before he left. "Not at first," he said.)

In addition to being a beauty, the girl was worth millions of dollars. Would you have accepted this in "The Harvest"— that the model was also an heiress?

It is true we were headed for dinner when it happened. But the place where you can see everything without having to listen to any of it was not a beach on a bay; it was the top of Mount Tamalpais. We had the dinner with us as we headed up the twisting mountain road. This is the version that has room for perfect irony, so you won't mind when I say that for the next several months, from my hospital bed, I had a dead-on spectacular view of that very mountain.

I would have written this next part into the story if anybody would have believed it. But who would have? I was there and I didn't believe it.

On the day of my third operation, there was an attempted breakout in the Maximum Security Adjustment Center, adjacent to Death Row, at San Quentin prison. "Soledad Brother" George Jackson, a twenty-nine-year-old black man, pulled out a smuggled-in .38-caliber pistol, yelled, "This is it!" and opened fire. Jackson was killed; so were three guards and two "tier-tenders," inmates who bring other prisoners their meals.

Three other guards were stabbed in the neck. The prison is a five-minute drive from Marin General, so that is where the injured guards were taken. The people who brought them were three kinds of police, including California Highway Patrol and Marin County sheriff's deputies, heavily armed.

Police were stationed on the roof of the hospital with rifles; they were posted in the hallways, waving patients and visitors back into their rooms.

When I was wheeled out of Recovery later that day, bandaged waist to ankle, three officers and an armed sheriff frisked me.

On the news that night, there was footage of the riot. They showed my surgeon talking to reporters, indicating, with a finger to his throat, how he had saved one of the guards by sewing up a slice from ear to ear.

I watched this on television, and because it was my doctor, and because hospital patients are self-absorbed, and because I was drugged, I thought the surgeon was talking about me. I thought that he was saying, "Well, she's dead. I'm announcing it to her in her bed."

The psychiatrist I saw at the surgeon's referral said that the feeling was a common one. She said that victims of trauma who have not yet assimilated the trauma often believe they are dead and do not know it.

The great white sharks in the waters near my home attack one to seven people a year. Their primary victim is the abalone diver. With abalone steaks at thirty-five dollars a pound and going up, the Department of Fish and Game expects the shark attacks to show no slackening.

THE MOST GIRL PART OF YOU

Jack "Big Guy" Fitch is trying to crack his teeth. He swishes a mouthful of ice water, then straightaway throws back slugs of hot coffee.

"Like in Antarctica," he says, where, if you believe what Big Guy tells you, the people are forever cracking their teeth when they come in from the cold and gulp their coffee down.

I believe what Big Guy tells you. I'm his partner in crime, so I'm chewing on the shaved ice, too. I mean, someone that good-looking tells you what to do, you pretty much do what he says.

Big Guy (he is so damn big!) can make you do anything. He made us become blood brothers—brothers, even though I am a girl—back when we were clumsy little dopes playing with jacks. He got a sewing needle and was going to stick our fingers, until I chickened out. I pointed to the sore on his elbow and the abrasions on my knee, and, in fact, what we became was scab brothers.

But this business with the teeth—I say Big Guy is asking for it. He hasn't done something like this since the seventh grade when he ate a cigarette for a dollar. Now when he brushes his teeth at night, he says he treats the gums like the cuticle of a nail. He says he pushes them back with the hard bristles of the brush, laying the enamel clear.

This is a new Big Guy, a bafflement to us all. The old one trimmed the perforated margins from sheets of stamps. He kept a chart posted beside his bed that showed how his water intake varied from day to day. The old Big Guy ate sandwiches with a knife and fork. He wore short-sleeved shirts!

That was before his mother died. She died eight days ago. She did it herself. Big Guy showed me the rope burns in the beam of the ceiling. He said, "Any place I hang myself is home." In the movie version, that is where his father would have slapped him.

But of course his father did not—didn't slap him, didn't even hear him. Although Big Guy's father has probably heard what Big Guy says about the Cubs. It's the funniest thing he can imagine; it's what he doesn't have to imagine, because his father really said it when he had to tell his son what the boy's mother had done.

"And what's more—" his father had said.

It may have been the sheer momentum of bad news, because in the vast thrilling silence after Big Guy heard the news, his father had added, "And what's more, the Cubs lost."

"So you see," Big Guy says these days about matters large and small, "it's not as if the Cubs lost."

Any minute now he could say it again—here, between the swishing and gulping, in the round red booth of the airport coffee shop, with his tired, traveling grandparents sitting across the table. They flew in for the services, and they are flying home today. Big Guy drove so fast that now we have time to kill. He thinks the posted speed limit is what you can't go *below*. He has just earned a learner's permit, so he drives every chance he gets. I have six months on Big Guy; this makes me the adult in the eyes of the DMV.

The grandfather orders breakfast from the plastic menu. He says he will have "the ranch-fresh eggs, crisp bacon, and fresh-squeezed orange juice." Big Guy finds this excruciating. More so when his grandmother reads from the menu aloud.

"What about the golden French toast with maple syrup?" she says. "Jack, honey, how about the Belgian waffle?"

Before his grandmother can say "flapjacks" instead of "pancakes," Big Guy signals the waitress and points to what he wants on the menu.

The rest of us order. Then the grandfather addresses his grandson. "So," he says. He says, "So, what do you say?"

"What?" says Big Guy. "Oh. I don't know. I don't know what I say."

The past few days have seen us in many a bistro. It hasn't been easy for Big Guy. His grandfather is always trying to take waitresses into his confidence, believing they will tell him the truth about what is good that day. Big Guy finds this excruciating. He says, "Gramps, have some dignity—snub them."

But his grandfather goes on, asking, with equal gravity, for more coffee and what Big Guy plans to do after high school.

Big Guy heads for a glass of water. *Ice* water. Then his hand moves in slow motion (this for my benefit) toward the refilled cup of coffee.

"Like in Egypt," he says, an aside, a reference to my telling him how Egyptians used to split stone—how they tunneled under a boulder and chipped a narrow fissure in the underside of the rock. How they lit a fire there, let it slow-burn for several days. How, when they poured cold water on top of the rock, the thing cracked clean as lightning.

We will have to eat quickly if the grandparents are going

to make their flight. While we wait for the return of the grandfather's new best friend, he teases his grandson about something that happened yesterday, something that Big Guy found excruciating. The grandfather says, "Come on, Jack, what's wrong with talking in elevators?"

For that matter, *I* could say it. I could catch my friend's eye, and *I* could be the one to say, "He's right. Look here, it's not as if the Cubs lost."

Big Guy is the person I tell everything to. In exchange for my confessions, Big Guy tells me secrets which I can't say what they are or else they wouldn't be our secrets.

Sewing is one of the secrets between us. Only Big Guy knows how considerably I had to cheat to earn the Girl Scout merit badge in sewing. It's a fact that my seamstress badge is glued to the green cotton sash.

So it had to be a joke when Big Guy asked me to teach him to sew. I cannot baste a facing or tailor-tack a dart, but I can thread the goddamn needle and achieve a fairly even running stitch. It was the running stitch I taught Big Guy; he picked it up faster than I ever did. He practiced on a square of stiff blue denim, and by "practiced" I mean that Big Guy did it once.

That was a week ago today, or, to put it another way, it was the day after Mrs. Fitch did it. Now I am witness to her son's seamsmanship, to the use that he has put his skill to.

He met me at the door to his room with one hand held behind his back. I had to close my eyes to create suspense before he brought his hand forward. I opened my eyes, and that's when my stomach grabbed.

Where I think he has sewn two fingers together, I see that

it is both worse than that and not as bad. On the outer edge of his thumb, stitched into the very skin, my name is spelled out in small block print. It is spelled out in tight blue thread. My name is sewn into the skin of his hand!

Big Guy shows me that he still holds the threaded needle. In my presence, he completes the final stitch, guiding the needle slowly. I watch the blue thread that trails like a vein and turns milky as it tunnels through the bloodless calloused skin.

I can't sew, but my mother you would swear had majored in Home Ec. She favors a shirtwaist dress for at-home, and she calls clothes "garments." She makes desserts with names like Apple Brown Betty, and when she serves them, usually with a whipped topping product, she says, "M.I.K.," which abbreviation means, "More in Kitchen."

Big Guy is in thrall to her, to her tuna fish sandwiches on soft white bread, to her pink lemonade from frozen concentrate cans. He likes to horrify my mother by telling her what he would otherwise be eating: salt sandwiches, for example, or Fizzies and Space Food Sticks.

Big Guy is a welcome guest. At my house, he is the man of the house—the phrase my mother uses. My father's been dead for most of my life. We are more of a family at these lunches and dinners where, once again, the man of the house is at the head of the table.

Big Guy cooks corn by placing the opened can on the burner. For breakfast, he tells my mother, he pours milk into the cardboard boxes of Kellogg's miniature assortment. Since his mother died I have seen him steam a cucumber, thinking it was zucchini. That's the kind of thing that turns my heart right over.

One thing he *can* make is a melted cheese sandwich, open-faced and melted under the broiler. It's what he brought to his mother for lunch when she was sick. He brought her two months' worth of melted cheese.

Big Guy says he brought her one that day.

"The last thing I said to her," Big Guy remembers, "was, 'Mom, guess what kids at school have?' I told her, 'Sunglasses,' and she said, 'Save your money.'"

Big Guy wanted to know, What about me?

"You were there," I remind him. "Remember about her hair?"

The last thing I had said to Mrs. Fitch was that I liked her hair. Big Guy had accused me of trying to get in good, but it was true—I did like her hair.

Later—it's a long story how—Big Guy got a copy of the coroner's report. The coroner described Mrs. Fitch's auburn hair as being "worn in a female fashion."

I'm doing my homework in bed, drinking ginger ale, feeling a little woopsy. I'm taking a look at a book on French grammar because is there anything cooler than talking in a foreign language? (*"Dites-moi,"* Big Guy says to me whenever I have a problem.)

I turn the page and see that Big Guy has been there first. In addition to reading my mail, he writes in the margins of my books, usually the number of shopping days left until his birthday.

Here in the French grammar, there is no telling why, Big Guy has written, "Dots is spots up close. Spots is dots far away."

I read this, and then there he is in my room. Big Guy can

do that—walk into my bedroom when I am in the bed. Years ago, at school, the girls were forced to watch a film called *The Most Girl Part of You.* I had gone home and told my mother that Jack and I weren't doing anything. My mother, who hadn't asked if we *were,* had said, "More's the pity."

In other words, it is all my mother can do to keep from dimming the lights for us.

The truth is—it does something to me, seeing him in my bedroom.

Big Guy does the female thing in a mood—goes shopping, or changes the part in his hair. So when I see his hair is puffed and no doubt painful at the roots for being brushed in another direction, I am tipped off.

I don't have to ask.

"No need to go to Antarctica," he says, and smiles a phony smile so I can see where his front tooth has been broken off on the diagonal.

"From *ice* water?" I say.

Big Guy says his bike collided with a garbage truck. "Actually," he says, "it wasn't an accident."

"And speaking of Antarctica," he says, to change the subject, "did you know that no matter how hungry an Eskimo gets, he will never eat a penguin?"

"Why is that?"

Big Guy, triumphant: "Because Eskimos live at the North Pole, and penguins live at the *South* Pole!"

And then he is gone, gone downstairs to eat more funny food, to fix himself a glass of Fizzies, or, if they have stopped *making* Fizzies, powdered dry Kool-Aid on a wet licked finger.

I see his schoolbooks where he left them on my dresser; I see my chance.

I skip the texts and make for his spiral notebook, there to

leave searing commentary in the margins. I find handwriting which only after a moment becomes the words that I am reading.

Big Guy has written: "If we had trimmed the cat's claws before she snagged the bedspread? If we'd had French toast for breakfast instead of eggs? If we had gone to the movies instead of Dad being tired?"

The bottom half of the page is filled with inky abstract drawings. On the next page he continues: "Am I thinking the wrong things? Should I wonder, instead, what took you so long?"

I reason that if he left it here, he wanted me to see it.

Big Guy takes me to a party the same day he goes to the dentist. There are refreshments for an hour, then the lights go out in the basement and the records start to play.

Big Guy says, "May I challenge you to a dance?"

I move into his arms—it is the first time we have danced—and the hand that is at the small of my back catches as it slides across the silk of my good new dress. I don't have to look to know what it is. It's the dry, jagged skin from where he pulled my threaded name out of the place where he had sewn it.

Big Guy leads me to the side of the room where a black light turns our white clothes purple. The black light does something else, I notice. When Big Guy talks, it turns the capped tooth dingy gray. Another girl notices; she says that is why you never see a black light used in Hollywood.

"Get it?" she says.

This is the birth of vanity for my date. Big Guy says it's time to go, and if I want to go with him, I can. Of course I do—it's so cheap to leave with someone who is not the person you came with!

To show that I can give it as well as I can take it, I say, "Big Guy, come on, it's not as if the Cubs lost."

He says, "Cut me some slack," and we get into Mr. Fitch's car. I tune in the Oldies station and mouth a Motown hit, the words of which clash ridiculously with Big Guy's and my frame of reference. When I stop knowing enough of the words, I hum along with the radio.

"We hum," Big Guy informs, "because people are evolved from insects. Humming, buzzing—you see what I mean?"

This is something he probably heard the same place he learned about the cracking teeth of Antarctica.

Big Guy drives me home. Nobody is there, not that it would matter if anybody was. I sit on the couch in the family room, in the dark. Big Guy finds the Oldies station on my mother's antique Zenith. The music comes in faintly; you would have to strain to hear the words if, unlike myself, you did not know the words already.

Then it's both of us sitting in the humid dark, Big Guy buzzing along with the radio, me scratching the mosquito bites I always get. A few minutes of this and Big Guy is off to the bathroom. He comes back with a small pink bottle. He sings, "You're gonna need an ocean / of calamine lotion" as he dabs it on the hot white bites.

I tell him he ought to chill it first, so he takes the bottle into the kitchen. He opens the refrigerator, and calls me in to look.

He shows me where a moth has been drawn by the single light. Its wings beat madly in the cold air; they drag across the uncovered butter, dust the chocolate pudding, graze the lipstick smear on the open end of a milk carton.

We try to get the thing out, but it flaps behind a jar of wheat germ, and from there into the vegetable Humidrawer. At that point, Big Guy shuts the door.

"I've got another idea," he says. "Wait for me on the couch."

He comes back with a razor blade. He says, "This will take the itch out." He drags the blade twice across a bite on the back of my wrist; the tiny X turns red as blood comes up to the cut surface.

I am too amazed to say anything, so Big Guy continues, razoring Xs into bites on my legs and arms.

Now, I think—*now* we could become blood brothers.

But that is not what Big Guy is thinking, and finally I come to know it. I submit to his crude doctoring until he cuts an X into a bite on my shoulder. Suddenly he lowers his head until it isn't the blade but his mouth on my skin.

I had only been kissed once before. The fellow had made me think of those kids whose mouths cover the spigot when they drink from a fountain. When I had pulled away from him, this fellow had said, "B-plus."

Big Guy is going to kiss me.

And here is the thrill of my short life: He does.

And I see that not touching for so long was a drive to the beach with the windows rolled up so the waves feel that much colder.

When I can get my bearings, I make light of what could happen. I say the cool thing I've been saving up to say; I say, "Stop it, Big Guy. Stop it some more."

And then he says the cool thing *he* has been saving, or, being Big Guy, has made up on the spot. He says, "I always give a woman what she wants—whether she wants it or not."

And that is the end of the joking around; we get it out of

our systems. We take the length of the couch, squirming like maggots in ashes.

I'm not ready for this, but here is what I come up with: He's a boy without a mother.

I look beyond my own hesitation; I find my mother, Big Guy's father. We are on this couch for our newly and lastingly widowed parents as well.

Big Guy and I are still dressed. I am bleeding through my clothes from the razored bites when Big Guy pushes his knee up between my legs.

"If you have to get up," he says, "don't."

I play back everything that has happened to me before this. I want to ask Big Guy if he is doing this, too. I want him to know what it clearly seems to me: that if it's true your life flashes past your eyes before you die, then it is also the truth that your life rushes forth when you are ready to start to truly be alive.

RAPTURE OF THE DEEP

I was the one they sent when it was Halloween night and Miss Locey couldn't move. I am not a nurse. I am barely a typist. But she didn't need me to type, or to take the shorthand I don't have, either. She hired me from an agency at an hourly rate to hand out candy on Halloween night.

Because look how it looked: a car in the driveway, a light on upstairs. But nobody answers the door. I know what I would have done as a child if there was somebody home on Halloween night who did not bother to answer the door. I would have come back later with shaving cream and eggs, with toilet paper and friends.

Even if she lay in her room in the dark, there was still the car in the drive.

And there were worse things even than shaving cream and eggs. What about "leaners"? Kids would fill a trash can with water, with worse than water, and lean it against your door so that when you opened the door, you flooded your Persian rugs.

Miss Locey had thought of all of these things. She said she feared a "lawn job"—where teenage boys drive a car across your yard and leave deep ruts when they spin out and drive away.

I come from a quieter place. I told her what we ever did

was to pack an extra mask so we could visit the same house twice, a house that gave Mars bars, for example. Even then, I told Miss Locey, there were those who saw us coming. The man who owned an ice cream franchise gave out Flying Saucers so if we came back for more, they would melt in the bottom of our bags.

We were talking in Miss Locey's bedroom. It smelled of new paint; the walls were a shade of deep raspberry.

"The Pepto-Abysmal Room," Miss Locey said. "It's never the color on the test card, is it? Always it turns out—bolder."

Miss Locey reached for a bottle of pills it turned out she couldn't reach. I offered to get them for her, but I didn't say her name when I did. She was only a few years older than myself. But she didn't say to call her by whatever was her first name, so I didn't, when I talked to her, call her anything.

"I was sure I was pregnant," Miss Locey was saying. "So I struck a bargain with God: 'Dear God,' I prayed, 'let me get my period and I'll do exercises the rest of my life.' Two days later, I had to keep up my side. I climbed up on that exercise bike, and right away threw out my back," Miss Locey said.

When she reached for the pills—it was a muscle relaxant she was taking—I saw Miss Locey's hands. She wore a ring on every finger. On some fingers she wore two. Not just bands, but stones, rings with jewels.

It was the age-old question Miss Locey put next. From her bed of pain she ran it by me—if you took only half a pill, did it work full-strength for half as long, or half-strength for the regular time?

I was a girl from an agency. I told her just as strong for half as long, but the way that I said it said what I thought, which was, Your guess is as good as mine.

"If I *had* been pregnant, I'd be having it in December."

Computation had Miss Locey laid up for nearly seven months. Was this woman a malingerer? Was she hurt worse than she said?

Miss Locey extended an index finger wearing an oval stone. "Turquoise is the birthstone for December," she said. "It's a sympathetic stone; it will save you from suffering a fall—it will crack itself instead."

She turned the ring around on her finger. "Turquoise turns pale when the wearer is sick. It loses its color completely when you die."

I told her I was born in the pearl month. But the ring that I wear does not have a pearl.

"On the plus side," Miss Locey said, "I don't have to go to a costume party."

I was back upstairs after the steady trick-or-treaters had slowed to the older kids every half hour or so. A horror movie, the sound off, was on TV.

"A friend of mine called to ask where he could find a wheelchair," Miss Locey said. "He wanted to go as George Wallace."

She said, "This is the fellow who had such a disappointment last year. He dressed up in pyjamas and carried a bottle of Diet Pepsi. He was supposed to be Brian Wilson, but everybody guessed Hugh Hefner."

Miss Locey lifted one knee to her chest, and held it there to a count of ten. Her knuckles went white above the rings.

"A ring for every hand on my finger," Miss Locey said. She corrected herself with a comic take. "It's just that I'm so relaxed," she said.

She let go of her knee and let her leg slide down.

"The rings belonged to my mother," Miss Locey said. "They did before I tricked her out of them."

She waved a jeweled hand slowly in the air as though she were helping nail polish to dry.

"My mother had the hands for them," Miss Locey said. "Long fingers and almond nails, no half-moons, no veins showed in her hands. My mother spoke five languages.

"One day I asked her how to say, 'You may have all of my rings' in Spanish. When she told me, I asked her how to say it in French. I made her say 'You may have all of my rings' in all five languages.

"My mother was a sport," Miss Locey said. "She gave me the pearls on the spot, the rest when she died."

Still flat on her back, Miss Locey held her arms straight out in front of her. It made her look like she was rising from a coffin to go haunting. Instead, she took inventory of her mother's rings and their powers, how garnet cheered the heart and strengthened the mind, how the emerald chased away stupidity and reconciled quarreling lovers, how her pearls, if ground up and boiled with meat, would cure a fever and chills. She wore a zircon, "an inferior diamond," to procure riches and honor. The red coral cured indigestion, is what she said.

The stones Miss Locey didn't wear were opal and onyx. The former, she said, was fatal to love, and onyx, the color of darkness, kept you awake.

I was thinking I preferred this to a horoscope when Miss Locey described her favorite.

"Topaz," she said. "It cures madness and brightens the wit. Powdered and put in wine, it cures insomnia. It was used by mariners without a moon," she said.

That's when I felt I should have been born in the topaz month. "Used by mariners without a moon."

"Let me see," Miss Locey said and reached for the hammered gold band that is the only ring I wear.

I didn't slip it off—I don't take this ring off—but I let her take my hand. She turned it over, so the palm was up.

"It's dented here and here," she said. "It's what—eighteen karat?"

I told her the dents were from a man's teeth. From where he bit the gold to show me how soft, then bit my finger, to show me how soft.

The ring was a gift from that man, I said. But it was never a wedding ring because he died before getting married was something we could do. On vacation, on an island, he took up scuba diving. He did it without supervision, although he had never done it before. He went down deeper than you are ever supposed to go; that is what made him giddy, I was told—and why he didn't think to come back up.

I told Miss Locey that I still needed to hear from the God that had betrayed me. An explanation would not be enough. An apology would not be enough. I needed for that God to look up to me, I said. I needed for him to have to tilt his head way back to look up to me, exposing his throat.

"Maybe you should take one of these," Miss Locey said. "You don't look very relaxed."

Then I told Miss Locey the name for what had happened, what the thing that happened diving was called, that divers called it "rapture of the deep." And she said what I had always thought, which is that it's odd—it's eerie—when a bad thing has a pretty name.

She said it herself. She said, "Rapture of the deep." She said it sounded to her "like a dive into Liberace's coat, staying under too long, and coming up coughing up rubies and pearls."

She twisted her rings.

She wore stones to guard against drunkenness and fear.

The doorbell rang for the last time that night. I went downstairs. Instead of handing the kids a candy bar each, I let them scoop out a handful apiece.

Before going up to say good night, I made Miss Locey a cup of tea. I carried it upstairs, and while she wrote out a check, I turned up the volume on a movie-of-the-week.

Miss Locey thanked me for coming and asked me to get the porch light on my way out.

I did one other thing on my way out first.

With the habitual kleptomania of temporary employment, I dropped the remaining Halloween candy into my purse, alongside boxes of paper clips and refills of Scotch tape.

I was home before I remembered where I had left the remote control, that it was beyond Miss Locey's reach. According to *TV Guide,* Miss Locey's channel went off at two o'clock. If she could sleep through the static, Miss Locey would wake at five to a televised exercise class. She would open her eyes to women in colored tights, all still working out their sides of deals with God.

DU JOUR

The first three days are the worst, they say, but it's been two weeks, and I'm still waiting for those first three days to be over.

One day into the program, I realized the only thing that made me smart was nicotine. Now I can't plan a trip from the bed to the bathroom. I don't find the front door 50 percent of the time. In my head there's a broken balcony I fall off of when I speak.

But better to be alive and well and not thinking than thinking and smoking and dead.

That is the point I've reached: Stop smoking, or else. The point is also: Stop smoking, or lose my job.

I make soup at a place that has fifty-two different kinds. I've made all fifty-two of them at one time or another; lately I only do the specialty of the day. I make Mulligatawny and Senegalese—the kind you would take a taste of for the sound of their names.

The owner called me over one day and showed me the bowls his customers had sent back. He said, "It's the seasoning, babe. It's the red pepper ratio."

I knew I was in the wrong on this; let's face it—three

packs a day will do it to your taste buds. But I don't take criticism, so the next minute I tore into it with Mr. Licalsi.

"So what?" I screamed. "So what! So they don't like the fucking gazpacho!"

And Mr. Licalsi, he said, "Jesus, girl—and you *eat* with that mouth?"

Sometimes I lose it personality-wise because I don't know what to do instead of smoke. I'm gaining weight of course; everybody does. But not because I'm eating more of anything. I'm gaining weight because I've stopped coughing. Coughing was exercise for me.

The weight problem is how I met Mrs. Wynn. She's in the weight-control section of the program, and I saw her at the weekly weigh-in. How could I miss her? She was loud and big, and she wore a powder blue T-shirt with navy letters that said LIFE IS UNCERTAIN—EAT DESSERT FIRST. I heard her explain bariatrics to another compulsive eater, how women gain from the bottom up and lose from the top down.

Mrs. Wynn and I got to talking because there we both were. She told me this was her first serious diet attempt since Metrecal was introduced in the 1960s. *That* had been a bust, she said, because it hadn't been clear to a consumer such as herself that Metrecal was what you had *instead* of lunch and dinner.

The program that is monitored at the clinic was guaranteed to leave you a broken husk, she said, "but a *thin* broken husk."

Mrs. Wynn is a singer in a supper club. Her husband owns the Club Volare, where three nights a week, after the band that plays Italian favorites, after the Greek dancer and the Bronx/Israeli torch singer, after the belly dancer and the bouzouki-player's solo, after the multitalented Spanish girl and

MURDER

"Something something something never / Love for an hour is love forever."

If that's true, I thought, then we're in business.

I showed the inscription to Jean, there in the used books store, and she said, "Maybe we should have married Jim."

Jean had five boyfriends, all named Jim. Aren't two of the Jims best friends? I asked. No, she said, this is a whole new crop of Jims. Isn't one of the Jims a scientist? I asked. She said I must be thinking of the Jim who had a Ph.D.

The Jim she thought we should have married was the Jim that got away.

Jean said, "Here," and handed me a newer used book, a book that, in its day, had been a best-seller.

She said, "This book gave me the will to live and have fun." She said, "I read this book and went right out and got myself asked out by a man—a man who liked me," she said, "and who didn't even have another girlfriend."

Jean and I are bridesmaids. At last night's rehearsal dinner, the bride spoke to us in the plural. She said, "You've been going ninety in a locked garage." She said, "We've got to get you out on the open road."

By "the open road," the bride did not mean the Stretch-mark. The Stretchmark is more of a locked garage.

In a biker bar called the Stretchmark Cafe, the tables of loudly muscled men ignore the strippers and leer at slides of choppers projected on the cafe walls. A chair in front of the stage is where the gals lob their T-shirts, bought in Laguna at Big Wave Dave's. The house cat wears a turquoise metal-flake collar and runs from the strippers' children, who are, quite naturally, back in the dressing room, playing slash fighting.

The Stretchmark is across from the used books store. Every time Jean and I make our entrance, the bartender sings in a Bugs Bunny voice, "I dream of Jeannie, she's a light brown hare."

Jean, the flutter of every male heart.

The bartender also has a crush on Sister Marianne, the former nun who moved to Phoenix for her health, then moved right back when she heard that the tarantulas there can jump eight feet, that some of them have landed on the saddle of a horse.

Sister Marianne, when her mind is someplace else, is not aware of the sound she makes there sitting at the bar—like a sprinkler kicker head going *kk-kk-kk-kk-shooshooshooshooshoo.*

Sister has her eye on the fellow from the post office. When you buy a sheet of stamps from him, he rubs the gluey side of the sheet across his hair. He says that the oil from human hair will keep the stamps from sticking to one another in your purse. It's a handy tip, and a gesture you want to remember when you go to lick a stamp.

The fellow from the post office wants to fix Jean up with his friend from downtown. I have met the friend from downtown. He tried to sell me some sort of coin that he said was owned by Alexander the Great and Genghis Khan and Bobby

Kennedy—"Only twenty dollars—okay, make it eighteen-fifty."

I warned Jean that the postal worker's friend was arrested one time for whipping taxicabs with a child's jump rope, the wooden handles rapping the windows and chipping paint off the hoods.

"Dust him," I said.

Jean could take him or leave him, she said, and I say it is a good way to be.

The day of the wedding, before a S.W.A.T. team of beauticians arrived to do the bride, the young son from the groom's first marriage gave his new stepmother a picture he had drawn of a scowling Green Beret with a sword through his flaming head.

The bride fitted the drawing into her vanity mirror. She looked beyond it and made a wedding face.

For her second time around, the bride chose ivory tea-length lace, better flowers and better food, better music and a better man. In the wedding suite, a.k.a. the bride's parents' bedroom, the bride reached for her earrings; Jean reminded her to put her jewelry on last so she wouldn't snag the weight-less Belgian lace.

The bride's first husband divided his time between Davis, San Pedro, and Encinitas. Say the word "home" and he could not stop talking about his rent, about the place he had for $37.50 when it was twenty years ago, and then, when the new owner raised his rent to $60 there at the top of Emerald Bay, he could not stop himself from telling us that he had said, "Fuck this," and moved out.

Say the word "home" and you can watch the bride's heart drop through the floor.

The new groom is like a Force-O-Nature. But the bride plays down his looks, his size. "It's about trust," she says. "And—yeah," she says, "it's about—who *knows* what it's about. We just go for these damn walks and listen to coyotes."

I dipped a finger in the prenup champagne and dabbed the cold fizz behind my ears, back of where Jean had pierced them with a kilt pin back in school.

Jean said, "Men." She said, "They hate you at first. But all you have to do is be funny and sad and tall and thin and short and fat and wear them down, wear them down."

"You can look on the bright side," I said, "but think of the men who have unexplainably fled after they got to know us a little."

The bride's parents' dog came in just then and offered a frantic display of devotion, leaping about our legs.

"I used to think I wanted to be loved like that," I said. "But I don't want to be loved like that."

Pushing the dog from her skirt, Jean said, "Would it help if you thought it was insincere?"

The bride, gowned, was called away for pictures.

Jean let a strap of her pink dress fall. "Oh, Jim—please don't," she said in a breathy voice.

"Oh, Jim—please," I said, all in my throat.

"Oh, Jim—" Jean said.

"Oh," we both said together.

Jean recalled the time she asked the bartender about Sister Marianne, if he had ever considered the *M* word, and the bartender had said back, "Murder?"

"Imagine that it's you," Jean said to me. "Imagine it's you that is getting married today."

I do.

I imagine myself waking in some Jim's bed.

His telephone rings. I imagine it is a woman calling, and because I am the wife, I answer in the voice that says, I've had it ten times today and *I live here.*

This is what marriage means to me.

THE DAY I HAD EVERYTHING

When Mrs. Lawton phoned in the threat, the threat was already a fact. Her estranged husband said that he could hear it in her voice. So he called for an ambulance, scheduled an appointment with the city's finest doctor, left his office early, and drove to the Lawton country home, where he closed up the house and boarded the dogs, then returned to the city and his hospitalized wife.

Mr. Lawton brought Mrs. Lawton flowers—freesia and yellow iris—and he brought her a bill for five hundred dollars, plus the cost of the opera tickets he had been unable to use, plus another hundred dollars for what he called same-day service.

At home a week later, Mrs. Lawton received callers. She laid an alarming buffet of Budweiser and crullers, and answered the question on everyone's mind—whether or not she had paid her husband's bill.

I heard Mrs. Lawton's story at the weekly meeting. My friend Lee brought me, six months after the Club was formed.

Lee died ten years ago; she can't stop talking about it. No reason *to* stop; that's what the Club is for, she explained.

When Lee and I got to Mrs. Lawton's house, the other members were already in Mrs. Lawton's living room. The other members were women, too. Lee told me there had used to be a man who came, a man who had died on the operating table. When it would come his turn, the man would laugh nervously and say, "I can't tell you what it was like—I slept right through it." After a couple of times of coming, Lee said, the man had not come back.

I watched a youngish woman with shiny black hair, who was leaning over Mrs. Lawton's baby grand, pick out a slow-as-a-dirge version of "Will You Still Love Me Tomorrow?" rather pointedly, it turned out, for, as Lee filled me in, the woman at the piano had just been deserted when she told her intended about the relapse and that this time she was going to really lose one, maybe even both.

I walked over and stood to one side of the piano in an attitude of listening. The woman looked up and past me, out the opened window.

"The devil is beating his wife," she said.

It was a sunny day, and a rain shower had begun, and I had not heard that expression—that explanation—since I was a child.

Outside was the kind of garden people want for summer weddings. I reached out the living room window and picked a plum from a tree. The sun made me squint, while the rain was cold on my wrist.

The plum I left on the windowsill. It reminded me of a time when I had not been dying, but had thought that I was, from nausea that ruled until I sucked the pulp from a dozen umeboshi plums, those pickled pits that are packed in glass jars and shipped to this country from Japan.

"How did you die?" the woman at the piano asked.

"Me?" I said. "Oh, no. Well, I mean, I got a divorce. Talk about *dying*."

I can be so lame.

"I was engaged," the woman at the piano said listlessly, and then said nothing.

Who knew what to say to that? Sometimes I play dumb when it would be so much better to—*be* dumb?

There was a bang of chords as the black-and-white cat jumped up on the black and white keys he was using as a launching pad to get himself onto the coffee table where he was going to skid into the tray of refreshments.

Mrs. Lawton looked in from the kitchen. "Lee's friend," she said to me, "will you keep Steinway out of the beignets?"

The women took their places on Mrs. Lawton's tailored white couch and side chairs as Mrs. Lawton carried in a tray of Mimosas. When the drinks had been handed out, Lee was the one who spoke first.

"Many men named Pablo entered my life this week."

It was always Lee saying, "Politics? *P.U.* Can't we talk about men?"

Or it was Lee saying, "Religion? *P.U.* Where are the boys?"

That was during Religious Emphasis Week, when ministers in the business of bagging souls would come to the schools and pass around, in jars, the brain of an alcoholic and the lungs of a smoker, show photographs from prom-night wrecks, speak diatribes against "jungle music," and screen a film advertised as Triple-X for attendance but which was, in fact, *The Birth of Triplets* and too disgusting to even neck in the dark to.

It was around that time, back in Colorado, that, until a short time before, I had last seen Lee, heading into a cemetery after midnight, there to make time on the grave of Alfred Packer, the state's famed cannibal. So when I got Lee's message, fifteen years after Lee had dropped out, I called back right away. I thought, This can only be good or bad news. The news, as Lee proceeded to tell the Club, was tango lessons, and what those lessons had yielded: a fiancé known as Pablo. Pablo the fellow taker-of-lessons, as distinguished from Pablo or Pablo, the instructors.

"He's very, as we say in psychiatry, 'inappropriate,'" Lee said.

"But he's nice to you?"—the words another woman put in Lee's mouth.

"He's nice to anyone who's around him," Lee said. "I just happen to fall into that category a lot.

"We don't speak the same language," Lee went on, "so we *assume* that we like each other. Cuts out a lot of the 'What did you mean by that?'s."

As Lee went on, there in Mrs. Lawton's living room, I recalled Lee's first husband, the one she had left school to elope with. Lee, the girl who was always very something I'm not, married a man who did not like dogs.

"Do you see," Lee was saying, "what can happen when you take your body and push it out the door?"

I saw the woman at the piano turn around to offer Lee a grim smile.

"Oh, Jean," Lee said to the woman on the piano bench, "come take a lesson. Come meet all these Pablos and Raouls."

And then Jean told a story about the man she would have married, about a dinner they had shared, the point of which seemed to me to be that things get worse before they get really terrible.

"I had just placed my order," Jean told the Club, "and Larry went, 'Ew.' '*That* was fast,' I said, and Larry said, 'What? What was fast?' I said, 'Why, only a week ago you would have said, "What a delightful selection,"'" Jean said.

"Next thing," said Jean, "I'm telling Larry what is really on my mind, that things with us are Out of sight, Out of mind, and he says to me, '*Please* don't talk in clichés—it's so not-you you wouldn't believe it,'" Jean said.

"And I thought, He knows me," Jean recalled. "He knows that clichés are not me."

Jean said she thought she might still hear from Larry but that hoping he would call was like the praying you do after the bowling ball has left your hand.

Several of us reached for our drinks.

"And the guy still breathes?" Lee said to the room.

Another woman said to Jean, "I'm reminding you that you asked me to remind you that if things got nasty, I was supposed to remind you that at first you found Larry a little bit boring."

Jean looked genuinely pleased. She said, "Larry is the kind of guy who says, Did I ever tell you about the time I was attacked by a pack of sled dogs in Alaska? No? I was in Fairbanks at the time, he starts out," Jean said, "and two years later you find out it was *one* sled dog and it was a puppy.

"And his family, my *God*," Jean said. "These are people so boring it would have to come from a gene."

I listened as Jean explained how scientists had already isolated a gene for shyness, so why not a gene for being boring?

"The deeply boring give themselves away first by the exchange of facts," Jean said. "It's a family reunion. It's been five years. Relatives walk in. 'Hey, how are you? How'd you get here?' 'We took 101 south . . .'"

"I just know he is going to call you," said a woman who had not spoken before.

"We'll see," Jean said.

"We've seen," said Mrs. Lawton.

* * *

The party was planned for a week before Jean was scheduled to go into the hospital. Mrs. Lawton canceled the male stripper, having had a brainstorm in the night. Mrs. Lawton telephoned the members of the Club and asked each woman to bring a piece of lingerie. She gave out Jean's measurements over the phone.

"You remember the last time she went in?" Mrs. Lawton said to Lee. "She wore that old white faux-quilted robe that looked like a panty liner?"

Mrs. Lawton instructed Lee to buy something in satin— tap pants, maybe, or what she called a "pop-up bra."

We learned that she had made Patsy Kendrick the designated photographer (she would have to stay in focus in the face of white wine spritzers) and told her to bring a jar of Vaseline to smear, centerfold-style, on the lens.

Mrs. Lawton had figured the Club would have to get Jean tanked to agree to the pictures. But after only one spritzer, Jean was lounging on Mrs. Lawton's sofa in a champagne teddy and marabou-trimmed satin high-heeled slippers. She slipped a strand of pearls into her mouth, made as though biting them, and pouted for Patsy Kendrick.

"This one is for the surgeon," Jean said and dropped a strap, exposing the breast she was going to lose.

"I was once given a teddy," Lee said. "A man I had been out with only once gave me half a dozen teddys. Some were banded with Alençon lace, some were embroidered with seed pearls. I know I should have returned them in a huff," Lee said, "but you should have seen them. So I *kept* them in a huff."

"Don't shoot me from that angle!" Jean cried out. I saw

her motion Patsy Kendrick to aim from above, not below. Jean sucked in her stomach. "Three months in a gym and I'd weigh what I lied on my driver's license," she said.

None of the women seemed to be expected back home. The luncheon was heading into its fifth hour when our pixillated hostess told us the story of the love of her life, which was not, it turned out, Mr. Lawton.

It seemed to be a story she had told before because for one thing it had a title: "The Day I Had Everything."

Mrs. Lawton began. "The man told me a story about the day he had everything. He was eight years old, he said, and was spending, in a hospital bed, what his parents believed was the last day of his life. And his parents brought from home every one of his toys, plus new ones bought for him just for that day, everything the eight-year-old boy had ever wanted.

"The next day, the man told me, the doctor said he was not going to perish, after all; that he instead had another, a highly contagious, disease. The boy would live, the doctor said, and then ordered all the infected toys destroyed.

"'One day I had everything,' the man said, 'and the next day I had nothing.' He said this as though he were giving instruction.

"'But your life,' I said to the man. 'You had nothing but your *life*,'" Mrs. Lawton said.

She waited a beat, then went on.

"Now, I wish that that man had told me something that began, 'No one else knows this . . . ' so that I could tell the thing to every one of you. What is the point of these hot collisions if not to be able to prove you were there?

"Listen to what he said to me," Mrs. Lawton said. "He said he almost fainted from not touching me," she said. "He said that to me the first time I saw him and the last time I saw him. The day was the same," Mrs. Lawton said. "The day I had everything."

I wish I could say smart things just by saying them. Because Mrs. Lawton's story made me feel something. But the moment was lost; the story seemed to be a sort of cue, or simply a conversation stopper. The Club members were on their feet, not exactly reeling, but neither were they moving with dispatch toward the door.

Jean, the soft-porn guest of honor, was changing in the open into another of her gifts, a black lace camisole and matching tap pants. Her face was flushed. She no longer looked as though she found the world intolerably apocalyptic.

I heard a perfectly groomed blond woman talking to Jean while she was undressing. "A facial didn't seem like enough," the blond woman was saying, "so I pointed myself toward the jeweler. When people ask me how I'm doing, I say, Look at these pearls! Later," I heard the blond woman say, "I put the necklace on the living room floor because what I really need is a new Oriental."

In the kitchen, I happened onto a sort of "You think *that's* bad" contest. "Him?" a woman said. "The only book he ever read was the first chapter of *Iacocca*."

In a little while it was just Lee and me and Jean and Mrs. Lawton. Jean was talking about Larry again, and looking the worse for it. "I pictured us stewing apples at Christmas, all that cozy Currier and Ives shit . . . all that time thinking, What we have—love sometimes passes for it, when I should have been thinking, Love passes."

Mrs. Lawton told Jean to tell Lee and me the last thing

Larry had said before he left, and Jean said that his last words to her had been, "Everything I did with you was love."

"That was awfully sweet of that fucking idiot to say," Lee said.

That cracked Jean up, and then she seemed to think of something that cracked her up more. What she thought of, she shared with the three of us, and I ran straight to the bathroom and wrote down what she said; I wanted to be able to pass it along.

Jean was trying to describe what she felt it would be like to be married to Larry; she said it would be like staying in a bad hotel and being forced to send postcards of it to your friends with arrows pointing to "my room."

I'm glad I wrote that down.

When I came back into Mrs. Lawton's living room, the women had recovered. Lee's mascara had smeared. Everyone turned to me.

"What kind of luck are you having, Lee's friend?" This from Jean.

It came back to me why the Club had given Jean this party, and I felt ashamed for my answer. But I told Jean the truth.

"I met someone," I said. "I'm happy. I'm probably in love."

Jean didn't know me, and Mrs. Lawton didn't know me, but that didn't stop them from shrieking with glee. Mrs. Lawton asked how we met. I told an unexceptional story.

"And he called you?" Jean said.

"He called me that night," I said.

"Tell me everything," Jean said, moving closer. "Start from ring-ring-ring."

TO THOSE OF YOU WHO MISSED YOUR CONNECTING FLIGHTS OUT OF O'HARE

To those of you who missed your connecting flights out of O'Hare, I offer my deepest apology.

What they did I had no way of knowing they would do because the last time this happened it was handled without the fuss. The last time it happened it affected no one else—I just walked off the plane before the stewardess locked the door, and my luggage, not me, was what reached my destination.

Did I know when I walked off Flight 841 that my suitcase would have to be pulled from the plane, a black fabric suitcase the handler had to find amidst the hundreds of other bags, and all of you passengers waiting?

And how about the pilot checking the toilets for a bomb, a stewardess doing likewise in the overhead compartment above what was, for maybe two minutes, my seat—6C.

I'm right about this—it didn't used to be this way. The agents on the ground, the ones who check you in, they used to see you coming off the plane and they knew what it meant and they knew you were not to blame and the looks that they gave you said, Better luck next time, and We hope you try again.

Now they are angry. The looks and accusations—making hundreds of passengers late!

That is when I told them that my husband was killed in a plane crash, the one in Tenerife.

There is precedent here for a lie of this kind, or rather, a lie at this time. On a talk show once, a comic told the story: how he boarded a plane to make a headline date in Vegas, but the plane that he boarded was a plane bound for Pittsburgh. When our comic finds out, the plane has begun its slow roll into position.

This man, this comic, was able to persuade the crew to return the plane to the gate. And how did he avoid the collective wrath of the passengers? When the plane came to a stop and the walkway was stretched to the door, the comic stood up and summoned a tone of voice. "I don't know about the rest of you," he said, "but I won't take this kind of treatment from an airline!"

The comic, looking indignant, then walked off the plane.

But you, the passengers of Flight 841, I want you to know the truth.

Starting with 6B, my would-be white-knuckle neighbor, buckling tight your seat belt as if it makes any goddamned difference. I mean—Sir, let me ask you a question: Do the newspapers ever say, "Whereas the survivors—the list follows—are those who buckled their seat belts"?

I want to take you, the passengers whom I have inconvenienced, into my confidence. Because if you are like me, you know that some of us are not the world, some of us are not the children, some of us will not help make a brighter day. Some of us are the silent sufferers of a noisy disease. And that is all I have to say about fear.

But! By making yourself scarce at the nation's airports, by deciding for the grounded comfort of a train, you will find yourself traveling through the City of Spires and the cities of steel, the country's richest pasture land and the Santa Fe Trail, across the Purgatoire River near the Sangre de Cristo range—just big sky and small talk and rhyming to yourself from a catalog of sights: pale deer at dawn on the edge of a lawn.

Past low pink tamarisk and Ponderosa pine, and Shoemaker Canyon lined with cottonwood trees that are home to wild turkeys beside the narrow Mora River.

Past the Forked Lightning Ranch that was once Greer Garson's home near the Sandia ("Watermelon") Mountains—they turn bright red at sunset and the trees on the side look like seeds.

Do I sound as if I work for the railroad?

The tragedy of the settlers on Starvation Peak—the Kneeling Nuns, a formation of rock.

It cost me some money to see this. You walk off a plane and even *think* about getting a refund! You get one—one—one trip for the price of two.

A five-hour flight works out to three days and nights on land, by rail, from sea to shining sea.

You can chalk off the hours on the back of the seat ahead. But seventy-some hours will not seem so long to you if you tell yourself first: This is where I am going to be for the rest of my natural life.

AND LEAD US NOT
INTO PENN STATION

On the nicer side of not a nice street, between God Bless the Cheerful Giver and his dog, and There But for the Grace of God Go I and his dog, a wino engaged me in the following Q and A:

Miss, am I bleeding?

Yes, yes you are.

Where?

From the nose.

And the mouth?

No.

Just the nose?

Yes.

I wonder how that happened.

Everything you can think of is going on here. Plus things that you can't think of, too. Those things are going on in groups. Men who have sex with vacuum cleaners—these men are now outpatients, in therapy down the block.

Today, when a blind man walked into the bank, we handed him along to the front of the line where he ordered a BLT.

A boy on a tricycle pedals past a mother and son. "Why can't *you* ride a tricycle?" the mother says to her son. "That boy is younger than you! Why can't you even go to Harvard!"

Under a streetlight, a man and woman are talking. The man says he feels sure that the woman is going to shoot him and that he can't help but wonder what caliber she has chosen.

Women who live alone in fear of intruders call the local precinct for advice. "Keep your doorknobs highly polished," an officer tells them. "When someone breaks in, we can get clear prints."

The neighborhood drug dealer kicks out his wife. He moves in a girlfriend and the wife finds out. The wife lets herself back into the house and steals a hundred thousand dollars that the drug dealer can't report missing. The drug dealer's wife goes to India, where she sends her husband a cable: "The people here are poor so I gave them all your money."

On the occasion of a star athlete's accidental overdose, a TV reporter takes his questions to the street. "What do you learn from this?" he asks the truant boys in a vacant lot. "What does it tell you that a young athlete takes this drug and dies?"

The boys fight for the microphone until one of them grabs it away. He says, "Man, you have got to build *up* to that dose."

A man stops into a bar and rests his shopping bag on a stool. He waves the bartender over to see where inside the bag is the head of a man.

"Auction at the old wax museum," the man says. "All anyone wanted was Elvis Presley and Martin Luther King. I picked up Richard Speck here for next to nothing."

A beautiful familiar woman is escorted from a nightclub.

A visiting Southern girl says, "S'cuse me, ma'am, but aren't you a friend of my mama's back in Sumner?" "I'm Elizabeth Taylor," the woman says, "and fuck you."

A famous artist is approached by a student. "You don't remember me," the student says correctly, "but years ago you said something that changed my life. You said, 'Photography is death.' After that," says the student, "I threw out my camera. I began again. I want to thank you for changing my life."

"Leave me alone," says the artist. "Photography is life."

A man falls to the sidewalk in what looks to be an epileptic fit. A well-dressed woman throws her weight against a parking sign. When it bends to the ground, she forces a corner of the "Tow-away Zone" into the seizing man's mouth. "This way," she says, "he won't bite his tongue."

Women who are attacked phone a hotline for advice. "Don't report a rape," the women are told. "Call it indecent exposure. A guy who takes it out and doesn't do anything with it—cops figure that guy is sick."

I don't know what to say about this. *I* am as cut off from meaning and completion as all of these crippled people.

These are the things that go on around here. After a while these things add up to enough weight to wear a person down. I am wearing down.

IN THE ANIMAL SHELTER

Every time you see a beautiful woman, *someone* is tired of her, so the men say. And I know where they go, these women, with their tired beauty that someone doesn't want—these women who must live like the high Sierra white pine, there since before the birth of Christ, fed somehow by the alpine wind.

They reach out to the animals, day after day smoothing fur inside a cage, saying, "How is Mama's baby? Is Mama's baby lonesome?"

The women leave at the end of the day, stopping to ask an attendant, "Will they go to good homes?" And come back in a day or so, stooping to examine a one-eyed cat, asking, as though they intend to adopt, "How would I introduce a new cat to my dog?"

But there is seldom an adoption; it matters that the women have someone to leave, leaving behind the lovesome creatures who would never leave them, had they once given them their hearts.

AT THE GATES
OF THE ANIMAL KINGDOM

Ten candles in a fish stick tell you it's Gully's birthday. The birthday girl is the center of attention; she squints into the popping flash cubes. The black cat seems to know every smooth cat pose there is. She is burning for discovery in front of the camera.

Gully belongs to Mrs. Carlin. Mrs. Carlin has had her since the cat was six weeks old and slept on the stove, curled inside a saucepan warmed by the pilot light. Mrs. Carlin has observed every one of Gully's birthdays, wrapping the blue felt mice filled with catnip, wrapping the selection of frozen entrees from Mrs. Paul's, and photographing the birthday girl with her guests.

This year, Gully's guests include the Patterson boys, Pierson and Bret, fourteen and ten, and their cat, Bert. Though it would be more accurate to say that Mrs. Carlin and Gully are the *boys'* guests, as the party is being held in the Patterson home.

Mrs. Carlin is staying with the boys for the week that their parents are in an eastern city for Mr. Patterson's annual business conference. It is a condition of Mrs. Carlin's employment that Gully come with her. She had explained to Mrs. Patterson that one time a cat-sitter came to feed Gully, "and Gully—there is no other word for it—screamed."

After she serves Gully's birthday cake, Mrs. Carlin brings the boys their dinner. The boys examine their plates with suspicion, and then with disbelief.

Between the two halves of the sesame seed bun, where there should have been catsup on a hamburger, rare, the boys see what looks like catsup on a cassette tape. It is actually tomato sauce on a slice of sautéed eggplant.

"Didn't our mother tell you what we eat?" says Pierson, the older boy.

"We eat hamburgers," says Bret. "We like hamburgers and smashed potatoes."

Mrs. Carlin tells them that *she* is making the rules now. She says, "Meat's no treat for those you eat."

She waits to let this sink in. "While I am looking after you," she tells the boys, "we will eat nothing with parents."

The boys look at each other so that Mrs. Carlin will see the look. They wish that Scooter were still alive to eat from their plates beneath the table.

In Alaska, begins the voice, *wild gray wolves are flushed from hiding and shot with rifles from low-flying planes.*

Mrs. Carlin loses her thought. She excuses herself from the table and returns a moment later with a photograph album from her suitcase.

"Duncan's parties were always more lively," Mrs. Carlin tells the boys.

Duncan, asleep in another room, is her elderly long-haired dachshund, his muzzle gone white, a perfect widow's peak in the center of his narrow forehead. Duncan was another condition of Mrs. Carlin's employment.

Through the years, the photos show the dachshund born of a Christmas litter poised on a silver platter, an apple held slack in his mouth; Duncan, a hand-knit sweater covering his rump, heading down a snow-covered hill on a toboggan; Duncan grinning at his "cake" of steak tartare, his guests straining their leads to reach their party favor chew-toys.

Mrs. Carlin thinks that reminiscing may be why the voice starts up again. This time what she hears is: *A veal calf cramped in a pen in Montana is forced to sleep on its feet.*

Mrs. Carlin asks the boys if they would mind eating alone. She goes to her room and takes two aspirin.

The boys look at Gully, still bent over her fish. Pierson spanks her lightly on the back; her body twitches, but the cat does not leave her dish.

"Takes a smacking and keeps on snacking," Pierson says.

Mrs. Carlin doesn't come out of her room until it's bedtime for the boys.

"We can have Ovaltine," says Bret. But Mrs. Carlin pours them glasses of plain milk and gives them each a tablespoon of peanut butter to go with it.

"It stimulates your dreams," is what she tells them and promises a trip to the aquarium if they are good.

In their own comfortable room, in the Pattersons' soft bed, Gully and Duncan take their cat and dog places—Gully at the head, and Duncan at the foot of the bed. During the night, when Duncan stretches and moves to the other side, Mrs. Carlin's feet seek the warm place where he had lain.

She angles her face on a plane with the cat's and breathes in the air that Gully breathes out—air that she thought would be warm but which is cool.

In a research lab in eastern Pennsylvania, a hole is drilled in the head of a young macaque . . .

Mrs. Carlin draws Gully closer. She scratches the cat's stomach, then strokes the sleek flank that shines like a seal. She strokes the cat's fur for the cat's pleasure, then for her own, and back, and forth, until the pleasures run together and the two of them sleep through the night.

"The other sitters never took us on a field trip," says Bret.

Mrs. Carlin has taken the boys to the aquarium. The boys are warming up to her—she keeps them entertained. She tells them what she knows about the animal kingdom— that twenty newborn possums will fit in a teaspoon, that the female lynx automatically becomes infertile when the number of snowshoe hares decreases. From Mrs. Carlin the boys have learned that emperor penguins sometimes ride an ice floe as far north as Rio!

That morning, Pierson complained of a stuffy head. Mrs. Carlin had told him it was sleeping with a pillow over his face that had done it. She told him what he had was called a "turtle headache," and Pierson had asked her if everything had to be animals.

Mrs. Carlin leads the boys to her favorite part of the aquarium. It is a darkened hall with a green-lit tank that circles the room. You stand in the center, in the hole of the doughnut, and turn to watch the hundreds of ocean fish swim around you. It is called the Roundabout, and it leaves you dizzy and reaching for the glass if you turn around too many times.

The boys study the reference cards with pictures of the fish. They claim to be able to match the following in the tank: the stingray, of course, plus yellowtail, striped bass, red snapper, tarpon, and the seven-gill shark.

Always there are those few fish who swim against the tide. These are the ones that Mrs. Carlin follows. For her, the darkness and water and steady current of silent fins is immeasurably soothing. She gives herself over to the whirling sensation which, she believes, leaves her open to what she cannot control when it suddenly comes to her what day it is.

In North Atlantic waters off the Faroe Islands, it is the day of "Grindabod," the return of the pilot whales, when fishing boats herd the whales by hundreds toward the shore. There, fishermen swing grappling hooks into the whales' flesh to ensure that the others will ignore their own safety; a whale will not abandon an injured mate.

Knives are drawn, and cleave through to the spinal cord. The whales thrash once more; in a sea of blood, they snap their own necks.

A handkerchief held to her mouth, Mrs. Carlin urges the boys out of the Roundabout.

During the ride home, the boys poke each other and make fun of their teachers. They whine at Mrs. Carlin till she stops the car for ice cream. They eat it in the car, being quiet long enough to look out the windows and see lightning bugs spark the blue dusk.

"In South America," says Mrs. Carlin, a tremor in her voice, "the women weave fireflies in their hair."

And then one of the lightning bugs flies into the windshield. Mrs. Carlin has to sit up straight and lift her chin to see above the glowing smear that streaks her line of vision like a comet.

"Come here, Bert," says Bret. "Little Bert-Bert, little trout, little salmon."

Mrs. Carlin stands listening in the open doorway of Bret's

bedroom, where he is supposed to be dressing for school. He has lifted one side of his quilt and is calling for the cat under the bed.

"Where's that little naughty-pants? That furry soft furry darn thing?"

Bert stays under the bed.

Bret gives up, then sees Mrs. Carlin and knows that she has heard his string of endearments.

He tries to recover, says, "Dad calls him 'the cockroach.'"

His look suggests that someone else has overheard him like this and will not let him forget it—his brother, Mrs. Carlin feels sure.

The night before, while the three of them watched television, Pierson had made fun of *her* when her eyes filled with tears during a cat food commercial. The folks at Purina see me coming, was all that she could say as, privately, she was made aware that *at an animal shelter in Oklahoma, an attendant did not clean the feces off the bowl that he used to scoop dog food from a sack.*

Mrs. Carlin is not ashamed of what she has come to call "the Tender Vittles emotion." And she does not want Bret to be ashamed of showing affection. So she asks if he will help her groom Duncan.

Duncan lies across a pillow on Mrs. Carlin's bed; he doesn't move when Bret drags the brush across his back. When Bret brushes harder, Duncan closes his eyes.

"Takes a bruising and keeps on snoozing," says Bret, proud of the rhyme.

Mrs. Carlin laughs and smooths the dog's fur. "Takes an adoring and keeps on snoring," she says, and props Duncan up. She shows Bret how to draw the wire bristles gently down the dog's hind legs. Then she asks Bret to get Duncan's pills from the inside pocket of her suitcase.

Duncan takes lanoxin for his rackety old heart. Mrs. Carlin examines the small plastic bottle and—the Tender Vittles emotion—thinks how unbearably dear it is that her pet's medication is labeled "Duncan Carlin."

Bret watches Mrs. Carlin stroke the dog's white throat to help get the pill down. He says, "I wish Scooter could have lived forever."

Mrs. Carlin looks up quickly. She pictures a plastic bottle labeled "Scooter Patterson."

She says something that is meant to be of comfort. She says, "Try to remember that God is rubbing Scooter's tummy."

She is surprised when Bret starts to laugh.

In her mind, Mrs. Carlin says to Duncan and Gully: You have made my happiness for thirteen years. Gully and the three cats before her, Duncan and the two pups before him—she owes them her life. It is for them she writes checks and congressmen to try to protect the ones she will never know.

Mrs. Carlin gets the boys off to school, then stands distracted on the Pattersons' front lawn. She walks slowly to the mailbox that is empty of mail. Then she follows the gravel drive lined with ice plants back to the house, just missing the spot where a neighborhood dog has done his business.

Mrs. Carlin slips a section from the morning paper and moves to clean up the mess. But it proves, up close, to be a cluster of whorled bronze snails, glistening with secretion, stuck to curled dead leaves.

Mrs. Carlin carries the newspaper into the house and trades it for the car keys.

She drives with one finger on the wheel at six o'clock—what the Patterson boys call "the accident-prone grip." She is tired, and tired of the voices that are sometimes visions—marmosets whose eyelids are sewn shut with thick waxed thread. Mrs. Carlin is tired of knowing when a rabbit is blinded to improve the scouring power of a popular oven cleaner.

The aquarium hasn't opened by the time Mrs. Carlin gets there, so she waits in the car.

She is tired of the voices. She says *no* to the voices. It occurs to Mrs. Carlin that the voices take a no-ing and keep on going.

She is the first visitor of the day. When the aquarium is open, Mrs. Carlin has the Roundabout to herself.

The fish—do they never rest?—are streaming behind the glass. First, Mrs. Carlin spots the single hump-backed blue-fish. From the shadow of a stingray swims a pair of sand tiger sharks.

She pivots just fast enough to track a school of amberjack the circumference of the tank. Then she plays a game with herself. She makes herself see the fish frozen in resin as in a diorama, feels *herself* the moving figure, the way, when a slow train starts, there is that disconcerting moment when it *could* be the landscape moving and not the train.

Then she lets the resin dissolve, freeing the fish to sluice through kelp and waves of their own kind.

Suddenly there is sound in the room. But not in the room—in Mrs. Carlin's head. She stands still and concentrates on what she seems to hear: *An infant gorilla, orphaned in Zimbabwe, makes a sound in the night like "Woooo, Woooo."*

Mrs. Carlin leans against the glass tank for balance. They should limit your time in the Roundabout, she thinks. They should pull you out after so many minutes the way they do in a sauna.

And then she has a vision, clear as if she were there—a Korean family looking for a picnic site. At a shaded clearing in a bamboo forest a mat is spread, a fire built up. The family's dog, a handsome blond shepherd, is called by his master and gleefully runs to the call.

Mrs. Carlin sees the owner slip a noose around its neck. It is "Bok Day" in South Korea, "Land of the Morning Calm."

It is the picnic of death that Mrs. Carlin attends.

It takes two of this family to tug the dog to a height above the flames. The dog will be hung from a tree to strangle slowly as its fur singes over the fire. The point of slow death is to tenderize the meat.

There is an indescribable sound from the choking dog, and like a person who suffers the pain of an injured twin, Mrs. Carlin gasps and drops to the floor.

That is where the couple who come in from the Fossil Hall find her. The man touches two fingers to Mrs. Carlin's wrist, then touches the side of her neck. The woman calls for a guard, and stands back.

In Belize, the eyes of a fallen jaguar reflect the green of leaves.

THE LADY WILL HAVE
THE SLUG LOUIE

My dog—I found him on the dining room table, stepping around the bowl of fruit, licking the beeswax candles.

My cat is another one—eats anything but food. I watch her select a tulip in a vase. When her teeth pierce the petal, I startle her away with sharply clapped hands.

A moment later, and again the cat stalks. She crouches in front of the next flower over, tasting the four-inch petal of a parrot tulip as if she is thinking, *That* one is the one I am not supposed to eat.

My brother keeps a boa constrictor for a pet. The preying snake suffers from a vitamin deficiency, so my brother buys a large jar of powdered high-potency supplement. Before each meal, he dips live mice in water, then drops them in the jar. He shakes the covered jar until each mouse wears a healthy coat of vitamins A through E. Then he feeds the coated mice to the snake.

When my brother and I were young, I mixed dirt with his scrambled eggs. My mother let me feed him in his high chair on the porch. I would leave my brother alone and go off into the garden. I'd return with a handful of soil from under the pansies; with the dirt and whatever things lived in the dirt, I laced his eggs.

For years, in seafood places, my brother ordered for me. "The lady will have the Slug Louie," he told the waiter. "And please, if it's no trouble, she would like her roll *au beurre*."

All my life I have been afraid of milk. I thought that if you drank too much, your bones would outgrow your skin, your teeth overrun your lips.

There is a story that mothers read to their children wherein the little girl speaks and the mother answers back:

—Mother, what do witches eat?

—Milk and potatoes and *you,* my sweet.

UNDER NO MOON

My mother said she would die when she saw the comet.

This was not superstition; it was sixth sense, or second sight. Clairvoyance. It was something she said she knew the way she said she knew the moment her children were conceived. It was how she said she knew which song would be played on the radio next, how she knew to circle one more time around the block before a parking space would open along a curb solid with cars.

My mother believed she would die when she saw the comet.

She booked, for herself and my father, a cabin aboard the ship that would cruise to the mouth of the Amazon River at the point in the world where the comet could best be seen.

This was a trip my mother had to plan a year ahead. From several lines that were making the trip, my mother chose a Greek ship, the Sun Line's *Golden Odyssey*, first reading aloud from glossy brochures about the first-rate entertainment, the swimming pools, and the food—the recreational pleasures of elegant cruising at its best.

She said that the real draw was astronomers on board— and not just any amateurs, either, but world-class authorities on extragalactic astronomy and archaeoastronomy—even planetarium directors, specialists in star photometry and eclipse meteorology—even an American astronaut and the author of the popular science text *Did a Comet Kill Off the Dinosaurs?*

These would screen instructive films for the passengers and offer lectures every day ("The Flaming Star and Genghis Khan—A.D. 1222"), at sea.

Two weeks after it was put on the books, this particular cruise sold out. An information packet was sent out shortly after. In it was the news that eight of the scheduled passengers had seen the comet in its earlier manifestation. As that was seventy-six years ago, I heard my mother picture her shipmates in various stages of decrepitude.

Often, all my life, my mother took risks. She outsailed the storm, the stray dog did not bite, the wobbly ladder held.

"Don't worry," she always said. "I will live to see the comet."

If couples can grow to look alike, then my parents' ailments came to resemble each other. My mother took something for an arthritic condition. My father took something else for the very same thing. So that on the plane to San Juan to meet up with the ship, when my mother discovered she had not packed her pills, it made all the sense in the world for my father to say, "Don't panic," she should help herself to his.

But en route to see the legendary portent of disaster, my mother's luck ran out. Minutes after takeoff, her hands began to itch. Then her arms, and then her neck. Then her face and then her feet.

Your normally dignified mother, my father said, was scratching herself like a wild thing. As my father recollects, my mother managed to be flushed and pale at the same time. He said my mother's scratching became a dance when she began to itch inside. By the time they were leaving the plane in San Juan, my mother—still itching—was wheezing, too. Had they waited much longer, they learned soon after, my mother would have stopped breathing entirely.

In the local hospital they did what they could to set her back to right, advising her to squash the travel bug and lie low for at least a week. My mother agreed to meet the doctor halfway, promising to rest if she could rest aboard the ship.

After leaving San Juan, the *Golden Odyssey* stopped in the port of Martinique. In Martinique, there were $30,000 emeralds for sale at the end of the pier.

At the island of Grenada, the seas were too rough to transfer to land by boat. The astronaut was seasick right along with exactly 86 percent of the passengers. Those who did not succumb were encouraged to play bridge and to sip freezing tropical drinks.

Matters did not improve when the ship neared Trinidad. According to my father, a freak accident on the promenade deck left an elderly man more dead than alive. What the man had not seen when he reached for his can of soda was the bee that had flown in through the pop-top hole. When he drank from the can, he swallowed the bee, which then managed to sting him in the throat on its dark way down.

All this time my mother was reading trash in the luxury of her cabin. My father attended the lectures and would thereafter recite them to my mother down below.

*   *   *

Trinidad was the first site from which the comet would be clearly visible. The passengers had been briefed in deep-sky photography—tripods were a must, so were time exposures of at least one minute. And since the motion of the ship would mean a celestial event that was blurred, the good captain arranged for a nighttime expedition.

He rented forty-five taxicabs (out of the forty-seven such that were on the island) to pick up his passengers, five passengers to a cab, and to drive them for two hours along a one-lane jungle road to the other side of the island.

In one of the taxis, the crew had sent coffee and sandwiches; in another, the cargo was a portable toilet.

Speeding through the jungle at midnight, the taxicab drivers talked snakes. They said there *were* no more snakes on Trinidad since the government imported the mongoose. It had done its job so well—eating not only poisonous snakes but birds' eggs, too—that in the daylight they would see that there were no more exotic birds.

Where the jungle stopped, at a point of slippery shale dotted with patches of sisal, a group of stoop-shouldered stargazers set up their telescopes and tripods.

This is the part my father made me see—all those people stumbling in the dark, under no moon, unable to shine a light or strike a match because a time exposure would be ruined.

And because of the hour, no one had dressed; these were men and women in bathrobes and peignoirs crashing into each other in the dark, slipping on the rocky point of what the guides referred to as Tripod National Forest.

It became an adventure, my father said, to see anything that night at all.

And then one of the astronomers had pointed out a tennis ball in the sky, to the southeast of red Antares on the side of the constellation Scorpio. He told them the tail depended on the body's rotation in relation to the moon. Consequently, he said, they would not see a tail that night, just a faint pink fuzzy business like a wisp of cotton candy.

Alone in her cabin, my mother saw nothing from a porthole.

With approximately the same degree of difficulty, those passengers who were greatly motivated repeated the midnight excursion, this time by bus, at the mouth of the Amazon River, on the northwest shore of Belém.

Their pockets filled with souvenirs of voodoo charms and crocodile teeth, the experts agreed—it was the poorest sighting of the starry visitor in two thousand years, anywhere in the world.

But guess who went out for a second look!

One might as well do what one could, my father reasoned. "When in southern latitudes," he said, and loaded up his camera with 1000 ASA.

At the end of the voyage, a charter plane flew my parents home.

When his film was developed, my father passed around envelopes that contained photographs of the equatorial sky. He pointed to the minuscule dot that was the entire point of the trip.

Neither my mother nor my father seemed disappointed that the sighting wasn't more than it was. Did my father ever say, What kind of screwball operation *is* this? And did my mother once say, with regard to his pictures, Which of these specks of dust is the comet?

My mother was content with this thought: that the pills that almost took her life may actually have *saved* it by preventing her from seeing the incarnation of her doom.

The last envelope contained pictures of the captain's guests for dinner the final night: my mother, her arm around my father's empty chair, and two older couples who had promised to stay in touch.

Then there were pictures of a smiling Greek crew, several undistinguished views of the port at Martinique, and one successful close-up of a boy about five years old.

My mother said she had wanted a picture of the only person on board the ship who would get another chance to greet the heavenly apparition.

THE CENTER

For the price of a cup of coffee a day, my friend Deborah adopted a child. She adopted one of the children on Channel 5. Except the word I think they use on Channel 5 is *sponsor*. She sponsored one of the Sally Struthers children, or maybe it was one of the Linda Evans children. Maybe they are the same children. In any case, it was a child that my friend Deborah saw advertised late at night.

According to the profile sent to my friend by the agency overseas, the child had two living parents. Both parents held jobs. In the photo, the child appeared healthy, well-fed, and well—even fashionably—clothed. The report the agency included said that Deborah's sponsorship would provide the child with much-needed supplies for school.

My friend Deborah thought, school supplies?

She telephoned the agency's twenty-four-hour toll-free number. She asked them to reassign her cup-of-coffee-a-day money to a child who was not so well off as that child was. The agency obliged and presented my friend Deborah with a new child, whose need for food and medicine overtook the need for pencils and books.

Deborah encouraged her own two children to write letters to the new child, to the translator who translated back and forth between them and the new child and between the new child and them.

After a time, the new child's letters stopped. Alarmed, my friend Deborah made inquiries. The agency replied that the new child did not like to visit the Center. But my friend Deborah thinks that there must be more to the matter than this. The Center?

So I asked my friend Deborah, What if you got the new child a dog? What if to the price of a cup of coffee a day, you added the price of a can of dog food a day? Would the agency overseas—would someone there in his country get the new child a dog?

I was thinking about Pal.

Original Pal is buried in a flower bed, his whiskers pushing up as stems at the end of which are configured, each spring, marigolds and impatiens. Pal was a shepherd mix who had been trained for Search and Rescue. This was less a community service than an adjunct to family safety. My mother used to say she lived precariously, meaning through her children—though I was a girl who had never broken a bone; I had to make do with faking out the eye chart so that I could get glasses and wrapping bent paper clips around my teeth for braces.

Often enough, Pal would strike out into the hills and find someone with something broken or something torn. Original Pal was so happy to save someone that we were always taking up positions of repose and waiting for him to find us and lick us so that we could tell him, Good dog, Good dog, Good dog.

But I can't help thinking about Pal Junior.

No relation, Pal Junior would, in times of stress, lie on his back on the terrace in the sun until he had sunburned his stomach. Pal Junior would wade into a stream and sit down, just sit there in the middle of a streaming stream that divided at his shoulders as though around a bigger Pal.

Pal Junior was part something and part something. In a cardigan with leather elbow patches, with his white fur brushed into spikes around his face, Pal Junior was Albert Einstein saving man.

You see, in the beginning, in the garden of Eden, man and animals had perfect accord between them. But when man discovered sin, a chasm opened up that divided man, on one side, from all of the animals, on the other side. The chasm widened, our mother said, until at the last possible moment, it was only the dog that leaped across the abyss to spend eternity with man.

I said to my friend Deborah, What does it mean, the Center? Would Struthers or maybe Evans know?

TOM-ROCK THROUGH THE EELS

"Are you here for all the things that I don't have?"

The man who owned the nursery, that is what he said. He thought I had come for the specials, which he was out of, but all I needed was peat. I was planning to start a rock garden, someplace to put the rock.

The Tom-rock had been underwater, under thirty feet of clear water cut by red eels beneath a pier on Lake Ontario in 1963.

She bribed me, my mother, with praise—would I be the diver to retrieve it while she watched? From the deck of the *Jolly Roger* you could see the word *Tom*. The name. The rock on the bottom was rectangular, its corners softened to curves. There was a green line drawn like a television screen, and inside the screen the name Tom, in blue.

The Tom-rock, when I brought it to the surface, was, let's say, half the size of a shoebox.

The ice-cream cone I got for braving red eels held chocolate ice cream in cylindrical scoops. *Canadian* ice cream, Canadian rock, and no one in our family named Tom.

And now, in California, the rock that had sat on a glass coffee table in several states in several years was going to be "planted" beside slabs of granite, lichen-covered granite hauled down from the Sierras, and all of it bordered by white sweet alyssum. The Tom-rock would be as much a marker as a headstone. And hadn't I nearly died to get it, holding my breath for so long, and those eels?

In California, you are not supposed to sleep beneath book-shelves or paintings or mirrors on the wall. But in my father's house, when my father is away, I sleep in his bed and gamble that the painting of a potter's wheel will not shake loose and crush my skull in the hours of a quaking town at night.

My father's room has dimmers on the lights. There are speakers for music recessed in the walls. In my father's room I leave the lights as near to off as they can be and still be on.

In the evening, I hear foghorns on the bay. In the morn-ing—the dawn cannon in the army base at the head of the Golden Gate. When the fog is especially heavy, the smell that comes in through the open upstairs window under the scent of eucalyptus is the smell of wet clay, of wetted-down dust, from the bricks in the courtyard below.

When I sleep in my father's bed, I sleep on the same side my mother used to sleep on. Sometimes, when the cannon goes off at dawn, I wake up and find myself in the pose my mother died in—lying on her side, her arm reaching from under her head as though she were doing the sidestroke in a pool, the pills she had swallowed weighing her down like so many pebbles in her pockets.

I don't fall asleep with my body on the bed in the same way my mother was found. It must be a thing I go into when I am asleep. And still I cannot be sure that, limb for limb, I am in the same position. My mother's legs, when I saw her, were covered by the sheet; it is possible that my legs are bent where my mother's legs were straight.

This is where after this it stops being dawn and muffled cannons and waking to a morning of eucalyptus-scented fog.

This is where a death means something else to someone else. Because while I am resting easy, there is someone who needs help to get to sleep.

Neither my grandmother nor I can swallow a pill with water. When I was young and visiting my grandmother's house, she would crush my vitamins and aspirin in a teaspoon of apple-sauce or of jam. Later, my grandmother and I moved on to berries for the smaller pills, a mashed banana for capsules. Together, we discovered that grapes worked well, too.

Since her daughter died, my grandmother rinses off berries at bedtime. In the morning she peels bananas. She says it is not enough that a pill helps her sleep through the night—somehow, she has to get through the day.

And now she is buying herself boxes of prunes and putting them in a jar with a quart of boiling water. Because the pills that are supposed to lift her spirits during the day have a side effect—the one for which the cure begins when you open a box of prunes and let them soften in boiling water.

My grandmother sleeps beneath a portrait of her daughter.

A short time later, and her voice has lost weight. She is speaking so fast that her thoughts lose their breath catching up.

"What is the word I want?" she says, because the word that my grandmother wants has been lifted from her tongue and carried from her head by the treatments—eight in two weeks.

She says the treatments have left her fuzzy; she cannot

remember the name of the nurse, and the same nurse readied her for treatment every time.

When my grandmother calls, it is after the fact. She doesn't talk about a thing until it is done.

"Darling, can you help me?" my grandmother says. "Help me remember the good times with your mother?"

My mother said, "What?"

I said, "I forgot. I forgot what I was going to say."

"Then it must have been a lie," my mother said.

California to the Midwest is forty-eight hours by train. And don't you know that in forty-eight hours aboard a train, in probably only four, you will meet the extroverted youth with guitar who takes over the club car for spontaneous hootenannies. You will stand in line for snacks behind good clothes on bad bodies, behind the man who is so drunk he has lost his shoes, and so belligerent no one will help him find them.

A thing you would not think would be good, is—orange juice in a can. On a train, canned orange juice poured over ice tastes good.

On the Lake Shore Limited, I try to sleep in the day and take advantage of the cars at night when it is quiet enough to hear carbonation in a glass across the aisle, when you can wake from drowsing because—three rows back—someone is peeling an orange.

When the car lights go out, a porter brings me a blanket. He tucks it around my shoulders like—what else?—like a mother.

I see my face reflected in the window and face the sad

truth—that I happen to look my best when there is no one there to see.

My head against a small synthetic pillow, I think: Mothers. They teach their daughters to use pumice on their heels, and to roll a lemon inside its skin before slicing, to bring out the juice. My mother said men, unless they were sober, what they meant when they asked you to marry was that you looked nice in that dress, or they liked your hair that way.

Every so often we tried to shop together, tried to bake together, tried together to teach ourselves something from a how-to book. Mostly I did things *around* her, the way nurses change the sheets with the patient still in bed.

I think back to a certain Christmas morning. Back to a summer vacation on a lake. I go back further still, to the beginning of my mother and me. When I have to say something, here is what I can say—that when I was born, my mother wore me like a fur.

MRS. PRICE told me I didn't have to ring their doorbell. She said I could be in their house when Karen wasn't home, if she wasn't back from swim team. Mrs. Price gave me blueberry cobbler. She asked me which I liked better—blueberry or peach—when she put in her weekly order from the baker who delivered in a covered truck in summer.

When I defended Mrs. Price to Karen, Karen said I sounded like a mother myself.

MRS. GRIFFIN sang at bedtime, "Turn around and you're two, turn around and you're four, turn around a whole lot of times, and get your ass out the door."

MRS. KOGEN would open her refrigerator. She would look inside and say to her kids, "What do you *mean* there's nothing to eat? There's a tomato, an onion . . ."

MRS. BEAUDRY, when the family returned from Yellowstone, and you asked if they saw any bears, would fix a look beyond your face and recite, "Forty-four bear, thirty-two deer, twenty-six moose . . . " and end with "and a par-tri-idge in a pear tree."

MRS. STERN looked at Deborah and Rita and said that she made her two best friends.

MRS. SMITH, when our slips were showing, said, "It's snowing down South."

MRS. DREW sent Patty off to board with this advice: "Never tap your feet at the symphony."

MRS. ROSS let Susan keep her underwear in a fondue pot sprayed with Estée Lauder.

MRS. SNYDER let me call her Noel. Her hair went silver when she was young and she was always tanned. Men would stare at her when she took Carol and me for sundaes. Mrs. Snyder called the men *our boyfriends;* Mrs. Snyder would say to Carol and me, "Our boyfriends are still looking."

MRS. BRITTON taught Jill how to kiss.

MRS. NELSON administered SAT tests to students. She tried to impress upon us the importance of scoring high. She did an imitation of herself as a doctor, checking the patient's pulse, blood pressure, and SAT scores.

MRS. LINDEN was beautiful in spirit and in fact. Her wish, she told her daughter, was to be a beautiful woman and surprise people because she was a beautiful woman who was kind.

MRS. CASE undressed in front of Alice. She and Alice wore each other's clothes.

MRS. UPTON taught Kelly limericks:

> *There was an old man from Calcutta,*
> *Whose tonsils were coated with butter,*
> *Thus reducing his snore*
> *From a terrible roar*
> *To a soft oleaginous mutter.*

MRS. JOHNS, even after Danny was up in her teens, still threw out her arm across the passenger seat to protect Danny when the car was coming to a fast stop.

MRS. O'DONNELL, when Lindsay was older, was still saving egg cartons, from habit, in case Lindsay might need them for a project at school.

MRS. FARRELL, in church with Andrea at her side, would try to make Andrea laugh out loud. Mrs. Farrell would sing the words "in the bathtub" after the title of each Sunday's hymns. "Abide with Me in the Bathtub," she would sing in a whisper. "God Is Working His Purpose Out—in the Bathtub," Mrs. Farrell sang.

MRS. HOBSON. On Valentine's Day, the Hobson children woke to find hearts on the floor of their rooms. Tiny hand-cut paper hearts of every color made a path from bedside down the stairs to their chairs at the table. Some of the paper hearts stuck to bare feet and were tracked into the bathrooms. The colored paper hearts, when wetted, bled onto the tiles.

It takes me nearly the whole of the trip to come up with even these. Roll all of the mothers up into one and The Good Times with My Mother would not get me into even enough water to soak a box of prunes.

The next thing I know, I am leaving the train, shaking out my legs and adjusting a shoulder bag. I have slept the night sitting up in the seat, and I know that it shows on my face, in my clothes.

Sometimes it feels as though I won't be able to live until I can sleep in a position of my own—not in the way my mother's body was found on the bed, but in a way that is mine—even if it is only a sort of dead man's float where you don't use a muscle but clasp both your knees and let your head sink into the pillow, rocking gently as a baby, tipping your head to the side to take in air, conserving your strength until help arrives, or until you can save yourself, there in bed.

At the end of the platform, my grandmother is waiting. When I see her I forget. What I thought I was going to say.

Then it must have been a lie, my mother said.

THE REST OF GOD

For days there was nothing to say except, What a glorious day. Wildflowers galloped across thorn-free fields, stopping only when cut and placed in water. Shopping lists grew to include carrots for the horse next door, black but for a spattered-looking black-and-white rump—a horse who ran crazed around the paddock at dusk, and whose name was Fury. The men of the house would start to drink then, but only enough to be playful late at night. They gave the kids rides on power mowers, careening over the lawns in great loops in the dark, missing the two kinds of oaks—white and red—the one with its rounded leaves, the other's leaves in points, which the kids were taught to know by saying, White men shoot bullets and Red men shoot arrows. Mornings, robins robbed the ground. A rooster startled the cat that had been raised indoors. Nothing clever was said.

What did come under discussion when everyone met in the evening was why, when people go to the beach, they always lie with their feet to the ocean. Asking ourselves this question was the most work that most of us called upon ourselves to do.

We were women in one-piece bathing suits beneath faded loose clothes, walking across dunes to call on one another, bringing bouquets of Queen Anne's lace and goldenrod trailing roots, quoting the poet's hope that, "Through gleaming gates of goldenrod / I'll pass into the rest of God."

This is the lyric seizure that succeeds a close call. Or surge, lyric *surge,* from the name "black surge" that is given to the storm-induced seepage of sewage that closes the beach. Had the black surge come one day sooner, there would not have been this lyric surge because there would not have been the close call.

Fay's husband called it a sea-poose. This was later, after Fay and the kids were safely on shore, after Fay had described the circular current that had kept her from raising her arms to wave for help. After Dave had finally seen what was wrong, after Dave had lost his head but his fishing buddy had not, had managed to get a rope to Fay and play her in with the kids, one by one.

Within minutes the kids were bragging, and Fay—not the type to cry—had turned snappish at her husband, Dave. Fay trained horses and Dave farmed trees, and to Fay's way of thinking there was shame in being weak, even if the stronger was a freakish ocean wave.

We celebrated our friends' safety with a party that night, though, in fact, the barbecue had been planned the week before to take advantage of a high full moon. We chose a stretch of sand between the ocean and a pond, posted, by the local conservators of nature, as a home for egrets.

Empty of trees, Dave's truck hauled grills. We were each assigned a contribution; Caitlin brought hot dogs, which opened up discussion of possible past lives. Caitlin was Fay's right hand at the stable, and a vocal vegetarian for most of her thirty years. But early in the summer a psychic had regressed her, had told Caitlin that she had been a fox in a previous life.

The next day Caitlin was riding her horse when she saw a rabbit leap in a field. "My, doesn't that look good," she said she thought and found herself broiling a chicken for dinner.

While Dave heated coals Dr. Bob took the smaller boys off to the pond with nets. Just at dark, the boys began scooping up fish—tiny, flipping like silver dollars.

"My mother used to fry everything she found," Dr. Bob was telling the boys. "She'd throw a hundred of these into the pan, but everything always tasted like bacon," he said.

The shirkers got up a volleyball game while Pete and I got the bonfire going. Even with the fire, we had to put on sweaters, a fact that had Pete looking ahead already to fall. "The first cold snap," he said, "I get in my car and drive south till I can roll down the window."

Ben studied the steak he was asked to do black and blue for Jeff Taylor's date, a woman who showed real estate and who kept up her nails. She had brought a locally baked boysenberry pie and, inexplicably, a bag of candy corn, which I saw some of us bite off white-orange-yellow, and others of us bite off yellow-orange-white.

Two grills over, Dave turned hamburgers and suffered the children's humor, evinced in sidesplitting riddles such as this: What do you have if you have fourteen oranges in one hand and eight grapefruit in the other? and the children's shrieking laughter all but drowning out the answer, which was, I believe, "Big hands."

"I love barbecue sauce," Dave was saying, "especially when it's homemade."

"Yeah, that's right," Fay said. "I just put it in this Kraft's squeeze bottle for convenience."

Fay turned to one of Dr. Bob's flock. "How much you want on that chicken leg, Will?"

"Not too much," Will said, holding out his paper plate. "Just enough much."

The fire was drawing some notice by then. Jeff Taylor, a kidder you could count on at holiday time for gifts of coasters that said "Eat, drink, and remarry," announced that later in the evening we would gather around the fire and sacrifice a virgin, amending his remarks after the requisite silence to "sacrifice an old maid" instead.

That late in the season we had our timing down. We were the model of capable neighbors, filling our plates in an orderly manner, then scrambling for places in the sand close to the flames.

Dr. Bob waved Dave and Fay over to a pot of steamers.

"I didn't know you brought steamers," Dave said. "I'm warning you all, I inhale these things."

"Don't worry," Fay said, securing a few of the clams for herself. "I can stand on my own two feet and fight for what is mine."

A call went out to Dr. Bob to please start up a sing-along. Dr. Bob protested. "I couldn't carry a tune if it had handles," he said.

"Then come here by the fire and tell the kids a ghost story," Dave suggested.

"I don't want to scare anybody," Dr. Bob said.

"You already have!" said Will, and the other children screamed their approval.

Dr. Bob was something of a medical inventor, esteemed by every one of us although we could not say exactly what it was he had invented. He was the one who had tended to Fay two summers earlier after her horse, spooked by an umbrella over a roadside farm stand, threw her into a ditch.

Fay had complained only of a headache where her head

had hit the dirt, but Dr. Bob knew to take her in fast. In his car, Fay's eyes had crossed. Asked for her name, Fay gave her maiden name. By the time they got to the hospital, Fay's speech was down to sounds—the sounds of crows and owls.

There were lessons to be learned wherever one looked, which is not to suggest that those lessons were learned. Witness the Henkins' boy, Bill, who left a party drunk, then discovered he had left his glasses behind only after he had pulled out of the drive and was headed for the highway home. Rather than return for his glasses, he later explained he had driven home really fast so that he would make it back before he had an accident.

That was something I remembered when Caitlin told us what else the psychic had said, which was that, as a fox, Caitlin had been killed when she was struck by a speeding car on the beach access road. What Caitlin wonders now is, What if *she* hits a fox with her car?

Then Dave said, "Remember the deer?"

"Jesus, Dave," Fay said, and got up and walked in the dark direction of the ocean.

Dave dropped the subject, but everyone knew the story as vividly as if *we* had been the one who hit the deer, then knelt by the side of the road and held the deer's dying head in our lap, and shielded with one hand the eyes that blinked at each pair of passing headlights, affording the animal that tiny measure of relief until a state trooper showed up with a gun.

In what she must have perceived as an awkward silence, Jeff Taylor's date jumped up and began to collect our empty Coke and beer cans, stuffing them into a plastic bag for trash.

Then we heard Fay calling out to Dave to hurry. Dave threw his paper plate into the fire and *all* of us took off running toward the shore.

We found Fay standing in the surf, surveying a rare phosphorescence in the tide. She took a step and scattered sparks, then bent over and shook her flat hands underwater like a miner at a watery mother lode panning for gold with her hands. We watched Dave run into the glowing shoals and take hold of his wife from behind. We watched both of them go over so that they were sitting on the rocky bottom. When a stray beach dog ran in to join them, we could see—phosphorescence clinging to his fur—the outline of his legs as they paddled underwater. When Dave and Fay stood up again, holding on to each other, the sudden phosphorescence was gone.

What was left of the summer passed quietly, as if in deference to that night as one befitting summer's end. It was a time when the only pain was inflicted by bees, and an easy remedy—three kinds of weeds pressed together and rubbed on the sting—was right in your own backyard.

TUMBLE HOME

WEEKEND

The game was called on account of dogs—Hunter in the infield, Tucker in the infield, Bosco and Boone at first base. First-grader Donald sat down on second base, and Kirsten grabbed her brother's arm and wouldn't let him leave third to make his first run.

"Unfair!" her brother screamed, and the dogs, roving umpires, ran to third.

"Good power!" their uncle yelled, when Joy, in a leg cast, swung the bat and missed. "Now put some wood to it."

And when she did, Joy's designated runner, Cousin Zeke, ran to first, the ice cubes in his gin and tonic clacking like dog tags in the glass.

And when Kelly broke free from Kirsten and this time came in to make the run, members of the Kelly team made Tucker in the infield dance on his hind legs.

"It's not who wins—" their coach began, and was shouted down by one of the boys, "There's *first* and there's *forget it*."

Then Hunter retrieved a foul ball and carried it off in the direction of the river.

The other dogs followed—barking, mutinous.

*　　*　　*

Dinner was a simple picnic on the porch, paper plates in laps, the only conversation a debate as to which was the better grip for throwing shoes.

After dinner, the horseshoes were handed out, the post pounded in, the rules reviewed with a new rule added due to falling-down shorts. The new rule: Have attire.

The women smoked on the porch, the smoke repelling mosquitoes, and the men and children played on even after dusk when it got so dark that a candle was rigged to balance on top of the post, and was knocked off and blown out by every single almost-ringer.

Then the children went to bed, or at least went upstairs, and the men joined the women for a cigarette on the porch, absently picking ticks engorged like grapes off the sleeping dogs. And when the men kissed the women good night, and their weekend whiskers scratched the women's cheeks, the women did not think *shave,* they thought: *stay.*

CHURCH CANCELS COW

Pheasant feathers in a plastic jack-o'-lantern—this is the way people decorate graves in October across from my house. In winter they tie wreaths to the stones like evergreen pendants in December. The halved-apple faces of owls on a branch will spook you, walking at dusk as I do with my dog who finds the one real pumpkin, small on a stem, and carries it off and flings it and retrieves, leaving on the pumpkin the marks of her teeth, the only desecration in these rows of tended plots.

Or not, according to the woman at the wheel of the red Honda Civic that appears from behind the Japanese maple and proceeds past the hedge of arborvitae where she slows and then rolls down her window to say, "You should keep that dog on a leash." She says, "That dog left faces on my mother's grave."

When I realize she means feces, I say my dog didn't do it. She says yes, my dog did it. I say, "Did you *see* this dog leave feces on the grave?" She says, "I found faces on my mother's grave. I had to clean them off." I say there are other dogs that walk here. I say my dog goes in the woods before the place where the headstones start.

I leave her talking to me from her car. I walk away with my dog in the direction of my house, and she follows in her car so I turn back around and lead her through the cemetery and sit down on a random grave and take a wire brush from the pocket of my coat and begin to groom my dog, brushing slowly from the ends up to the skin so as not to tug and hurt her. I stay where I am until the woman drives away, and I stay until she reappears. When she leaves the second time, she leaves rubber in the road.

For days I see her car across the street, parked on the little-used access road, her at the wheel just watching my house where my dog patrols the yard, unmistakable dog. I write down her license plate number, so what. I pull weeds with my back to her. And after thoughts of worse things than bricks coming flying through the windows of my house, I pull off grass-stained gloves and cross to her car and say, "You know, I'm on your side about this. *I* have relatives buried here, and I don't want to find faces on their graves."

She says, "*You* have relatives buried here?"

For peace of mind I will lie about any thing at any time.

In fact, she says, she has counted three dogs the other day from her car. Like counting cows, in the game I played in cars when the family went out on long drives. My brother and I were told to count cows in the fields we passed along the way, me counting cows on one side of the road, my brother counting cows on the other. But if we passed a church, the person on whose side the church appeared had to start their count over again.

Why did church cancel cow? The question was not a question back then, and when I try to think why, the best I can guess is—because we were having fun? Until I mention it to my brother who says, "Don't you remember? You don't remember. It was cemetery, not church, that cancels cow."

And why it comes to me now.

THE CHILDREN'S PARTY

"Bye-bye," the baby said, his voice a little bell. "Bye-bye," he waved, as we arrived for the party at the lake.

We were stiff after driving from our house hours south in a town overrun by tourists. We put gifts on a table in the hall. The three children all had birthdays the same week.

The baby's father showed us to the porch. He poured us drinks, said, "*This*'ll change your handwriting."

The others were friends from across the lake who came up for a month every summer, tying their bull's-eye or turnabout to a cleat and hopping out onto a dock.

Between the back porch and the lake was a well-kept lawn with a grill, coals just lit, and a large decorated paper-bag piñata strung up in a shimmering willow. The baby's mother and a woman I didn't know called me over to join them beside the piñata. The woman I didn't know asked if I had a match. I didn't see the cigarette she held, and thought she meant to light the piñata. I told her, and we all doubled over picturing melting gummy bears dripping like hot wax onto the outstretched hands of the blindfolded children beneath it.

"Some little boy's scrotum get nailed to a tree?" asked one of the children's fathers from the porch. "I see three women laughing like this"—he bent over, knees pressed together, and held his crotch—"I look for a scrotum nailed to a tree."

Farther out, naked children pushed each other off a dock into the bracing lake. At the far end of the dock was a small child's slide poised above deep water. "I just put it there to scare his mother," said the baby's father, chuckling diabolically: "Look—he can go in by himself!"

Tony Peebles—handsome, hearty next-door neighbor—still had not arrived.

"Heart attack," someone said.

"Car wreck," someone else said.

"Heart attack then car wreck," came a chorus.

"Talking to someone at the store," said his wife. "He went there an hour ago. I was telling Judy, he goes to pick up the steaks, there could be a stuffed effigy of the butcher behind the counter, Tony'd engage it in conversation."

Only a couple of us knew what was taking so long. The children's dog had been killed the month before. The children felt it would be unfair to get another dog—unfair to their *former* dog. The children were in pain, and I felt I knew what to say. I said to their father, quoting a lovely poem, "Tell them this: 'The need for the new love *is* faithfulness to the old.'"

He said, "That's what I used to tell myself when I cheated on my ex-wife."

But he had agreed, and the men were picking up the children's new dog, a pup from a nearby camp.

"I hope none of you are allergic," said the baby's mother, moving aside a vase of wildflowers to make room for a cake on a plate. "It's an allergy-fest out there.

"This cake, by the way, is real chocolate," she assured us. "I'm sick of trying to force carob on you, and all of you spitting it out behind my back." Yet we saw that our health-conscious hostess was still serving the dreaded organic fig bars from the health food store in town. "Colon blasters," we called them. The baby's father had said that Colin Blaster sounded like the name of an English soccer coach.

"Tony's not back yet?" one of his friends asked.

"And he made Bruce go with him," Bruce's wife said. "Tony probably told him there was something in town he had to show him, and he took Bruce to town and the thing he had to show him was a stop sign."

We ate deviled eggs while we waited for Tony and Bruce to return with the steaks. On the drive up, I told a friend, we'd seen blueberries wild by the side of the road and birch bark peeling from the trunks of trees with towering crowns, but so far we'd seen no moose.

"If you come out with us in the canoe tomorrow, you'll see plenty of moose," she said. She described the stretch of river we would travel and the numbers of moose we would see. "But no males with antlers. They're shy. You have to wait. You see them come out to look for females in the fall."

The children called for us to watch them play with eggs. It was the game wherein you toss a raw egg gently to your partner a few feet away. Your partner tosses it back, and you widen the gap between you. The toss and retreat is repeated until all but one of the pairs has broken their eggs.

We watched, sipping drinks, until the baby's father called, "Eyes right!" and appeared in the yard to the right of the house carrying a baseball bat. The children screamed with laughter as they took turns pitching raw eggs.

"Jackpot!" they screamed, as the baby's father connected, splattering them all, including the neighbor's dog who had stopped by to cruise the grill.

Mr. Howell, emboldened by the display, retrieved from his

car a sack of sheathed hunting knives. But other of the parents blew the whistle on this—high-stakes pin-the-tail-on-the-donkey not the same as batting eggs—and we strained to hear his gnarly utterances as he returned the knives to his car.

"Deadlines," one of the birthday girls announced, excusing herself from the games. "I have deadlines," she said soberly, inexplicably adjusting a gorilla mask over her face.

On the porch, in a high chair, the baby sent a bowl of Cheerios sailing off the tray.

"Dinner is shoved," said his mother, kneeling to wipe up the mess. She returned from the kitchen with a jar of baby food and a clean spoon. "What's he eating now?" asked the baby's father. He picked up the jar and mimed alarm as he "read" the label: "Deadly poison?!" This made the children spit potato salad till their parents said get a grip.

Down on the dock, a brother and sister began yelling at each other until the girl ran to their mother crying, "Dan hit me back!"

"Dan has a temper. He takes after me," said their little brother sagely.

"You mean *you* take after *him*," said their mother. "He was here first."

The baby's mother picked up a small inflated raft in the shape of a giraffe. She pointed the long spotted neck at her husband and winked at him through the two small holes in the seat. "Imagine being able to fit your legs through these," she said.

"I thought they were for your breasts," her husband said.

Bruce's wife shushed him. We heard the distant, slightly hysterical cry of a loon on the lake.

"People think they're related to ducks," said a local for our benefit, "but they're really much closer to penguins."

"You go in the lake," said Mr. Howell, "watch out for leeches. *Giant* leeches. I had to nudge a moose this morning with my boat—he was eating the lily pads I planted, and he didn't move when I yelled at him to stop. When you ram a moose from behind, you got to be prepared for more than contact. He had a row of leeches on his butt swung like fringe."

"You see the fox last night?" a neighbor asked.

"I seen a fox grab a leech off a moose's butt—" said Mr. Howell before we could shut him up.

In the absence of Tony and Bruce and the steaks, we refilled our glasses and shared the children's hot dogs. I heard the baby laughing from inside the house, and followed the sound to where he was having his bath. His mother made an ice-cream cone of suds and pretended to lick it. "Aaaagh!" she said, and the baby laughed again. I knelt beside the tub and scooped up a handful of suds. I brought it to my mouth and licked. "Aaaagh!" I sputtered to the baby's delight, squinching my face in dismay.

From outside, someone called us down to see. In the road, beneath a streetlight, was the young moose the children had named Moosifer. As we watched, the moose went down on its front legs, kneeling in the road like a camel, its tongue slowly rolling across the spot where, earlier, a clump of crows had pecked at the soft parts under the crushed shell of a box turtle someone hadn't stopped for.

"It's Moosifer," one of the children whispered to another.

Moosifer was a female, said our moose-butt expert. You could tell by the absence of antlers.

"Eyes right!" the urgent whisper of our host.

We looked to the woods where something large was making its way through the trees toward the road.

In the moment before Tony and Bruce drove up—the children's new dog barking in the car—locals and guests, we held our breath as branches broke, the magnificent rack an emblem of need that could not wait another day.

SPORTSMAN

By rights, Jack should have headed west when his wife, Alex, left him, but they lived in California so he drove east, folding down the visor each morning against the sun. He didn't wait to find a cheap motel at night, just pulled off the road and slept cramped in the car a few hours. At dawn he thrust a stick of Right Guard up under his shirt—the rock 'n' roll shower—and drove until he found coffee. He thought that traveling alone was like being in therapy—the things you found out about yourself.

Speeding across the Bonneville Salt Flats, Jack played car golf, weaving in and out of the lanes trying to roll the Ping-Pong ball in the passenger seat well into the Styrofoam coffee cup that was on its side after spilling out most of the coffee. Jack was good at this.

Not that he'd been invited, but he was, he realized, going to New York, to the home of his friend the doctor, the closest thing to rehab he could find.

Jack signaled and changed lanes at the exit for the Long Island Expressway, and remembered Alex's directions, the way she would say "then turn left six blocks before the liquor store." He'd phoned from the last gas station. The doctor said they would be glad to see him. Jack had to ask, "Does Vicki still talk about feelings all the time?"

Vicki had given him a diary one Christmas, a blank book that stayed blank, and which Jack had titled "Jackie's Log of Feelings." Vicki was a good mimic and did a dead-on imitation of Jack as if he were a psychiatrist wincing at a patient's confession, ordering a depressed person to "just snap out of it" or leaning forward in his therapist's chair saying, simply, "Handle it."

Jack had offered to take them out to dinner, but the doctor wanted to barbecue, so Jack stopped at a market and bought three big steaks on the way. It was too soon for even Vicki to try to fix him up is what he told himself when he considered buying four.

In summer, the town was a beach resort. In realtor parlance, Vicki and the doctor lived on the wrong side of the highway, but it was still only a five-minute drive to the water.

At the door, Vicki gave Jack a kiss and a bath towel, and pointed him down the hall, which made a thick gold bracelet slide the length of her forearm to her wrist. "It's one of those 'Honey, I'm sorry' gifts," she said, and Jack said, "Nice. Get him angry again."

The doctor had a cold beer for him when Jack came out of the shower smelling of mandarin orange–scented soap. They showed him around the house, an Arts and Crafts cottage built in 1932. Since his last visit, they'd replaced the previous owner's insane wallpaper (shelves of books behind chicken wire) and pried off the bedroom floors' linoleum, the pattern of which was a photograph of carpeting, revealing wide planks of clean pine.

"We put up a detached garage," the doctor said, adding, for the nth time, "it doesn't care if you park in it or not." The tour concluded on the redwood deck the doctor had built himself.

"Things are looking pretty swep'-up around here," Jack said.

Vicki, in faded cutoffs, kicked off espadrilles and took the red butterfly chair. She observed that Jack always said he was on his way out when he called. "It's like you can't make an entrance until you've established your exit."

Jack hated for people to analyze his behavior. He hated for them to notice it. He moved to give the doctor a hand with the steaks and managed to fork one off the grill and into the coals. "Oops," he said, fishing for it. "Mine."

"Doctors can't say 'Oops,' " the doctor said. "Doctors say '*There*.' "

Jack had resisted the temptation to run his latest symptoms by the doctor, but when the doctor asked him how he was, Jack told the truth about the shoulder that had betrayed him. The doctor was in orthopedics and so gifted at treating sports injuries that he had become a team physician, retained to see to football stars. It looked glamorous to Jack—his friend going out onto the field and examining the swelling million-dollar knees. But it was really "like veterinary medicine," the doctor had told him. "You can't get a history from those guys."

"I'll give you a shot of cortisone after dinner," the doctor said.

Jack was glad Vicki had gone to check on the corn and hadn't heard him use the word *betray*. When she joined them back on the deck, Jack asked Vicki if she would get him another beer.

"Why? Your leg broken, hon?"

"Bring me one, too," the doctor told Jack.

They ate around a redwood picnic table with a pole poked

through the center for an umbrella. There were pink flamingos on the plastic tumblers and chili peppers painted on the rims of the plates. "In a year or so," the doctor said, "we'll have a swimming pool to look out onto."

Their aging dog, Banker, grayed at the temples and muzzle, with his air of a retired cruise director, got up from under the table to check out the new dog that had moved in next door. Jack and the doctor got going about the Knicks until Vicki mimed the act of sawing, sawing off her place from their part of the table. She had learned the gesture from Jack. When she had his attention, she said, "I want you to see my friend Trina. It's not like that—she's a psychic."

Vicki's favorite subject after feelings was the paranormal.

"You know, I bribed the doctor here to go to a hypnotist to quit smoking," she said. "If he'd have given it a chance, it might have worked."

"The guy didn't swing a watch on a chain," the doctor told Jack. "He just talked to me really slowly. He *bored* me into a half-trance, something you know I can get at any goddamn dinner party."

"Trina has movie star clients," Vicki said. "She looks like a movie star herself. She'll come to your house."

"I had an out-of-body experience before I left," Jack said, playing with her. "And it was good," he said, reflective, " 'cause I could help myself pack."

Vicki stood up to clear the table.

"It looks like Vicki here is doing all the work," the doctor pointed out.

Jack leaned back in his chair and drawled, "*I* have no problem with Vicki doing all the work."

"Jack?"

"Vick?"

"I used to think a lot of you."

She brought out a stack of dessert plates and a string-tied bakery box. "You want to do a line of pie?"

"Dogs heard you," the doctor said. Banker had returned from telling off the neighbors for starting their car. He had with him the puppy from next door, a clumsy mutt named Boss that it had fallen to Vicki to train.

"He's been gaining a pound a day," Vicki said, admiring.

"He's a miracle of cell division," the doctor said, scooting him over to Jack.

Jack examined the pup's chest and belly. "Where do the batteries go?"

Over bourbon-pecan pie, Vicki asked about the breakup and Jack tried to change the subject. When she prefaced a remark with "She wasn't nice enough to me not to tell you this," Jack could tell she was in his corner.

None of it was news to him, but he could hear what Vicki was saying. Not understand "where she was coming from"— he could literally hear her voice. Toward the end, he hadn't been able to hear his wife. When he asked her a question and cared about the answer, he could not seem to keep his attention fixed on her. "What do you mean?" he would say to Alex and hope she would repeat the gist of it.

Jack didn't have to say anything to Vicki because, at their feet, the puppy let pass audible gas.

"The bloom is off the rose," Jack said.

"The plug is on the nose," the doctor said. Both men waved their hands in front of their faces.

A beetle flew into Vicki's cleavage; she stood to flick it out, and the doctor said you couldn't blame it for trying.

Jack said, "What movie star does your psychic friend look like tomorrow?"

*　　*　　*

Jack woke to the sound of his car alarm. He went to the kitchen to look out onto the driveway and found Vicki leaning on a counter, laughing.

"You missed it," she said. "Boss went over to pee on your tire? He lifted his leg and set off the alarm and toppled right over."

Jack disconnected the alarm—Boss had hidden in shame—and went back inside the house for coffee.

Vicki was running a roll of masking tape up and down an arm of her cardigan, picking up fur. She handed it to Jack to do her back. She said, "Breakfast?"

"What've we got?"

"If we had some ham we could have ham and eggs—" Vicki said, and waited for Jack to join her on "if we had some eggs."

Jack looked at her samples of countertop materials—a kitchen renovation was next—and watched her chop a pepper for an eggless omelet.

"There are appliances that do that for you."

"But I hate to move into the twentieth or twenty-first century, whichever this is," Vicki said, and reached to turn up a song of busted romance that was on the kitchen radio. Jack listened until an ad for some lame kind of career came on. He had a small graphics business that ran itself; every ad he saw or heard made him think: Is this what I'm supposed to do next?

Vicki worked three days a week at the hospital as a physical therapist, sometimes carrying out her husband's instructions. She taught people how to walk again, helped them recover a grip. She gave a surpassing deep-heat massage, the doctor told Jack, and Vicki herself had several times offered this to him. Jack had been afraid he might *respond* and embarrass them both, so had always begged off. But this morning, when she saw him straining to look over his shoulder at the dogs, he let her work on the back of his neck.

When she finished, he said, "I've got something for you."

He opened his gym bag and took a tiny box out of a zippered nylon pocket. Inside, under a layer of cotton, were gold earrings that each framed a piece of round onyx in the center.

"You have pierced ears, right?" he said.

"I love them," Vicki said, putting them on. She moved to a hallway mirror and pulled her tangled hair away from her face.

"They came with blue stones or red ones, too," Jack said. "The salesgirl kept pushing me to get a color, but I'm a big black man." He snorted and said, "Yeah, I'm Denzel Washington."

Vicki touched her ears and turned from side to side for Jack to see. "Trina's coming at two," she told him. "I'll be out of the way."

"What do I do with her?" Jack said.

"*She'll* tell *you*," Vicki said, and left for the hospital.

Jack was wearing a T-shirt Alex had brought him from last year's sales conference. It said across the front: THE DANTEL GROUP COMMITMENT TO EXCELLENCE 1993. His gym bag said: the DANTEL GROUP THE LEADERSHIP ADVANTAGE 1992, and—no telling why since they didn't have a child—there was a baby's bib in the glove compartment with another go-getter slogan. (Nineteen eighty-nine—BUILDING ON THE BEST—was the only year in their years together that Alex hadn't brought Jack back a souvenir. That was the year the company had tried to cut corners. Alex's budget for the conference had been reduced, and the motivational speaker she'd been able to afford was the backup quarterback for a losing team. He had, it turned out, one speech for all occasions and had earnestly urged the management team of The DanTel Group to "stay in school.")

Jack hoped he had one clean T-shirt left. He had packed up a box of his clothes to take along, but instead of loading it into the car, he had left it beside a Dumpster, saying, "This'll show *me*! This shirt I wore last summer?—I won't be wearing *it* again."

Jack shaved and put on an old blue shirt that Alex had told him played up his own blue eyes. He worked a snakeskin belt that belonged to the doctor through the loops of his jeans, then took it off in case it scrambled signals to the psychic. He practiced a clear countenance in the mirror, reminded himself that this was not a date, and smoked a joint while watching a sports roundup show on TV.

The psychic, who was only as spooky as any beautiful girl, had barely had time to begin when Alex called from California to tell Jack that her mother had had a stroke. Jack asked if she wanted him to come back, but Alex said no, she wanted to talk to him was all.

Jack apologized to the psychic as he walked her to the door. He asked if he could take her to dinner the next night in lieu of a reading.

"What are you doing with a psychic?" Alex asked.

"Vicki set it up," Jack said.

"She say anything about us?" Alex said. "Not Vicki, the psychic?"

"Trina," Jack said. "She said my departed cousin Barry is still looking out for me."

"You *hated* Barry," Alex said. "*Barry's* looking out for you?"

"She said he was in the room with us," Jack told Alex. "I told her to get him out of there!"

Jack didn't tell Alex that he had invited the psychic to dinner. They talked about her mother, who had been as much his mother as hers.

"Alex," Jack said after a while, "we've managed to talk for an hour without either one of us crying."

And Alex said, "Hang up right now."

When she had recovered, she phoned Jack back. She was wistful and reminiscent, as though her mother's life had already ended. Alex said her mother was the oldest person kids called by her first name. She said she had so many friends, and always remembered which sorrow went with which person. Jack said their friends from high school, when they came back to visit their parents, always called on *her* mother, too.

When the conversation ended, Jack thought about all the things he hadn't seen coming. He walked the residential streets until dark, saw timed lights lighting and dimming, controlled by preset clocks.

The next day: "What did you think of Trina?" Vicki said.

"High marks," Jack said, "but there's still the long program and the free skating." He almost told Vicki what he hadn't told Alex, that the psychic had predicted a turbulent year ahead with the love of his life.

Vicki was assembling an ambitious salad of smoked trout and red lettuce and grapefruit—substituted, she said, for a citrus type of fruit you couldn't get in this country.

Earlier, Jack had heard her on the phone with the doctor; he heard her say "setback" and thought they were talking about him till he could tell they were talking about a patient.

"Me, me, me," Jack had chanted to himself.

He looked at the French cookbook she'd left open on the counter, and said, "Cauliflower *Grenobloise?*"

"I've made it before," Vicki said. "It's not as throw-uppy as it sounds."

Without looking up from her work, she said, "Not that I'm pushing you out the door, but I was thinking we should get you some books on tape for when you drive home."

"You don't think they're kind of dangerous?" Jack said. "I'm listening to the book and it's a really good part when I reach the house, so I pull into the garage and close the door and keep the car running to find out what happens and they find me in the car the next morning dead?"

Vicki handed him a jar of seedy mustard sealed with wax. "Can you do this for me?"

Jack opened the jar, then poured himself a scotch. He tore off the corner of a bag of cheese-flavored popcorn, summoning Banker and Boss. The dogs had been napping in the herb garden, and came inside wagging thyme, basil, and dill through the kitchen. Jack flicked kernels at the older dog, who caught them with a snap in the air. *The clean way a dog enlists your heart,* he thought.

Vicki mixed a vinaigrette and joined him, minus the scotch. She tried in vain to control the pup. "You can't train a dog with popcorn flying through the air," Jack said.

"Then give it a rest," Vicki said to Jack. "Watch this."

She got the puppy to sit but couldn't get him to lie down. She tried to ask a question about Alex's mother, but the puppy wanted to play, so her question was spliced and punctuated with commands—"Do you DOWN think you will NO go to California SIT to be with Alex?"—a kind of canine Tourette's.

"Everyone's out there now," Jack said. "It's later she'll maybe need help."

"What about you?"

"I always need help," Jack said, and reached across the table for the smaller of the local papers. He turned to the "Tide Table" and, with a couple of hours before he had to pick up Trina, asked Vicki if she wanted to take the dogs to the beach.

Jack picked up the car keys when Vicki came out of her bedroom pulling on a large faded work shirt over a modest one-piece bathing suit. Vicki opened the tailgate of her station wagon, and Banker jumped in. The puppy whimpered until Vicki bent over and lifted him.

It was late enough in the day that they had most of the beach to themselves. Jack surveyed the surf as they hopped across still-hot sand; he said, "Look—the bluefish are running!"

Bluefish churned the water in a feeding frenzy. Closer up, Jack and Vicki could see two-footers leaping, roiling in the waves not six feet from the sand, scaring up bait fish onto the shore. There was no stepping around them, the sudden numbers of them, so that fish wiggled inside sandals, fish were under their feet, inside of their shoes and they had to unbuckle those shoes and make squeamish faces as they held the shoes away from their bodies and the thin silver bait fish, inches long, rained to the sand.

"The bluefish in a school, do they know one another?" This from Vicki, who did not wait for an answer but hooted at Jack to look at Banker, who was sitting at attention a few feet out to sea with the tail of a fish waving up and down in his mouth until with one intake of breath the dog sucked the fish in and gulped it down.

Jack was instantly giddy with fish. He scooped up handfuls of fish and, fast as he could, hurled them back into the water as though their lives were not already over.

Vicki gathered shells that she scattered in the garden when they got home. She threw wet towels across the picnic table to dry.

In the shower, watching sand wash down the drain, Jack recalled the psychic's prediction of a turbulent year ahead, and it struck him that the psychic had not said that Alex was the love of his life. He had *assumed* that was who she was talking about.

This made him happy. "I am started," he quoted the old poem, "the tugs have left me."

He was ready for whatever the psychic could tell him. He wanted to be told what was coming and where he had been. And if you had to, he reasoned, there was nothing wrong with faking your way to where you belonged.

Trina was shorter than Jack remembered. She had, therefore, to look up at a man, exposing her throat, which was unadorned but for the deep V of a V-necked dress to entice the eye down.

"I thought we'd go into the city," Jack said, and headed back onto the expressway where, for the ten remaining miles, they had a view of the skyline at dusk.

Jack said, "The city looks pretty good."

The psychic said, "Give it a minute."

HOUSEWIFE

She would always sleep with her husband and with another man in the course of the same day, and then the rest of the day, for whatever was left to her of that day, she would exploit by incanting, "*French* film, *French* film."

THE ANNEX

The headlights hit the headstone and I hate it all over again. It is all that I can ever see, all that I can ever talk about. There is nothing else to talk about.

It is right there out in front. I mean the cemetery that is out over there across the street from our house. With the headlights turned off and the car parked outside the garage, there is enough of a moon to see that there is no missing it over there across the street in the part of the cemetery the people around here call the annex.

The annex is for when the cemetery fills up.

Anyway, there is a stone there that has the baby's name on it. And there was a week-old bouquet of something all dried up past knowing what it was that was tied with wide white ribbon out there until the time I came home today. There was a white ribbon on it. I could have taken the ribbon away. But the woman would have come and put another one, I suppose.

This is a cemetery which has its shapely tended trees and flowerful shrubs and Halloween headstones that go back two hundred years. The thing that is different about the annex is that the annex is not landscaped. It is a wild grown-over field of scrub oak and dune grass that gets bulldozed and plowed under as the need, in somebody's mind, arises, one row at a time. Except that the men who run the bulldozers and things don't call what they are clearing a row.

I made a point of finding out.

They call it a plot line.

From every window in the front of our house, when you look out, that gravestone is what you see—from the sunporch, from the living room, from the dining room, from the bedroom upstairs, from the garage where my husband and I have been cleaning out the junk that belonged to the previous owners, which is why I cannot now find the shovel when I reach up to the place where it should be.

There is every other kind of tool hanging from nails pounded in. My husband is good at all the housey things that require these bucksaws and shingling hammers and extension ladders, the pitchfork and pruning shears, the lazy boy, the pick.

You see what it is? It is a two-car garage with a loft where we haven't had time yet to make the big effort to clean out the crap from the previous owners, why didn't they clean out their own crap, is what I want to know. The oversized stuffed animals, the rotten throw pillows, the mildewed best-sellers from other summers, everything cheap and ruined and left behind.

Where is the shovel?

Can you believe it? The flowers were baby's breath.

I wanted to ask my husband if you call it a baby at the age of five months.

I mean five *unborn* months!

According to him, my husband, the date on the stone is only the month and the year. But I have not crossed the street to see if that is really what the stone says.

I can tell you it's got an arch across the top. But no cherubs that I can see.

And I can see.

For days after the burial, I would go inside the house, leaving weeds unpulled in the border of portulaca; I would leave the hose coupling loose and spitting, and hide out in the kitchen while the woman visited the site. I would pour myself a glass of lemonade and carry it into the dining room and look across the street to where the woman had parked her rental car and was standing there looking at her dead baby.

She came with some new flowers today. I saw her come with them. They are a big bunch of purple cosmos. Local—what's in bloom right now.

The other thing she did was plant a row of impatiens that I happen to know will not last any time at all in this heat.

She would know it, too, if she actually lived around here.

Well, she doesn't, thank God.

Something else, which is that she was wearing a sweater that I could tell was from a catalog that I had just been looking at that I myself get in the mail, too. I could see the ribbing at the neck and wrists. She was wearing it in plum. I was going to order it in black.

Was.

Although black is not a very smart color to wear around here. Not with the dust that is forever finding its way onto everything I wear. Not when you have to go into a filthy garage with its leftover heaps of plastic crap.

What did he use the shovel for last?

To move our scraps onto the compost pile, chances are. But he would not have left the shovel outside, would he? He is careful with tools. He is careful, and he has a good eye. He was the one who kept me from throwing out the one good thing the previous owners left behind—an ice bucket with a procession of penguins marching right around the middle of it.

There was a high chair left behind in the garage, too. It was a pretty good one, I suppose—if you could get yourself not to see Donald Duck saying "Let's eat!" painted on it. The lousy thing was that he cleaned it up and drove it over to the house she was going to rent for the summer. I suppose he thought it would be a useful thing for her to have for when she had the baby. Well, she never had it!

Maybe he should have also taken over the chess set the previous owners left behind. I mean, you never can tell about babies, can you.

I bet we never get the high chair back. Someone who buries her baby in your front yard is not going to think to give you back anything you ever lent her. Not that she'd have to go out of her way to do it. I mean, she's there every day—at the annex, that is.

And now our dog goes over there to bark at her when she comes.

She's usually happy to just tag along with us around the yard as we garden. She likes to dig in the dirt, nap in the sun. The usual. At the end of each day we walk her across the street and through the annex to a pond beyond the cemetery where she swims out under a covered bridge to fetch her ball and sticks. We don't want the dog to cross the street without us, but that is what she does when there is a person who gets out of a car and stands there so close by.

When we first moved here, we didn't know the streetlight

was going to shine in our bedroom window. Is this why we're up so much—because of the light? Or is it because we know that I have what she already had and still wants?

I can almost believe that somewhere is the person who could look across the street and see a vision of perfect peace, the resting place of someone who, unlike the rest of us, was only encouraged and adored.

When sunlight hits the headstone so, it flashes through the branches of the copper beech we planted to obscure it. If I stare long enough, it will burn a hole through my head.

For the rest of my habitation in this house, in this marriage, her baby will be buried in my life unless I can make my way to back behind the stacks of shingles and to back behind the row of storm doors and to back behind the rolled hammock—and maybe find the goddamn shovel.

THE NEW LODGER

One of the locals said at the bar, "I hear you've got a new lodger." I thought, Word travels fast—I only got here last night.

In a corner booth of the Soggy Dollar, an old beach bar that also serves food, I can listen to other customers without seeming to eavesdrop; I've got postcards fanned out on the table. I'm trying not to say the same thing on every one.

The best is an aerial view of the road you take to get here. Seeing this ahead of time, you would choose to go somewhere else. Hugging the inside curves of the road, taking steady deep breaths, I can drive myself here, but not back. I hire one of the locals to drive my car down to the junction of the road where I can take over. I arrange for a taxi to meet us there, and I cover the large fare back.

"It's imported," the bartender says, and pours a glass for the guy at the bar who meant *lager.*

"What do you think?" the bartender says. "Should I order more?"

It is not easy to get to this beach. The one road is dangerous even in good weather, even during the day. It winds around the hills on the edge of a cliff, climbing above the ocean until it suddenly grades down. People have lost their lives on the way to this beach, or on their way home from it. Heading home puts you in the outer lane where there is no guard rail, not that it would help. There is only the occasional turnout for a scenic lookout point, and people mindful of others pull over to let them pass.

It's a moody beach, more often foggy than bright. It is rarely warm enough to take a swim. It is pretty to look at, the cove a perfect C, and there's the haunted house tour if you're that hard up. For excitement: the peril of a storm that washes away a residence, fire in the dry hills, a fight that breaks out among bikers passing through. The new lager.

I hadn't been to this town since the time, years before, when I nearly drowned. I credit the pancakes I'd had that morning for giving me something to draw on to fight the current, until I remembered not to fight the current, but to swim parallel to land until I had swum past the current and could then turn in toward shore.

I took a room in the annex to the Soggy Dollar that had not been built the last time I was here.

The first time I saw this beach was with a man who, during our stay, compared himself to Jesus, so the trip had not been a waste of time for him. Someone else brought me the second time. We rented, for a day, a cabin across from the beach with atmosphere and damp chairs. I told him it was my birthday. He left me in the cabin, and came back carrying a piece of chocolate cake. There were no plates or forks. He watched me as I ate the cake. I said, "What—am I covered with frosting?" "Every day of your life," he said, and went home to his wife.

The third time I had those pancakes.

I'll stay for as long as it takes. I will not get in touch with anyone on my list. Not the friends of friends who live nearby, whose gardens I must see, whose children I must meet. Nor will I visit the famed nature preserve, home of a vanishing tern. Why get acquainted with what will be left, or leaving?

Farther up the coast is where you have to go for stuffed plush whales and orange rubber crabs, for T-shirts and mugs, placemat maps. Postcards are what the store can manage. That's okay with me. I don't have to hunt up souvenirs. It is enough to feel the pull of the old home, pulling apart the new.

TUMBLE HOME

. . . I would have traded
places with anyone raised on love,
but how would anyone raised on love
bear this death?
                    —Sharon Olds, from "Wonder"

I have written letters that are failures, but I have written few,
I think, that are lies. Trying to reach a person means asking the
same question over and again: Is this the truth, or not? I begin
this letter to you, then, in the western tradition. If I understand it, the western tradition is: Put your cards on the table.

This is easier, I think, when your life has been tipped
over and poured out. Things matter less; there is the joy of
being less polite, and of being less—not more—careful. We
can say everything.

Although maybe not. Like in fishing? The lighter the
line, the easier it is to get your lure down deep. Having delivered myself of the manly analogy, I see it to be not a failure,
but a lie. How can I possibly put an end to this when it feels
so good to pull sounds out of my body and show them to you.

These sounds—this letter—it is my lipstick, my lingerie, my high heels.

Writing to you fills the days in this place. And sometimes I long for days when nothing happens. "Not every clocktick needs a martyr."

The trees are all on crutches, on sawed-off braces of deadwood notched into Y-shaped crooks for support. The birds that nest in these crippled trees line their nests with the clumps of fur that come loose to float over brambled grass when the house cat is groomed out of doors. The birds are fat on seeds that did not flower. Seed packets mark our places in books. Everyone here is better than they were there, "there" being anywhere else. The fact of someplace else means we are not native. Not one of us started here first.

What got me here was a six, according to the nurse who had devised her own scale. And I remember thinking, What must be the sevens and eights if this is only a six?

I have killed two of the wrong things to kill. It is not like the city where you know what to kill. First a preying mantis (they will eat the other bugs if you give them a chance to do it) and then a firefly which, without its glow, was just a beetle in the bathroom.

Some of those of us who stay here appreciate the trend toward doctors calling their patients "guests." But I think I would be happy to wear a plastic bracelet and a white gown that fails to cover my backside. Patients, guests, we are expected to get well enough to leave, even if it is only for an afternoon drive. When I get a pass and a car comes to pick me up, what I have the driver do is park across the street from the gate so that I have this place in sight until it is time for me to come back. The driver can keep the radio on if he likes—or if she does. All I want is to see where I'm going next.

A pass is a formality; we can leave anytime we want. I usually call a car, but others take the bus into town. The time I took the bus, I felt sure that if the side of my face were to touch the window glass, the skin would be abraded, and I spent the duration of the ride leaning into the window.

At a famous institute of technology there is a room filled with scale-model trains set up to run in perpetuity through a scale model of the town that is home to the institute. You can watch the trains power along the tracks and through the tunnels and avoid near-collisions before you notice the clock on the wall and its madly spinning hands.

The clock is on scale time, of course.

Those of us who have to leave here, even briefly, feel, I think, that time, anywhere else, is like this—like scale time.

What goes on when things go well: I see Warren pushing the house cat "out to sea" on the Styrofoam cover of the ice chest on the pond. I brush a shed hair from my collar and the hair turns out to be cornsilk.

There is the unidentified object that flies. When any one of us spots it hovering above the house, we all grab a book and run to the lawn and hold up the books to show them what kind of people we are.

Shakespeare and Tolstoy!

Run get Jane Austen!

If you take the highway to get here, you will pass our favorite sign. Posted at the entrance to the housing development a few miles back, the sign says, RESIDENTIAL HOMES. Some of the residential homes are under construction still. We like the smell of cut lumber, the way post and beam meet, the men working so fast, cobwebs can't form in the eaves.

The Southerner among us is Chatten Gaines. She will take a chair in the sun and produce a bottle of lotion, her Swiss Performing Extract, and Warren will ask, "What does it do— cartwheels?" Chatty will say to watch out he doesn't become an outpatient.

The definition of outpatient here is: a person who has fainted, who has passed *out.*

I believe that moisturizing has become as important to Chatty as accessorizing—that retail verb. I can tell you that both activities are crucial to me.

The vegetable garden is open to us all, and all are encouraged to cultivate something in it. Consequently, there are rows of trendy lettuce, beans climbing poles tied up like tepees, tiny yellow tomatoes shaped like lightbulbs, kale not even the moles will eat, and my own contribution—nothing so literal as a vegetable, but row after row of perfect dwarf zinnias. This is not bragging; given the soil here, you can shake the seeds out like salt on a baked potato, tamp not a spicule of soil on top of them, and up they will come to a height greater than you would want.

I am not quite myself, I think.

But who here is quite himself? And yet there is a way in which we all are more ourselves than ever, I suppose.

I have made friends with the Southerner. Chatty is not one of those ironic nicknames as when a fat person is known as "Tiny." Chatty says that when she was a girl away at school and the holidays were coming, her mother would ask if she was bringing home any listeners. Chatty talks about the poltergeist and what will it do next—turn up the stereo in the music room, run an upstairs shower, turn on the fan above the stove if it doesn't like the smell of our dinner cooking?

The nearest neighbor is not so near. Still, you can hear his country music, faint from down the road, till all hours of night. The nearest neighbor is from the South, and how he knows if he likes you is he puts on Hank Williams and do you know who that is singing? Coming in so low when you are lying in bed awake—it is the pleasure of keeping the radio on all night when you were just able to have a friend stay over, and all you cared to drink in the dark was ginger ale.

Sometimes in the dark a person will call out, "Where am I?" and really want to know. What must be the nines and tens?

Have you noticed there are no second sheets? I use the blue letter paper with my name at the top of *every* page. I do this because of a dream I had the first night I was here. In the dream, I went to pick up the stationery I had ordered for myself in waking life. But in the dream, there was a different name at the top of each sheet.

I did not have to puzzle over what this meant. Those people whose names were on my stationery? It seems to me that I am every one of them.

Writing to you, I am myself. And what that self is I will tell you: a graveyard. I can be a graveyard. But that is a thing you would have to find out for yourself. A person cannot tell you a thing and have you just believe them. A person has to prove it. You would find out, if you cared to, that I have told no one about you. As if anyone would believe me if I had! As

I think you would be the first to agree, it is hard to know what to believe anymore.

Although this is the kind of place that can call your bluff. It's like—let's say you are at a mixer in high school, and a boy you don't like keeps asking you to dance. Let's say he keeps coming over, and each time he asks, you say, "Let's wait for a good one." Then "Great Balls of Fire" comes on, and what are you going to say—"I'm waiting for 'Color My World'?"

This place was once a school for girls. For one hundred years a tony school for girls in the Georgian style with a circular drive, then mounting fiscal problems and a merger with the corresponding school for boys, only the name retained in the hyphenated name of the new institution.

After many years vacant, what was once a parlor hung with portraits of the founder, the place the girls received their guests, is now a lounge we call the Hostility Suite. The paint is fresh, the armchairs inviting, the wood polished; it stops short of fussy. It is easy to imagine mattresses being pulled off the beds upstairs, and teenaged girls in baby-doll pajamas surfing them down the stairs.

And how about this for the way life works—one of the patients used to be a student. When Chatty was away at school, this was the school she went to until she was kicked out, that is, for drinking. She plays the drinking down, says she monitored herself using the Jimi Hendrix test: Am I choking on my own vomit? No? Then I can have another drink.

Chatty has lost nearly all of her short-term memory, and she loves it. Wasn't that the point, she asks, of drinking? But she says her recollections of school are untouched. She said a platinum screen goddess had attended in the thirties, and had sneaked out through the chapel to elope. Chatty said that every girl in the school for years after claimed that the screen star's room was her own.

Chatty remembers jumping out of her window and running to the beach where, under a full moon, you could make shadows on the sand. She said she sabotaged convocations, substituting vegetable seeds for the flowers in the Centennial Garden, so that where should have bloomed hollyhocks—corn stalks. And in place of delphiniums, butternut squash.

School had not been, for me, the place of unalloyed joy and fulfillment that it was for her. When the other girls squealed, "Let's jump in the car and go have hijinks," I was the one who asked, "How far is the car?" If deferred to in any way, I would go up in a bonfire of self-immolation. Now here we both are. And I am writing to you.

I have to roll up my sleeves to do so.

Did you wonder why my clothes were too big? Why I kept having to push up the sleeve of my sweater to lift my cup of tea? This is a holdover from high school, from when I read in a women's magazine that to make yourself look small, you should wear your clothes too big. The column went on—it said don't stop there! It said buy yourself oversized furniture so as to look small and delicate when curled up in a chair.

Are you wondering why a person who is already small would want to make herself look smaller? That should become clear. Not everything I know is something I want to see. Though on highways and, once, on a mountain road, I have strained to see things I didn't want to see. The worst I ever saw was a body without a head. That was when I realized that I don't mind seeing everything as long as everything is there for me to see.

The person I strained to see on the mountain road was

myself. A paramedic wouldn't let me. He cut away my jacket and sweater, then he scissored off my shirt. It seemed to me he could have covered me up faster than he did. In the hospital, a doctor laid his hand on my shoulder. Does this hurt? he asked. Moving his hand to my collarbone, What about here? And lower. Does this feel good?

It felt like that joke that I can't exactly remember, but that has to do with a woman being examined in a doctor's office. I think the way it goes is that after the naked woman has been thoroughly examined, she asks what is wrong with her. And the man in the white coat says he wouldn't know, he's not the doctor.

When someone starts heading for the life they had before, Chatty says, "Steam your face." She herself will lean over a pot of boiling water with a towel held tented over her head and over the pot. She puts chamomile leaves in the boiling water and says the effect is soothing. But chamomile is the tea you drank that day, and the scent of it here is too much for me.

I lost my watch the day we met. Without a watch, to find the time I pick up the remote and turn on the weather channel. Trying to find the time, I track tornadoes in the plains states. A lost watch is something I will have to look up. I, who above and beyond the normal precautions, make fortune-courting gestures such as placing my shoes at my bedroom door with one shoe pointing in and one shoe pointing out—this to prevent nightmares—although it makes me look as though I don't know whether I am coming or going. I am superstitious, and never change the bedsheets on a Friday (it gives the devil control of your dreams). When I wanted to measure your intentions when you agreed to meet me for tea, I threw apple pips into a fire and said, "If you love me, pop and fly, if you hate me, lay and die." A lost watch is something I will have to look up. I am superstitious, and sometimes con-fused, opening an umbrella before I leave the house, but never, ever, wearing sunglasses inside.

A fetish for me, sunglasses, so I was glad that you said you liked the green ones. "Show me what else you've got in there"—when I put the glasses back in my bag, how nicely you cued me up. Show me what else you've got in there. Because the last time someone said that to me, it was a gorilla that said it, the one who talks in sign language with her hands. She said the same thing to me—I sat as close to her, a famous gorilla, as I sat to you—after she, too, admired my green-rimmed glasses. I think you could see that, had you let me, I would have talked about that gorilla till brooms were thrust under our feet. The situation is this: If you stopped people on the street and asked how they felt about gorillas, I would be among the ones who lighted right up.

And she said with her hands, "Show me what else you've got in there." For her, I took out everything I had and held it up so she could say to me with her hands, "Pretty"—the green-rimmed glasses, and "Put on"—a tube of lipstick! And when I held up an invitation to an opening (not one of yours), at a gallery, held it up so she could see the side of the card that showed the artist's work, "Lousy painting" is what she signed! Because she paints, too. I wish I could tell people here that you said to that, "They all do."

I would have told you about how, when it was time for me to leave, she asked me with her hands to stay, but it was enough that you said, "I envy you your gorilla."

I warn you: Don't get me started on dogs! Volunteers from the shelter arrive with orphaned dogs to walk. Karen has become loquacious, but only when a dog is present. On the days the dogs come, Karen sings the same song, only changing the words to fit each newcomer: "Sad-eyed Mongrel (Mastiff, Shepherd) of the Lowlands."

Since the dogs began to visit, Karen has been going to chapel. There, although she does not have religion, she lights a candle—"for Saint Bernard," she says, her only joke.

The dogs from the shelter take a great deal of pleasure in pissing on pine needles and lapping at mud puddles when you volunteer to walk them in the woods behind the pound. We can do this sometimes. Karen has become enamored of the shelter's mascot, a dog who, because of his age, is unlikely to be adopted. Banker came to visit once, but frightened another guest, so every day that she is allowed, Karen drags a vinyl chair across the concrete floor and positions it in front of Banker's cage when the weather is too bad for her to take him outside.

In the first flush of companionship, Karen and Banker had rolled in the woods, and Karen, careless in a sleeveless blouse, had found patches of rash from poison ivy crusting into epaulettes on her shoulders.

Sometimes I go with her to the shelter, and that is how I heard about the job that she lost. She said a dove was walking north on Madison Avenue, walking with a limp, when it turned left at 73rd Street and entered Pierre Deux. Karen was on her way to a job interview, but she followed the bird into the store. The bird was hurt, that was clear, so Karen said she wrapped it in a remnant of French challis and took it to the hospital known as the Mayo Clinic for animals. She said she wrote out a check for the bird's costly treatment, then put it in a cab for Brooklyn where there is a sanctuary for such cases. She took the driver's number, told him the person at the other end would call her when he arrived.

She said she missed her interview. So did this make her compassionate, Karen asked, or just ambivalent?

Banker had gone from a sit to lying down. The dog's eyes remained on Karen the entire time. When she finished speaking, he thumped his tail.

"Good boy," Karen said.

A young woman came over to the pen with a large plastic scoop. She opened Banker's kennel and removed his dish, filled it with food and put it back in the part of the kennel that was unroofed and open to the air. The woman left to tend the other dogs, and Karen spoke to Banker; she said it was exhausting to always have two jobs—your job, and the job of being able to do your job in the first place.

A blue jay dove into Banker's bowl and flew off with a kibble from his dinner.

"How do you do both?"

My guess was you worked twice as hard, but I wasn't the one she asked.

Only Warren can pull her out of a mood. Last night she told us she was going to go look at a litter of puppies. Warren told her there was no such thing as "just looking" at puppies.

"Often you *do* see puppies that just aren't cute enough," he said. Then he wondered aloud what kind of puppy did we think Karen could pass up. "Let's see," he said in Karen's voice, "all the internal organs are on the outside? I can live with that."

"I like golden retrievers," Karen said.

"You don't think they've kind of got that Stepford thing going?" Warren said.

Warren is pronounced Warn, or Worn.

You know how most of us don't say things in a memorable way? The way everything sounds already *handled* by everyone else? But Warren says, when he is angry, that he's as mad as all outdoors. He says do I want to meet him after dinner and chew the rug? He says he can't always follow the threat of my conversation.

When Chatty sees Warren in her old school dorm, she says she nearly calls out, "Man on the floor!"

I think you would like Warren. He drinks Courvoisier in a Coke can, and has a laugh like you'd find in a cartoon balloon.

Sometimes we go into town together. Last time, we got a ride in with the gardener. He had to stop at the Ford dealership to pick up a part for the van, and I followed Warren into the car repair dock. Warren took a cigarette out of his pack, and a uniformed employee said, "No smoking, sir. They don't let us smoke here." Warren took out a pack of matches and lit his cigarette. "But *you* can smoke. You're a customer," the mechanic said. Warren flicked his used match into the lube bay and looked straight at the guy. "I guess if *I* buy a truck here, I can smoke, too," the guy said.

That was the day before Warren's parents came to visit. They were coming from a small town in Texas. I told him I looked forward to meeting them, even though it always seemed that the very things others find charming about your parents—the feyness, the provincialism, the odd takes on everything—are the things that make you want to rustle up a firing squad.

Warren smoked his cigarette, held it low on his lip. At dinner the first night, Chatty had said in my ear that if Jean-Paul Belmondo had not been born, Warren would not have had a personality. She said it was hard not to notice that it was a long way from Belmondo to Warren Moore.

He pulled a folded snapshot from the pocket of his canvas pants. It was an aerial view of a small island. The island was shaped like a heart.

"They came to my island in the spring," he said, of the last time he'd seen his parents, "when everything was in bloom and I had cleaned up the house. They were supposed to stay a week, but after two days, my mother said they had to go home. She hadn't liked anything about it," Warren said, "not the ride on my boat, not even that I had rigged a pot at the end of the pier and dropped the shrimp into boiling water the minute I fished them out of the ocean. I called her back in Texas. I said, 'Dad was here last week, and he brought your evil twin.'"

The gardener had dropped us at the plant store. Warren had said he wanted to find a book on bulbs. Did he plan to be here to see fall-planted bulbs bloom next spring? The plant store is next door to a shuttered-by-day gay bar called Man-handlers. The owner of the bar also owns the plant store, which is why Warren calls it Planthandlers. He said it made him feel funny when he went in to buy tomatoes, and had to ask the owner for "Big Boys" and "Beefmaster."

Warren paid for his book. I looked at the back of his hands where intravenous drips had left tiny scars like age spots. We all have them.

The gardener came to fetch us that day toting a paper bag filled with dozens of packs of gum. He handed a couple of packs to each of us. He said it was for the moles in the garden, that we had to chew the gum, then put it down their holes because the moles like the taste and would eat it but couldn't digest it and it would kill them. He said he was also going to try those plastic pinwheels that you can get at carnivals, that those were supposed to work, too. Vibrations sent into the ground by the pinwheel spinning at the end of the stick.

We left Planthandlers with gum in our mouths. Outside, at the entrance to the greenhouse, a dog licked crumbs of fertilizer off the blade of a shovel.

When he is ready, Warren will return to his heart-shaped island. He says he can't wait, but he is waiting.

A thing I haven't told anyone is that *this* place is the place where I feel the way you would feel on a heart-shaped island, glad to open my eyes from dreams of the place I live where the boys next door are dim malevolent twins who ride their bicycles onto my lawn and say, when I go out to shoo them away, "We know you from somewhere." "You know me from right here," is what I tell them, and go back inside.

Tumble home. It's a shipbuilding term I learned from Warren. It's the place on a ship that is, if I understand him, the widest part of the bow before it narrows to cut through water—it is the point where the water parts and goes to one side of the ship or the other. To me, the tumble home is the place where nothing can touch you.

I have walked barefoot on floors so badly cleaned I had to brush off my feet before sliding them between the sheets at night. Floors cleaned not at all is what I mean, because the cleaning was left to me.

Here it's not my job so the floors are clean. Our rooms, Chatty says, are the same as years before. There are no college pennants tacked up on the walls, no posters of rock stars, either. Just serviceable furniture—a maple chest and desk, a single bed refreshed by the linen service weekly, and hangers that cannot be removed from the closet, a hotel touch. At the end of each hall is a kitchenette with baskets of apples and oranges, and packets of hot chocolate mix.

We can personalize the rooms to the extent we care to. Chatty hung curtains of crocheted lace, but I like a room that doesn't give a person away. Though I do display a collage I made. It is a photograph of a Great Dane looking at his leg where I strapped on a photo of a Timex to his wrist. The title of this piece is "Watchdog Watching." We're all artists here.

Would it make you uneasy to know that I have seen the inside of your house? Anyone who bought that magazine did. It surprised me. I would have guessed you lived in spare rooms done in stinging whites and grays. But there you were by a cozy fire in a house more lodge than stage. And in the studio where you paint: orderly racks of canvases, the wood-burning stove to heat the place. But is it a good idea to have an ax in the room where you work?

And a swimming pool in the backyard. I never had a swimming pool; I swam in a willow-ringed pond. My favorite thing was staying in the longest when a thunderstorm struck (*She is the smallest child who swings the highest* my mother once wrote in a letter to my father). What can I say about myself today? That I am the last to close a window when it rains.

I am writing now beside an open window in Little Egypt. When this was school, Chatty said, they called the smoker Little Egypt because of all the Camels in it. They blew their smoke out the window that overlooks the circular drive and from which we can see everyone arrive and leave.

Little Egypt is to the second floor what the Hostility Suite is to the first floor, only gamier. I can write to you here on an old school desk, the kind that is desktop and chair in one. There is a vending machine Chatty swears is the same one whose lineup the girls used to memorize when they were snowed in and bored. She said nobody ever ate the Good & Plentys because that is what they called the Trustees, the monied donors of laboratory and pool.

There is a television in here now. I'll watch whatever is on, such as the swimsuit special that I watched with Warren. It was actually about the *making* of the special, and it intercut footage of the models arching their backs in the surf with segments in which the photographer described what he had had to do to get that shot. Warren became irritated by the photographer's intrusion. He said it was like being a teenager and trying to masturbate to *Petticoat Junction,* moaning, "Betty Jo, Billie Jo, Bobbie Jo . . ." and all of a sudden there's—*Uncle* Joe!

My watching whatever Warren is watching is overcompensation for Chatty telling Warren what I said about his habits—that he watches too much, and what he watches is dumb. I have done this all my life, insisting, when caught out, that, "I *do* want to be your partner, and I *like* your ideas, and let's do *many more* projects together." Karen calls this syndrome "Tour of the Lodge." Her family bought an old fishing lodge on a scenic lake in Maine. It had been shut down for many years before they cleaned the place up and moved in. Karen said she would be riding her bike in the nearby hills and meet people on vacation who would stop their cars and ask her if the old fishing lodge was still open. No, Karen would say, the place has been shut down for years. And the disappointed travelers would begin to reminisce about the happy times there when the family was together, and Karen would wind up saying, The truth is *we* bought the fishing lodge, and if you've got the time, why don't you come on over and take a walk through. And then forfeit half a day to give nostalgic strangers a tour of the lodge.

I have left this place only one other time, to go into town with Chatty. She took me into the jewelry store—accessories. I usually wear silver (I did the day we met, you might recall), but the earrings Chatty was urging me to buy were gold domes embedded with small fake jewels.

"They look like a gift from someone who likes me but doesn't know me very well," I said.

"Like when you see men in pink sweaters," Chatty said.

I turned the counter mirror, put the earrings on, hooked my hair behind my ears.

"What would I wear them with?" I asked Chatty. "They don't go with anything I own."

"Then you'll have to start life anew," Chatty said.

I think you would like Chatty, though she can be a strong cup of tea. She has hit the change of life, and told me about a niece's wedding where she had to step back from the carved-ice swan—she thought she was going to melt it. She is given to asking leading questions ("How many feet do *you* use when you drive?") and making pronouncements with which you cannot argue: "I would rather buy a lot of presents for ten dollars each than a few for a hundred dollars that *look* like they cost ten."

I am the only one who seems to like her jokes. She tells them wrong, and I think her way is better. The one about Christa McAuliffe and Donna Rice both going down on the *Challenger*? Chatty told it this way: They both had sex all over Florida.

Chatty is surprised I like her. She says women who have only met her in line at a movie don't like her. She says she had always acted as if she were God's Gift, and then it had turned out—she *was* God's Gift.

Chatty seems content here. She says what is there to rush home to except threatening stacks of third-class mail.

Chatty believes in poltergeists, and I am the only person

here who does, too. I believe in it all. Can I tell you about London?—how outside of London, in a manor house run by the National Trust, I saw the ghost of a girl throw the ghost of a ball in an orchard for her little ghost dog? The girl was skipping soundlessly; the dog's jaws worked but there was no bark to hear. I saw them through an upstairs window, on the pane of which was scratched the date the mistress of the house had jumped. The date was the 1600s, and I knew to look for it from the guidebook to the house. The book said nothing about a ghost girl and dog.

The hair did not rise on my arms beneath my coat. The ghosts were a bonus and a comfort on the third and final stop of the tour I was on. I had lagged behind the group that had gone on ahead to look at ebonized, gilded armchairs in a dead duke's bedchamber.

We had stopped first at a cathedral whose famous spire was hidden under a tower of scaffold. The cathedral's famous choir was in concert in another country, so I bought tapes of their anthems and an evensong service, and breathed musty incense as the hour was marked by carillon. Grazing nearby were sheep descended from those whose wool, the sale of it, had built the cathedral. There were cows in the fields, too. I had just learned what the ancients used for shovels, that the trenches surrounding the site were dug from chalk with the shoulder blades of cattle.

The guidebook said that the mistress of the house had scratched the date in the window with the diamond in her ring. This is something I have always wanted to do—scratch on glass with a diamond.

A heavy fog had opened and then filled itself in. I wanted to stay at the window of that house, and never mind the veneered pianofortes and the lacquered candlestands. The girl and her dog were still visible below, keeping to the gravel path inside the court, then pausing for the girl to sit and rest on a weathered goblin-carved bench.

I watched until the girl stood up and led her dog, a kind of spaniel, to the South Gate of the garden. I could see, on the overthrow, the family coat of arms, and then the girl and her dog were gone. I looked up the gardens in the guidebook. There was a view from the South Gate of the formal avenues, the labyrinth of boxwood and yew. Close up, I could see the family motto as well as their coat of arms; translated from the Latin: No man can harm me unpunished.

The girl had not seemed to see me watching, although maybe ghosts know? Without having to turn to look up at you? These ghosts were not the first ghosts I had seen, but they were the first ones I saw that moved, as when the girl, who was dressed in a long white pinafore and short leather lace-up boots, threw the ball and her spaniel dog let it bounce on the ground before he jumped up to catch it in the air.

The ghosts I had seen before were at Stonehenge. They were the ghosts of roads—the long pairs of parallel lines leading up to the site, barely visible in the sod of surrounding fields. The roads of prehistory—dents now like the tracks a vacuum cleaner leaves in thick carpet. They made me think of American baseball fields and of the men who mow them daily, criss-crossing the green in different patterns every day, and of how—if the home team won—the men would repeat the pattern they had mowed the winning day.

On the bus on the way to our third and final stop, there was the cicada sound of automatic cameras on rewind.

And then the ghosts. And the stopped clocks. Stopped at the moment the duke had died.

The watch I lost the day we met was a cheap watch with

twelve dots of radium green for the numbers, but with none of the stuff painted on the hands. Knowing this did not keep me from looking in the dark at my arm, where what I could see was my watch but not the time.

I'm glad for the poltergeist here, the one that unscrews lightbulbs in the lamps, that leaves them loose in their sockets.

One day I asked the gardener what had gone wrong with my tulips. The last time I planted tulips (I am going back years here), they had bloomed right out of the ground—they had bloomed without stems, and had looked like ground cover. The gardener said the problem was low self-esteem. Then he laughed at my expression and said the bulbs had been confused, they must not have been planted deep enough and so had gotten warm, then cold, then warm again, until finally, confused, they had given up and bloomed.

I didn't tell the gardener that I had planted them half as deep as recommended to save them the work of pushing up through all that dirt. It seems that there is a lesson here, staring me in the face. I told you about the tulips to tell you something ordinary. The way, watching a movie, you find you want to scream, "Doesn't anyone eat or sleep in this film?"

All I remember of church when I was a child is a part of a sermon about the ordinary. The title of the sermon was "The Blessing of Dailiness," and had to do with why we should thank God for our toothbrush in the morning. We should thank God that each day must begin with an ordinary ritual, and not go immediately into crisis. It's a time-honored fact that after a close call, we all embrace the ordinary. But that is because it has become miraculous. Or *we* have—alive to see it.

In England, in another century, the "ordinary" was a clergyman appointed to prepare criminals for the death penalty. The clergyman would wind up his day in a house whose every fixture and appointment sprang from, and paid homage to, a politer way of living. How did he prepare them, the criminals, do you think?

You know, I often feel the effect of a place only after I leave it.

England!

Outside of London, a surprise I got was: the site was roped off. You had to view the site like an exhibit in a museum. It made me give up to learn that until a few years ago, you could hire a man in the village to chip off pieces of Stonehenge for you, to keep as souvenirs.

The guide gave us twenty minutes. Those of us on the tour found out that you cannot walk the circumference of the site and return to the bus in twenty minutes. You could walk the roped path, mud through the sheep-cropped grass, until the anxiety of being late and missing the bus turned you back around. At a point on the path, I held out my arm and cupped my hand so that it looked as though I was holding the site in my hand.

The highway you drive in on is very close to the monument. It is possible to pull over onto the shoulder and lean out a window and take a picture without leaving the car. I watched people do that. It was jarring, like finding the rope-laden stanchions holding us back.

I have seen things my mother never saw.

I often feel the effects of people only after they leave me.

In a locked metal box I took when my mother died, there is a button she would pin to her jacket on the days she led tours as a docent at the museum. "Art Has Drawing Power"—she never got tired of it.

My mother took me to the art museum once on a day she worked as a guide. I followed her on her rounds; it was a sunny day when few people wanted to be inside. I tagged along with a couple of stragglers who insisted they be given a tour.

Her remarks that day were perfunctory. I suspected her of cutting back the usual presentation. And then it became obvious. Who was there for her to impress? She showed us into the Seventeenth-Century Gallery. She motioned toward the portraits mounted on darkened walls, and said, "Dutch. Seventeenth century."

She was going to lead us into another wing!

But I had studied in secret to surprise her. I got the attention of the visitors, and before my mother could usher them out, I offered up the history of Protestant Baroque. How I loved what I had memorized—with neither Catholic churches to embellish with religious images, nor a court to foot the bill for grandiose art, with the Calvinist edict not to corrupt God's majesty with fantasy, "So it was to the objects in the world around him that the Dutch painter turned," I intoned.

Apple-polishing toady.

"You're in my way," my mother said through her teeth when I came to the end of my speech.

The button I wore at the time said, "You Look the Part."

Warren rides a bike to the dining hall wearing a T-shirt that has printed on it, "One Less Car." He got it in town at the place whose best-selling T-shirt in summer says, "So Many Tourists, So Few Bullets." Tourists are the ones who invariably snap them up.

Summer slows us down. Does it slow you down, too? I like to close a book I've been reading on the porch and picture you swimming in your backyard pool. I see you swimming alone, with no one waiting to wrap you in a robe when you climb out. This letter is a robe I hold out to you.

The article didn't say if you swam before or after you work. Wouldn't the chlorine bother you if you swam before you painted? But maybe you have that new filtration system, the one that uses ions. I don't feel like I've been in a pool unless I come out with eyes red and stinging.

I told you I never had a pool, but that gives the wrong impression. My best friend was a champion swimmer. We wanted to be wet, and every weekday we were. Even after a shower, our skin smelled chlorinated. With a strainer on the end of a stick, we would flip the turtles, moles, and frogs from out of our neighbors' pools. The builder of these pools had since gone out of business, and no longer honored his service contracts. Sometimes we would have missed a frog from the time before. Trapped in the filter, floating in chlorine, the frog would bleach out white. Green or white, the frogs' eyes were open as we sailed them over fences into other people's yards.

Warren caught me on the porch with a catalog of your work. He leaned over my shoulder and said, "What does he get for a painting like that?"

I didn't answer, and he practiced the trick he swears he can do where you flex your arm when a mosquito lights on it so the mosquito can't detach itself until the sheer force of your blood pressure makes the mosquito explode. He has not succeeded yet, though earlier I saw him rid Little Egypt of a hornet, luring it out with a dead fly placed on the offered straw of a broom. When proud of himself, he chants tongue twisters for us. He made up "Shoes and socks shock Chatty." Sometimes when I pass his door at night, I can hear from behind it the rapid refrains of "sifted thistles" and "mixed biscuits."

*   *   *

Last night I was in the library waiting to go in to dinner. I shifted my legs away from Warren, and snagged my stockings on the wicker chair. As though it had been his fault, I shot Warren a sour look, so he went on to dinner without me. I opened the book in whose margins he had scribbled, "How foolish we were to fear loneliness!" and next to a particularly Latinate passage, "Oh, get off your stilts."

Dinner was one of those times when the past gets a good going-over. Chatty and Warren and Karen all have access to their pasts. Does it matter that I can't remember if the living room couch I built a fort behind was black or tweed or plaid? Or if something I think I did turns out to be in *Jane Eyre*? So much of the time, what I came away with from a day was the shape of my mother's barrette, and not what she said to me. They were always made of tortoiseshell; some of them were oval, some were square. The barrettes were large, and held a low ponytail. It is the easiest way to keep hair out of your face, but I won't do it—it makes me look too much like her. Warren has a heart-shaped island, and I have a heart-shaped face. Karen has the face I would want if I could choose, but maybe you would say that the unconventional face is the one you would rather paint? Forget about her—just keep thinking about me.

Didn't you think it was odd to find raisins in your "fresh" fruit salad?

When I was in school, I often got sick from the fear of classes. I fought off the feeling by keeping a fistful of raisins with me. Before going into a class, I would shake part of a box of raisins into my hand, and close my fingers tight around them. Steadily, throughout the hour of class, I would take a single raisin—now warm and plump with sweat—and slip it into my mouth when the teacher couldn't see. I never chewed the raisins. I would swallow each one as a hedge against the nausea, and so get through each class. I needed the most raisins in math, the fewest in English. I kept this up until I finished junior high, just as, years later, I swallowed pills, tranquilizers, to get me through a day, no longer staving off nausea but a feeling of approaching doom. For me, raisins are still so completely pharmacological that I'm surprised when I see them in grocery stores, in cellophane-wrapped "lunchbox" packages of six.

I can't stand raisins now, and was relieved when you separated them and left them on your plate. As you might imagine, folks here take exception to what is on their plates, too. My first night here, Chatty warned me away from the fruit drinks, concocted as they are in the blender the gardener used once to whip up a frothy pitcher of mole repellant—equal parts cod liver oil and dish-washing detergent—which he painted along the rodents' corded trails in the garden.

Despite Chatty's success with the long-gone Centennial Garden, she says she can't bring herself to spend any time in this one. Warren said, "It could be argued that you do not get the full measure of the experience here if you don't take advantage of the garden," and Chatty told him, "*We're* what's going on here, so by having dinner with you, I'm taking in the attractions." She took a small pouch out of the pocket of her smock and emptied it onto the tablecloth. "Coquilles sucre," she said, sliding one at a time across the cloth to my place with her finger. Sugar shells, hard as rocks, in scuffed colors of coral, white, and blue, like pieces of sea glass, their shine tumbled off in salt water.

"One of the attendants gets them for me in town," Chatty said.

Other people bring their own food to the table, as long as it has been approved ahead of time. Chatty told me a woman had gagged when she tried to swallow but instead inhaled a dry spoonful of Spirulina, a faddish powdered supplement that was meant to be stirred in fruit juice and would turn it an evil green.

Karen swallows Gore Vidal. Then she swallows Donald Trump. She takes a blue capsule and a gold spansule—a B-complex and an E—and puts them on the tablecloth a few inches apart. She points the one at the other. "Martha Stewart," she says, "meet Oprah Winfrey." She swallows them both without water.

My first night, unsolicited, Warren leaned across the table and confided, "The way to keep an ice-cream cone from dripping on your shirt? Before you put ice cream into one of those pointed cones, put in a miniature marshmallow to plug up any leaks. You can eat it at the end," he pointed out.

I don't really care what is on the table, as long as it isn't raisins. Tonight we ordered in pizza, and the pizza-with-everything looked like a bad neighborhood. It is after dinner that I think about home. Across the way there are beer bottles lined up alongside the grave of the young man whose motorcycle stalled on the tracks. Not empties, but full bottles of Budweiser, capped. The malevolent twins steal in and drink them warm, hiding behind a towering hedge that encircles a trio of well-tended graves—the doctor who took two wives, sisters. The twins drink their bottles of stolen beer and think no one hears them snorting at dusk, then they put on wigs—black Afros from the sixties—and pretend to have sex in the hammock back of their house.

A woman on horseback walks the gravel paths. She is someone the twins have spied on, watching from the woods as she mucked stalls dressed in a string bikini, muttering "Perverts" at the yardmen who stared. In summer, in the cemetery, she climbs down and clips the white French lilacs that grow in one spot, spliced by rotting cedar. In the fall, she helps herself to dried hydrangea clusters, voluptuous, no doubt, on her dining room table. Her horse lifts its tail, and unleashed dogs escape nearby yards to come and feast, snapping, the way they scramble for clippings from hooves in her stable.

High winds redistribute bouquets, and Alice Parker's roses blow to Grace Hall one row over; carnations intended for Henry Hand work loose from a vase and are trapped by the stone of Red Howell, Senior, interred at Indianapolis.

At dinner this evening, Warren talked about his pet. He said he had had a spider monkey named Elmer and Chatty interrupted, having heard it as "monkey spider," to tell the table about the one she and her ex-husband had seen (from where they lay beneath mosquito netting covering their bed) climb into a wardrobe in their rented villa in Nevis.

"We left the island without our clothes," Chatty said.

Warren continued. "My parents rented a place in Hatteras where we were supposed to spend the summer. Me and my sister and our parents and Elmer and about a million crazed mosquitoes. My dad read where you could order chameleons through the mail, so he bought two dozen of them, and let them loose in the house. My mother called it a harmonious solution, until we got home from the beach the next day and Elmer met us at the top of the stairs with what turned out to be the last two chameleons, one in each fist. When he saw us," Warren said, "he waved them over his head like pennants. When my mother screamed at him, Elmer brought one fist to his mouth and bit the head off the chameleon. Then he did the same thing with the other."

I asked him if monkeys know right from wrong, and Warren said, "Elmer was a goblin from hell. He used to jump on the dogs' backs and make them carry him around the house until they learned to duck under the coffee table and knock the bastard off."

Warren burned himself putting out a cigarette, and Karen began to cry. Warren took a long drink from his Coke can.

"Thought you quit," Chatty said.

Chatty looked beneficently around the table. "I am getting better," she said. "So the others are starting to fail."

That time I was in London, I went to an elegant dinner for which the chef assembled a roast turkey inside of which was lodged a goose, inside of which was a duck that housed a chicken that contained a game hen—all of them boned and served with a dark, tart currant sauce. I think of that dinner, of the chef slicing through the five fowl, when I imagine what kind of woman you like. A woman who contains a series of surprises? There are clues in the women you have had, though the thought of asking you what you like is like the team of artists who hired a marketing firm to find out what Americans want in a painting. The artists painted the result of the poll which found that what we want is a blue painting the size of a dishwasher with a biblical figure and landscape.

I am so suggestible. When Chatty asks if I am hungry, I say, "I could be." I would try to become the woman you wanted without even knowing I was trying. As it is, I am barely the woman I am.

And what if you don't like the person you are? Where do

you find the parts to make yourself into some other kind of person? Can it be something you read in a book, a gesture you see on the street? Half-smile of a teacher, the walk of a girl on the beach.

I would like to go to a matinee with you. Any afternoon, any theater, I would not care what we saw. I would like to sit next to you in the dark in a public place and lean over from time to time to better hear your caustic asides.

I want to ask the questions I failed to ask that day when all I could think was: He is sitting across the table from me, and he has ordered fruit salad! I was like the woman who met Anaïs Nin and walked with her in Central Park, and couldn't help exclaiming that Anaïs Nin was eating a hot dog. The woman's incredulity bothered Anaïs Nin, just as I am sure my behavior bothered you. But surely you are used to it.

I want to know everything about you. So I tell you everything about myself.

A psychic once told me that I was too honest. It was the first thing he said to me before he had turned over palm or card. He was not urging duplicity; I think he meant for me to be what a certain kind of woman calls "clever."

The psychic was right, yet I am such a fraud:

"Are your parents still alive?"

"My father lives out West."

"And your mother?"

"My mother is dead."

"Of what?"

"She did it herself," I said, and let you think that that was hard on a girl, a tragedy.

Is this where I exhibited a ruinous lapse of judgment? Asking if you had known my mother when you were both in art school? You might have known each other. Yet is this an instance where I might instead have been clever, and not pointed out how much older than me you are? Worse, did you think I was suggesting that you knew my mother *well*? That maybe she posed for you?

The truth is, it was hard on me. Not her death—her life. The only surprise when she killed herself was that she had killed *herself.* I said to my father, "I always thought if she killed anyone, the one she killed would be me." And my father said, "I know."

My only job was not to get killed. At home, at school, at the movies, at a party, riding a horse, rowing a boat, skating on ice, raking the gravel drive, getting the mail, swimming in a lake, hiking in the mountains, on a bike, in a tent, in a church, in a car, eating breakfast, lunch, and dinner, on Halloween, Christmas, and Easter, awake and asleep, I had no other job.

Two slips of the tongue: I said to Chatty, "In all important ways, I believe I am her evil," instead of "equal." And when Chatty voiced an opinion, I added, "I feel the shame."

She has been dead twenty years, and listen to what happened to me on the street. Of all the things I could have said to the woman on the sidewalk, the woman I had never seen before, the woman who, unprovoked, had made a fist and brought it down on the side of my face, what I had said was, "Get out of me!" As though the demon was not an overweight woman in an out-of-season straw hat who had said as she swung her fist at me, "*This* is what you want!"

The other day I was playing Scrabble with Karen. I saw that I could close the space in D-E- -Y. I had an N and an F. Which do you think I chose? What was the word I made?

Sometimes, in the kitchenette here, I open a French cookbook so as not to think about her. Better to try to find out, what is a pomelo? Where could one find lemongrass to crush with a mallet for eggplant?

Before I came here, I asked my father a question and gave him a year to answer. The question I asked him is: What is it about me that most resembles my mother?

And I will wonder during this year that follows, did I do the right thing? What will come of it? Will I get something valuable to have? And know that he will make something up, most likely, to give his daughter a gift. And in the year of waiting I will answer the question for him. The way you are most like your mother? You play tricks on people's minds. You are unlovable. I see in your eyes the love of death.

I'll give you one year, I said.

Have you detected a curious lack of medical authority here? It is only missing from my letter. There are counselors for us, wise and complex people who do not intrude but are always available—why have I not written about them sooner? They are one of the consolations, here in the present. They live in a separate wing of the main building, and drop in throughout the week. We can call them at night if we need to. Some are young and still in training. They follow the doctor, and are courteous and kind. They take it as an article of faith that bad things that happen are "occasions for transformation," that creating distance from them is different from denying they were bad.

They are not averse to joining us in games. One time we all played charades. We were uniformly bad at the game. I pulled a hard one that no one could guess, no one came close to this person's name. In a private session several days later, when my counselor asked if I had any questions, I said yes—"How would *you* have done 'Nancy Reagan'?"

At the same time each evening, a counselor checks to see that no one is going out. What he asks us sounds like, "Urine for the night?"

One night last week we had a bad moment. One of the guests—she's new—has the same name as a well-known actress. Chatty began to tell a story about the actress and as soon as she said the woman's name, she glanced at the one in the Hostility Suite with us and said, "I mean the *real* Anne Bancroft."

Our Anne Bancroft is not so crazy she didn't recognize an insult. She sat up straight in her lounger, and then she left the room.

That is not a bad way to handle an insult if you don't have a ready comeback. I learned my lesson in a foreign country. I was visiting a friend in Paris. We were riding to the Louvre in a cab. I insisted my friend let me handle the transaction, though I knew I didn't know enough French. By accident I undertipped the driver. He turned on me, an American *touriste*. I recognized the word *putain*—the driver had called me a whore. I remember that I tried for a French *hauteur*, and said, "Je *suis, suis*-je!" I realized that what I was saying was English with French clothes on, and slunk away in defeat. (A saleswoman at a pet store later neutralized the cabbie. I went to a fancy shop on the Rue de Trop Cher to buy a friend's dog a collar. The saleswoman, before she would show me the collars, asked, "What kind of dog is he?" I said, "He's a beagle," and the saleswoman said, "No, no—I mean, what's he like?")

The first time I walked one of the nearby shelter dogs, I broke into futile tears. I said to one of the counselors, "There are twelve million others in this country alone that I am not able to help!" And she said, "It doesn't have to be complete, your help. The goal is not to erase the problem. You do it to make the choice, to give and get joy in this life."

And I said to her, still in tears, "But it is not enough!" And then I asked her, "What is enough? Enough energy, attention, effort, et cetera." She said, "The answer lies in the practice. In balance with what comes naturally." I said, "How can I, a six, help anyone else until I am better?" And she said, "Helping someone else can *make* you better."

In large part, we are meant to heal each other. The garden is a metaphor. Seeding, tending, weeding, watering—all leading up to the harvest. Although leave it to Warren to point out these words that are synonymous with "plant": hide, secrete, conceal, bury, entomb.

Warren says, of the place he was before this, "My counselor was a moron, and he helped me."

There is one counselor here we suspect of being something more. She gives such encouraging and optimistic guidance that one day I asked if I could tape her. We set a time to meet for a talk on the patio off the parlor. I turned on my pocket-sized tape recorder and showed her where to speak into the mike. She delivered a kind of pep talk, one I could now replay and refer to as the need arose.

The need arose the very next day, so I grabbed my tape recorder, fitted in her tape, and went up to deserted Little Egypt. I pressed the "On" button, and closed my eyes. I let myself believe her good words; they displaced my bad thoughts for the length of an hour. When it was over, I pressed the "Off" button. Nothing happened. The tape continued to wind in its cartridge. I held the "Off" button down with my thumb, and still the tape played, though there was no more voice to hear. I ran downstairs with it, found Warren in the

Hostility Suite. I handed him the tape recorder, said, "Can you turn this off for me?" Warren was not able to turn the machine off until he had smacked the recorder into his palm and then against the table edge to empty the batteries out.

Not graduating is how Chatty left this place the first time. This time, all she will have to do is call a car, just as I have done. I have learned to specify *town car* so the company does not send over a limousine. I remember to tell them to tell the driver to bring along something to read.

With my bags packed and in the car with me, it is like the concert I went to—a chamber quartet—at what was once a private home, a Victorian mansion. In the music room there was a birdcage that had finches in it. The cage was a replica of the house it was inside of, down to the mansard roof and broad-stepped porch. That night I arrived early and heard the musicians already playing. Thinking my watch was slow and I was actually late, I hurried in. The musicians were playing— not tuning up, but performing the evening's program—to an empty house. And the finches were singing along! When they finished, the cellist explained to me that before every concert given in the house, the musicians played first for the finches so the birds would tire themselves out singing, and would then remain quiet during the concert that was scheduled.

Chatty assures me I will know, I will "just know" when to leave. How does she come by such certainty?

Who said sanity is free? *That* is the answer to Karen's complaint about always having to do two jobs.

*   *   *

Don't you find that there is no right place to begin? When you try to make sense of a thing that has happened? That everything is as important, or as unimportant, as everything else? A poet writes, "He opens a book at random, and consults randomness." To me, this is what it seems. To me and, Warren has pointed out, a million other people.

I pretend I know you well. I say to Warren, "I have a friend who—" and Warren says, "You have too many friends."

I waited so long to write to you. I liked knowing, as it came to me throughout the course of a day, that I would be writing a letter to you. It made me think of a doctor here, a man who said he'd have liked to have treated Marilyn Monroe, what a lift it would have given him to look in his appointment book and see her name. He had lifted up for a moment on the toes of his shoes.

Warren taped a one-word sign to his wall. The word that he wakes to is: Headlong. Writing to you, it is my word, too. And, hey—here's hoping you like blue! This is the color my mother used to use, though she chose the stock with a ragged edge, and I prefer my edges sharp. She fit what she had to say on a thank-you note.

The pond is surrounded by winter-stripped trees, packed so close together the lack of leaves doesn't matter. There is no seeing through them to the single man and woman who proceed across the cracked black ice on borrowed skates. No crack of the puck. No Rock 'n' Skate, no Rap 'n' Skate, no programmed medleys threatening disco. The sound of speed on blades. Turtles float below. We are humming "The Nutcracker Suite."

My consolations are many, their power no less for not including you. I said to a psychic just after our tea, "There is a person I met," and the psychic cut me off, saying, "He is a thief. He will steal your soul."

The man ran groups. He took a token fee from people wanting to quit—smoking, drinking, eating too much. "Picture the thing you want to live without." "My husband," one woman whispered to another. I shut my eyes with the rest of them and tried to conjure fear, what I want to live without.

The counselors here say we often mistake excitement for apprehension, for fear. They say it is up to us, that we can forcibly jog ourselves from one state into the other. But it sounds to me like my favorite joke when I was a girl: What is Pollyanna's epitaph? "I'm *glad* I'm dead."

The psychic said I would have two children. This makes me shake my head. I know you are not supposed to leave a baby alone. Not even for a minute. But after a while I think, What could happen to a baby in the time it would take for me to run to the corner for a cappuccino to go? So I do it, I run to the corner and get the cappuccino. And then think how close the store is that is having the sale on leather gloves. Really, I think, it is only a couple of blocks. So I go to the store and I buy the gloves. And it hits me—how long it has been since I have gone to a movie. A matinee! So I do that, too. I go to a movie. And when I come out of the theater, it occurs to me that it has been years since I have been to Paris. Years. So I go to Paris, and come back three months later and find a skeleton in the crib.

No one has ever told me that I am good with children. Shortly before I came here I went to a dinner party. The hostess was setting the table—there were eight of us that night—when her daughter, a barefoot seven-year-old, demanded we play the game.

I had not played the game before. You had to build a tower out of narrow cross-placed pieces of wood, then pull away the pieces one at a time without making the tower collapse.

I am not good at games, and the girl was sure of her moves. Yet somehow I was good at this, and when the girl removed the piece that made the tower fall, she ran to her mother screaming, "I didn't lose!"

The mother put the child to bed and lay beside the child for a while in the bed.

When I go to sleep, I sleep on the side of the bed my mother used to sleep on. Sometimes, at dawn, I wake up and find myself in the pose my mother died in—lying on her side, her arm reaching from under her head as though she were doing the sidestroke in a pool, the pills she had swallowed weighing her down like so many pebbles in her pockets.

I don't fall asleep with my body on the bed in the same way my mother was found. It must be a thing I go into when I am asleep. And still I cannot be sure that, limb for limb, I am in the same position. My mother's legs, when I saw her, were covered by the sheet; it is possible that my legs are bent where my mother's legs were straight.

Sometimes it feels as though I won't be able to live until I can sleep in a position of my own—not in the way my mother's body was found on the bed, but in a way that is mine—even if it is only a sort of dead man's float where you don't use a muscle but clasp both your knees and let your head sink into the pillow, rocking gently as a baby, tipping your head to the side to take in air, conserving your strength until help arrives, or until you can save yourself, there in bed.

*   *   *

Consolation is a beautiful word. *Everyone* skins his knee—that doesn't make yours hurt any less. The standard line here.

Karen's consolation is a dog. Mine, too, some of the time. In the lobby of the shelter you can buy a bag of biscuits and pass them out through the kennel bars while an attendant readies a dog for you to walk. Last time I went I collected the loose fur from the dogs just groomed to make a present to the gardener to stuff guess where. Then I walked Shauna. She is a young shepherd mix who had a litter of ten that had to be weaned early, at the age of five weeks, because the mother developed mastitis from nursing so many.

The attendant handed me Shauna's leash, and Shauna leaped into the air. Her belly sagged, and was covered with long scabs, but once outside she ran for a mile, pulling me along at the end of a leash. When I finally had to rest, I said, "Shauna, shhh," and she sat down and leaned against my leg, waiting.

When I brought her back to the shelter, I went to see her puppies in a private room. They were no more than eight inches long. I sat on the floor and they moved as a single mass onto me. They were crying and mewing like kittens. They licked and bit and tried to suck as they moved up my arms and chest, clinging to my neck and reaching up to bat at my face and nose, around my ears.

Once I walked Shauna in a nearby park where a group of people holding leads stood huddled in conversation while their dogs, off-leash, played close by. Shauna and I stood at the edge of both groups, and I heard a woman brag, "Barney makes on command." Another woman observed her dog as it was mounted by two others in succession; she said that her dog's social life was better than her own.

I was watching TV in Little Egypt with Chatty when a dog

food commercial came on. A litter of tumbling pups crossed the screen, and Chatty said to me, "I guess *you're* happy."

I've never heard it said of you that you had dogs as pets. Though surely when you were a boy, a boy on a working farm, there must have been a dog that you befriended?

Do you find consolation in a person? In a woman? I found it once with a man, but I lost my combs. This was the last time I saw him. In the cab going home is when I saw the combs, one on top of the other on the table beside his couch. It would have been better if he had been the one to remove them, but when they interfered with the travel of his hands, I was the one who reached up and slipped the combs out. They are just cheap plastic, their job not to ornament but to secure and vanish in hair. It is not like leaving behind an earring, something that needs to be joined with a mate. The combs cost nothing, so he did not think to return them. But they're the only ones that work in my kind of hair, and you can't often find the ones that blend in with your hair. They tend to be packaged in assortments of a dozen, in garish bright primary colors. Before I left that night, I used his hairbrush when we finished. I left long hairs caught in the bristles, making of his hairbrush a kind of reliquary.

Where is the consolation in this? It is in humiliation, which brings the softness of heart that allows you to listen to God.

"You a student over at the college?" The cabdriver, gunning for a tip.

I still want those combs back. I need all the things I left behind back. Better to find consolation in a place. At the beach. A day at the beach when everything rhymes: crabs picked clean, one thong—green, flies blown in on a warm land breeze, parking lot rainbow in a pool of gasoline; diving seagulls, blasted boat hulls, sea-scarred plastic, rusted bedstead, rotting refuse, fish now dead.

Sometimes I worry that we don't talk about ideas. But Warren says, "I hate ideas," and Chatty says, "Ideas, sugar, are not sexy."

So a lot of the time it's moisturizers and accessories, physical fitness and hair. And still so many ways to go wrong, as when I said to Chatty, hadn't she colored her hair, and Chatty's frosty reply, that she had not *colored* her hair, she had *enhanced* it.

We talk about clothes. On the theory that generic elements improve with repetition, Chatty wears two identical cashmere sweaters, layered one over the other. My own closet, an ugly-dress bonanza, yields sacklike black washed silk. Chatty can wear what she likes; she eats two desserts a night and you would never know it. Whereas the rest of us would gain weight even if we had food poisoning.

Karen presents herself in tooth-torn shirts. She showed up in the Hostility Suite with a miniature dachshund from the shelter. She held the dog in her lap, and while Chatty went on at some length about the plans she had for her wardrobe, Karen ran her opal ring down over the dog's ears—ears she had made stand up like a rabbit's—the way you thread the ends of a silk scarf through a scarf ring. Karen said that she had had this kind of dog when she was just out of college, and had taken the dog to restaurants where she would wipe out an ashtray with her napkin, and crumble part of a hamburger into it for her dog. She said she would get her dog's leash and ask the dog—not, Want to go for a walk? but, Want to go out to lunch?

Chatty told Karen that one thing's for sure—when you

have a child, your dog becomes a pet. That would not happen to me. I can't stand the sound of a person eating, but I love the sound of a dog crunching down on kibble. I love a dog's appetite. The appetite of a baby is a frightening thing to me. I watch a mother spoon food into her baby's mouth, then spoon back in what the baby spits out; to me, it is the job of spackling. If I had a baby, I would change overnight from a woman who worries about the calories in the glue of an envelope to someone who goes to the corner for coffee, a nightgown showing beneath my coat, the hem of that gown clawed to shreds by a cat.

My mother gave away my dogs; when she died, she died with cats. A calico cat sat tucked like a hen on her chest, as though it were hatching her death. A Siamese cat, when my mother was gone, yowled in her empty room.

I don't know that I have ever seen a cat in one of your paintings. Or a dog. All those paintings, portraits of friends, and not one friend that was dog. *My* first friend was a Labrador retriever. His name was Needles, and I would saddle him up with a folded bath towel held on with my father's belt. Needles obeyed only one command in the house. He would run into the living room and you would have to call out, "Swerve!"—one of us would have to call it out—and he *would* swerve just before he would have crashed into the glass-topped table.

My mother gave him away.

I was at school. When I came home, there was on my desk a dimestore turtle swimming the shallow moat around a ramped plastic island—island of the plastic palm—in search of specks of lettuce.

*　　*　　*

Surely it is in part the medication, but we have hung our libidos on hooks outside the door. Do men play a version of the game women do, when a woman asks herself in, say, a shopping center, If I had to go to bed with someone in this store, which one would it be? Here, Warren is the best of the lot. If I can return to the high school mixer, a girl would go up to another girl and say of one of the boys, "He's really cute." And suddenly the girl to whom this was said, a girl who had not previously noticed this fellow, was taking another look and thinking to herself, "He *is* really cute."

Where was I going with this? I mean to say that if Chatty said such a thing to me, I still wouldn't see it, given a push.

That gorilla I met, the one who signs, was given a push, but it didn't work. The people with whom she lives wanted her to mate. They brought in a suitable male, younger and larger than she, and set them up to cohabit. The female gorilla signed to him things like, "Hurry up" (and give her more bananas), and "Truck not yours" (a Tonka Toy truck). Neither gorilla would make a move, so the people rented an X-rated film and screened it for the primates. It held the gorillas' attention, and when the film was over, the female gorilla signed to the male, "Climb up my back." But he did not have her language skills, and did not otherwise take the hint.

My libido, what is left of it, flows in your direction. By the time I recognized you in the bookstore and boldly asked if I could buy you a cup of coffee, I had already constructed you in my mind, even though a voice in my head cried out: Don't confuse the painting with the painter—let's not forget the example of Picasso!

Given the hours I think of you, given the hours in my white-sheeted bed, you would think I could cook up a scene or two. But I can picture nothing that has not already happened.

And so I am stuck with: a cup of tea in a public place on a winter afternoon. A failure of imagination? Or a self-protecting check, a screen blacked out when the home team plays.

Except I let myself imagine that you are painting my portrait. I offered myself as model to a teacher when I was a teen (having just read *The Prime of Miss Jean Brodie*). I worked up my nerve to do this—didn't he sometimes paint nudes? But he painted me fully clothed. He painted me looking out a window, looking away. Yearning? The painter had just quit drinking. *I* was not what he was interested in.

When you paint me, I sit in a darkened room. I lean toward a dark desk, quill pen in my hand. I am dressed in a fur-trimmed yellow satin mantle; my hair is beribboned and pulled back from my face. Does this sound familiar? Are you with me on this? "Woman Writing a Letter," by Vermeer.

Look at me. My concerns—are they spiritual, do you think, or carnal? Come on. We've read our Shakespeare. "There's no art / To find the mind's construction in the face."

And what are my chances of enacting "Young Woman Reading a Letter at an Open Window"? I have, as you can see, no wiles or guile, the things I would need to elicit a letter from you in return. I would change this if I could, this curse of earnestness. Am I out of my mind?—putting my cards on the table! A woman should conceal, not reveal. Now my lipstick is chewed off, my lingerie is dingy, my high heels scuffed and broken.

There was reportedly a painting of a woman writing a letter that was found in Vermeer's studio at his death.

I would like to know—did you see me that day as a woman? Did you think of me just as a fan? The way you have painted women—do you see us that way in the flesh? Do you ask permission to paint someone, or does she offer herself to you? Or do you paint a woman from memory, taking her without her knowing? Are you clinical as a doctor, or do you fall in love a little? Do you start out painting one woman and end up painting another?

This is what happens to me. I start out being myself, and end up being my mother. It isn't something I try to do. In fact, I try hard not to. That is the crucial difference: I don't want to end my life, but I can't keep myself from trying.

The pills that she swallowed were mine. They were pills prescribed to me because I couldn't sleep. With as much thoughtfulness as she showed me in her life, she left one behind in the vial. Presumably, it would be hard for me to sleep the night we found her.

I have never slept better.

I saw a movie in which two girls share an apartment. One day, one of the girls opens the other's diary and makes an entry in it as though she is the diary owner. It scared me, that scene, because what—except for dying—could be scarier than merging?

Men are afraid this will happen with women. Often, after an intimate visit, a man will pick a fight. Have you done this yourself? I find you can count on it. And the closer you have been, the more snappish after. To separate himself, to keep from being pulled in. I have learned to head this off. I find an excuse to take myself away. I find this is easier all around. Even if where I take myself is into the next room, to sit and listen to music.

Do you listen to music while you work? I would if I were a painter. You know the way children ask which of your senses you would give up if you had to make a choice—your hearing or your sight? Before I saw your paintings, I would have given up my sight. It is the choice I used to make.

*   *   *

Warren and I watch reruns in Little Egypt, seventies sit-coms. A man tries to teach his friend a lesson. He says, Do you see what happens when you *assume*? You make an "ass" out of "u" and "me." But what is a life without assumptions?

Failing to engage us with clothes, Chatty makes us talk to her about men. As many men as we remember. Some, like you, have been painters. Maybe *all* of them have been painters. Even the gardener here, when he isn't numbing our minds with endless talk of bud count and petal length, will set up an easel during his break, and produce a passable landscape. He will tell us the story of the Chinese paintings in which the time of day could be ascertained by the dilation of the cat's pupils and the degree to which the peonies had opened. Happy pastime, painting. And when it is a man's work, it is work he will enjoy. Although Warren feels it isn't work if it isn't hard. "Why do you think they call it work?" he says. With no need of segue, Chatty is off on Edward, the man she says we will meet when he comes to call on her here.

"Edward is bad," Chatty says, not without pride. "But he doesn't think he is bad. He thinks I can't see things clearly."

"And you can't," Warren says.

"You think the moment he behaves untenably, you'll leave," Chatty says. "But you find yourself saying, 'He's been *so* nice until now . . .' So you think, 'I'll ignore it,' and pretty soon you're ignoring New York City. And then watch—he'll have to put *me* out the door."

"He could change." My tentative entry into the conversation.

Chatty looks at me as though she does not know where to begin. She says that instances of change are anecdotal, deep-seated fantasy. "The New Testament has versions of it over and over: the whore becomes a saint, Paul on the road to Damascus. I mean," she says, "Christianity acknowledges that for a person to change his nature is *miraculous.*"

"It's not as if *we* change, either," Karen puts in.

"What I think," Chatty says, "is that if a man loves a woman more than a woman loves a man, then they're even. The thing to remember," Chatty says as though reminding herself, "is that a man is not obligated to love you. Once you reach that philosophical state, *he* feels your grip loosening, and *you* retain your dignity. Otherwise, you go nuts, you're subject to the dark undertow of it all."

And I say, "Can't a normal person take a walk on the dark side? If she watches where she took her last step?" Thinking of you, and thinking this is the moment when Chatty will ask, What is the *deal* with this guy? And knowing if I told her your parting words to me—"We'll see each other again"—she would look at me with pity, not giving your words the right spin.

But Chatty just passes a bowl of bitter scrotalized olives. "When I get out of here, Edward wants me to visit," she says. "He's fixing up his house, and I'm afraid he will want me to help. He'll open a section of Sheetrock—there'll be clouds of bees and rotting honey. I call his house The Hive. I told him to hire help, but the local help is Lawrence Home Improvement—Larry and his scrap-hoarding teenaged son. Larry's motto is: Pound to Fit, Paint to Match."

"But you're good at all that," I tell her. "You know what goes with what."

"It's hopeless," Chatty says. "I'll say, Paint this trim *lobster bisque,* and I come back and they've made it *terra-cotta.*"

Which brings me back to the question, How does she come by such certainty? How does anyone? My mother, believing she could give away my dog—and she could!

And what about the certainty I feel regarding you? You could say that an hour is not a lot to go on. But always, before, a thing didn't work because I was too young and too old. Too dumb and too smart. But I learn from my mistakes. The certainty I feel—it is something to hit back with. So in a manner of speaking, I now have a stick that is bigger than the stick I was beaten with.

Except let's not think of it as something larger of the same type. Maybe, instead of a stick, it just looks like a stick. Maybe it is really a snake. And it moves like a river. Maybe it *is* a river, and we can go someplace on it, someplace new.

"You still writing that letter?" Chatty says.

Warren: Why do dogs roll in dead animals? (Because live ones won't let them.)

Warren caught sight of a mouse in Little Egypt. He traced its path back to a nest of Raisinettes, the chocolate gone chalky in the dust beneath the couch. He told us he had caught mice as a boy, that once he skinned a trap-killed mouse and made a mouse-skin rug for his sister's dollhouse. And then he was telling us again about Elmer, about Elmer his little spider monkey, climbing to the top of their Christmas tree, pelting the family with ornaments he had pulled from their places on the branches.

"We yelled at him to stop," Warren said, "and Elmer threw them harder."

That was Elmer's last Christmas, Warren told us. Elmer caught cold on New Year's Eve. He died in Warren's arms in the car Mrs. Moore drove along icy streets to the vet. Is there an animal story that doesn't end in tears? This one. Warren said the family gathered to bury Elmer in the backyard. "The dogs came, too," Warren said. "They stood with us at the edge of Elmer's grave, and kicked in some of the dug-out dirt. They couldn't wait to see that sucker in the ground."

Chatty has been having her insights again. A fall from a horse, a blow to her head some twenty years ago, left her able to approach a stranger in the park and say, I'm sorry about your husband. How did you know? the woman would then say to Chatty.

She says she can't predict when a thing like that will happen. She says sometimes she will meet a person and know then and there how and when that person will die. She knows these things for facts, but she says she would never say as much out loud.

I have heard Warren try to get information out of her, saying, "You see any reason I shouldn't get a Harley?" I have done it, too—watched her closely as I unveil plans for next year.

I know her insights are back because of last week in Little Egypt. It was the two of us in there, Chatty dozing in the rocking chair, me reading a book about—what else?—dogs. Then Chatty sat up straight; she opened her eyes and said in a firm voice, "Get back in your body right now!"

Who are you talking to? I said.

She had a letter from a cousin days later. The cousin's husband had had a heart attack. He had flat-lined in the CCU, until to everyone's amazement he had suddenly come to life, conscious. He told the medical team that he had left his body and gone to visit his wife's cousin. The day, the time, corresponded. "I was talking to my cousin's husband," Chatty had told me that night.

Without faith or courage, I hope she would do the same for me.

I told her about the dream I had the night my last dog died. I was out of town that night, asleep in a small hotel. My dog came to me in the dream, and he said aloud, "It's time."

I didn't tell her about the night my mother died, a night I dreamlessly slept through the night in the room right next to hers. But then, my mother never slept with her head on my stomach, or licked my face awake.

"Tell you about my neighbor," Chatty said. "We all of us despised him, the way he cheated us out of water when he tapped into our lines to fill his swimming pool in summer. When he sent his children over to collect for a cause, it seemed to us unlikely that the money his children collected ever left his house. He ran for the school board to keep blacks out of the schools, and sold faulty garden equipment to a young couple new in the community.

"So when he was taken to the hospital by ambulance one night, the only flowers that followed came from his immediate family. He lay in a coma for weeks. Then he was back, seen leaning on the arm of a nurse, walking the shaded paths through the woods wearing a surgical mask—an affectation, most of us thought—waving at his neighbors along the way.

"One who didn't hold a grudge had a conversation with him, and passed along the news that since the coma he often couldn't think of the word he meant to say, and the word that came out in its place was *government.* He was not aware that he said it, according to the neighbor who had heard him say that he would like to put his boat in the government and do some fishing.

"And we took it up, inviting each other over for government and coffee. Children were told that when a man and woman loved each other, the government brought them a baby. At backyard cookouts, the neighborhood refrain was, 'Put another government on the grill.'

"And we wondered why 'government' was the word that he said. Couldn't the word that came into his head as easily have been grasshopper? Or galoshes? Or ghost?

"Some of us saw it this way: there was a morning we walked our properties, taking in the damage the 'government' had done in the night. We saw broken trees and downed lines, flooded gullies and drowned flowers. And as we cleared away debris, it seemed to us that even though he didn't realize what he said when he thought he was using the word that he meant, when he invoked for protection from all that was ungovernable the word that he did, the son of a bitch was right."

A sign of getting better: without getting larger, we seem to take up more room in a room.

"Where are we?" I one day asked Warren, who said, "In a little country south of Canada, and just this side of Mexico, in a state the size of this table, in a town the size of this ashtray."

I still couldn't tell if Warren liked me. Always there is a point when you can tell, when most people can tell. It takes longer for me. And then I'm angry with them, for it being so hard to tell. And whose fault is that? I think this is another assumption I have made a life without. I am like those people who hold grudges for what someone has done to them in a dream.

Always, we are asking here, What does a thing mean? And being asked back, What do you mean? Whereas I like to say things just to say them, because they are pleasing to say, to remember and say, "There is a tiny cove on a lake in the Sierras and I sat in its sand one late summer night when the air didn't move but was clear and dry and the lake barely lapped and the only thing that moved was a passenger ferry set forth from the other side that was strung with lights like a flirty Parisian barge and made no noise but kept coming closer," a consolation then, and now.

In the library, I found these words in the margin of an old copy of *Vogue*:

> *Why, then, did you engender me?*
> *We didn't know.*
> *What didn't you know?*
> *That it would be you.*

Warren again. In approximation of Beckett.

A clipping from a tabloid paper: A woman in West Virginia carried her unborn baby for more than forty years. It calcified outside the uterine wall. When questioned by reporters, the woman said, "As long as the child is inside me I haven't lost it."

A friend of mine tried to get pregnant and found out she

could not. I said, "The world doesn't need more babies," and she said she wasn't going to do it for the world.

The only time the word *baby* doesn't scare me is the time that it should, when it is what a man calls me.

I brave shower after shower in which the stacks of gifts divide clearly into gifts from moms and gifts from non-moms. The moms give practical items with safety as a theme: a net to keep a crawling child from slipping through the railing of a deck, a mirror that affixes to the dashboard of a car so the driver can see the infant in the car seat behind, a dozen earnest gadgets to "babyproof" a house.

Whereas I will have chosen a mobile to hang above the crib, baby animals painted on china discs—a breath sends them swinging against one another with a sound to wake a baby down the block.

Here's a good baby story; it happened in the Caribbean sea. A woman went into labor after her husband's small fishing boat sank, and the current pulled them apart. He would later be rescued and reunited with his wife, but there was no sign of him yet when the woman's life preserver was not enough to hold her above the water. She panicked, scanning the horizon where she thought she saw a squall, the water churning with storm. It moved toward her, closing in till she could make out leaping forms; it looked to her like hundreds of leaping fish. She bobbed in the waves, enduring contractions, and the school of dolphins moved into formation around her. Later she would learn that they can locate a BB with their sonar, so it was no trouble for them to detect her daughter, about to be born.

The woman screamed when a phalanx of dolphins dove and then surfaced beneath her, lifting her above the level of the sea. But as she pushed her baby out she saw that they were there to help her, and because the dolphins were there, her daughter didn't drown.

The dolphins held their position, a buoyant grid beneath her, and kept the mother and daughter safe until human help arrived. Had help not come so soon, might the nursing mother dolphin have offered her richly fatted milk to the baby?

"They were sent to me by the Holy Father," the woman would tell her husband. "He wanted our baby to live.

"The dolphins chattered like little children," the woman said. "When my baby was born, the dolphins went wild. They bobbed up and down; their smiles were so beautiful!"

In gratitude, the woman named her daughter Dolphina Maria. The dolphins slipped away through the waves, intercessors supporting humankind on the sea, allowing us to return to land cleansed of our sins. Deep inside their bodies float the few bones left from the hind legs they once had on land.

It is such a pretty story, told to me by a Cuban woman I met in a bar at the beach. She left the bar before I did; a drunken man took her place. He leaned into me and said, "I see in your dark eyes that you have suffered, and you have compassion, and *I* have suffered, and *I* have compassion, and I see in your eyes that I can *say* things to you—"

"My eyes are blue," I said.

At the beach with Karen. Seed pods, corn cobs, smashed clams, horseshoe crabs, starfish, cartilage, bird tracks, "sea snacks."

A passing thought: "Can a woman hurt you as much as a man?"

"Worse," I tell her. "They understand you better, so they can hurt you worse."

"That's what I thought," she says.

"Nothing pulls weeds faster than frustration." I walked the rows of vegetables in the garden, and without having planned it, kneeled to pull up weeds, the right way, by the roots. It is a satisfying task—a tangible improvement, an instant fix. I fell into a kind of trance moving along the rows, improving the lives of beets.

In the drawer of my mother's night table, under the emptied bottles of pills, were two pages torn from a women's magazine. One page was a kind of consumer's guide, a chart of deadly combinations, which pill taken with another would make you sick, or worse. Depending on your point of view, it was cautionary or how-to. The other page was what I quoted a moment ago, a list of suggestions for chasing off a gloomy mood. "Spend time in your garden. Nothing pulls weeds faster than frustration."

But wait—maybe I am confusing this page with the page I found in her night table drawer the time she tried to quit smoking. And she *did* quit smoking, and what a time that was. I was in the seventh grade. I would ask her for permission to do something, and before I could get the question out she would have snapped back the answer—No! Years later, I heard a joke that brought this back. I say to you, "Ask me what is the secret of comedy." You get as far as, "What is the secret—" and I cut you off with, "Timing."

Yes, I went through her night table drawers, her dresser and closets, too. What simple taste she had. Everything she wore was unadorned. A cable in a cardigan came to seem festive. Plain black pumps. Unfrilled slips. Not drab-classic. She wore a lot of white.

You told me you had dressed the same since you were back in college, the khaki pants and Oxford-cloth shirts. Never bohemian, certainly no beret. Cast against type. One is tempted to say you don't look like an artist, but that is like the man who introduced me to his friend and told him I was talented, and his friend said back, "She doesn't *look* talented."

Did you ever paint a portrait of a woman you didn't like? There is a portrait I saw—the one that hangs in the Tate—where I thought you must hate the woman. Hatred is a passionate involvement. It's worse not to care for a person at all. Or is this a notion I hold onto to flatter myself?

My mother picked out all my clothes. We never went shopping together. Often what she bought was too small for me, too tight, as though she thought of me as being smaller, or wished that I was.

I said to her once, "My friends all wear their mothers' clothes," and she said, "Ask me when you're older." I got older, and asked again.

I only ever wore one thing that was hers, not that you exactly wear a purse. I carried an old brown purse she had thrown away. I took it out of the trash and hid it in my closet. On weekends, I took it, empty, to department stores. I brought it home filled with tightly rolled clothes of my own choosing. "I'm going shopping with my mother," was my private joke on a Friday; I'd come to school on Monday in a stolen sweater set. If she asked where a dress had come from, I had friends my size. I wore the stolen clothes maybe two or three times, then stuffed them in the donation box at the church on the way to school.

When my mother died, I was her size. I could have worn

any of her clothes at any time. Instead I packed them in shopping bags, and drove them to the Goodwill drop. Then I had only the fear of seeing derelicts wearing my mother's clothes, her ghost in neighborhoods she didn't visit, alive.

One of the counselors here asked a single loaded question. She asked me if anyone deserved that kind of loyalty. The loyalty that would require the end of my life, as well. And it was the first time I believed the claim that you can help a person more by asking the right question than by giving them the answer.

And didn't one of your paramours do the same thing? Was that the woman you painted, the one I thought you hated in the portrait in the Tate? You didn't give her a name in the title of the portrait. You gave reporters no comment when your lady friend was found. I read she left no note—that is, if it wasn't an accident. But maybe she sent *you* a note, not that it is my business.

My mother wrote her note on a page of notebook paper, from a notebook I had used to do my homework in. Her note was four lines long. She left behind directions for what to do with "the body." She insisted there be no memorial, no mention of "this death." The note was signed and dated. There was no salutation; it was a document, nothing personal. It must have been taken by the coroner or by the police. The note was eventually returned to my father. And now it belongs to me.

I have not told the staff that I am writing this letter to you. Not when they are keen to get me talking about her. Might not a counselor gently point out the irony of our letters? Mine too long, hers too short. Might not a counselor suggest that the letter I am writing to you is the letter my mother should have written to me? Letting me get to know her. Trying to win me over.

My favorite suicide note has been fairly widely reported. It was left by a fellow who jumped from the Golden Gate Bridge: "Th-th-th-that's all, folks!"

"San Francisco," my mother once said, "is the only city that demands you love it." And she did. She wanted to keep other people alive to see it. She wanted them to have her organs, transplanted. Apparently she didn't know that the pills she took would destroy them.

I wonder what makes you angry, what happens when you are. Have you ever destroyed a canvas? You are not, I have heard, or I have read, a drinker. Does it take its toll in silence? Do you get angry with yourself? Are you, like me, your own worst critic? How do you let something out into the world when it's a sure thing someone out there won't like it?

You're good, my mother seemed to say to herself, in fact, you're *very* good. You're just not good *enough.* My mother refused to show anyone her paintings. After a while, she stopped painting at all. What was left of her gift was the argument she had with the painter who came to paint our house and was unable to mix "her" blue.

Chatty's gentleman caller was due to arrive. Back in her room, I brushed green eyeshadow on her, but she said it made her look like she ate colored babies for breakfast. I painted on the palest lip color. "I'd sooner ride a hog to Memphis," she said.

"The Hindus have a word for this," Karen said, watching the makeup lesson. "Overexcitement. They say that when your pulse races and you get flushed and anxious, the person is bad for you."

"He was *trained* to get us overexcited," Chatty said. "By keeping himself still? By holding the best part back, and suggesting it? The best actors do that."

"Three dogs are put in a room," Warren says, and the rest of us hunker down.

"An architect's dog, a doctor's dog, and an actor's dog. Each dog is given a pile of bones and told they'll be given one hour."

Chatty blots her lips as Warren continues. "The architect's dog arranges his bones into a Cape Cod saltbox house. The doctor's dog arranges his bones into separate piles by species. The actor's dog—"

"Hand me that eyebrow pencil?" Karen says.

"The actor's dog eats all his bones, fucks the other two dogs, and asks to go home early."

"He's not an actor anymore," Chatty says. "He teaches. In a university."

Suddenly I am no longer jealous of her; I wilt at the thought of the earnest exchange of information, explanations of the way things work and who invented what.

Karen tells me about *her* trip to town with Chatty. "I found a ten-dollar bill on the grounds," Karen says, "and she told me you said it's bad luck to keep found money, I should spend it right away. So we sign ourselves out and call a cab. We get the only slow cab in the history of cabs. We miss three lights in a row, and the driver says into his rearview mirror, 'You'd better buckle your seat belts.' And Chatty says, 'Why? If we have an accident, I'll be out of the car before you hit anyone.'

"I didn't see anything in town I wanted to buy, but Chatty insisted I spend the money," Karen says.

Karen and I have the same shopping problem. You could set me down in Paris, I would not find a thing to buy, if what I was there to buy was something for myself. To shop for yourself requires you to know yourself. I shop for myself by default, dressing in black (though the day we met for tea I had taken a chance on gray), buying only things I have bought before that fit. I can't even think about the choices posed by makeup. To try to pick a shade of foundation is to end up in a place like this. What is peach and what is pink, what is sallow and what is fair? Skin is skin, to me, though of course you would disagree. You would know what shade of lipstick a woman should wear—a blue-red or coral, a brown-red or frost. I wonder what color you would dress me in. The moment I think a thing like this I no longer need to rouge.

But send me to find a gift for someone else, I'll show you what I can do. Christmas is never a problem for me. Most years I finish my shopping in the fall and throb until December. Although there was one year I did no shopping until December, and that with my father, in a leather store in San Francisco, for a person we had never met who was going to be our host for the holidays three thousand miles away.

My mother had died in November, on the day the United States shot off a five-megaton nuclear blast underground in Amchitka, Alaska. It caused the largest earth tremor ever produced by man. It registered 7.4 on the Richter scale, and I felt the shock in our hundred-year-old house.

People had been good to us; we had seen a lot of casseroles. We had offers of a ski house in Tahoe, of a beach house in the dunes on Monterey Bay. Someone offered us a boat—a new sixty-five-foot Chris Craft—and his captain for as long as we liked.

That was the plan, Christmas on a boat cruising the

inland waterways of Florida. Then my father and I attended a lecture on American art of the postwar period. The speaker illustrated his talk with slides. Nothing, given time, is random; one of the slides was a painting of yours. Another of the slides was a painting by Arthur Brookmyer. This particular canvas hung on a wall of our living room. It was one of a series that was the artist's self-proclaimed obsession.

The lecture ended, and my father introduced himself to the speaker. They spoke about Arthur Brookmyer. The speaker confided that he was worried about the artist—he was said to be depressed following *his* wife's death.

Driving home from the lecture, my father had an idea, the kind you can only explain as the partial result of shock, the shock of my mother's death. He wanted Arthur Brookmyer to join us for the cruise, to put on boating togs and hoist a "sea breeze" with us.

"You don't know me," my father said on the telephone, "and this may be impossible. But the invitation is given in concern and passionate admiration."

The artist said he could not join us on the boat, he had to sign new prints in Europe. So he suggested we come to *his* house, he would put us up in the guest quarters.

My father and I chose a simple shirt, classically tailored in fine toast-colored suede. It looked like the kind of thing an artist could wear in the fancy Connecticut suburb where he lived.

I did not want to spend that Christmas with a stranger, a reportedly depressed stranger who was an intellectual and aesthetic titan who would, I feared, nail me to the floor with pointy-headed lectures on modern art. I forgot to set my alarm clock for the morning we were to leave; we were the last to board the plane for New York after a race to the airport that cut through corner gas stations so as not to hit red lights.

Brookmyer owned several houses on the property. It is not so far from your house. Since he did not own the manor house itself, he referred to himself as the tenant farmer.

In his library upstairs, I found volumes of poetry, philosophy and erotic drawings, plus catalogs from his friends' shows, including several of yours. In the guest house, the bedroom ceilings were painted the uncannily beautiful color that was, according to the tubes of paint we found in his studio, "cerulean," but which we had always called Brookmyer Blue. We'd painted the ceiling of our kitchen this color, and it was comforting to find it here, as well.

We took long walks on his property, and met up with our host at lunch and dinner. My father was in his element, but I felt immeasurably awkward. Brookmyer was thoughtful and gracious, and suffered my questions with patience. If I had known that I would meet you, I would have asked additional questions. How did he feel, I wanted to know, when a person looked at his work and said that a child could do as well? He said that it meant something when an artist arrived at a single line late in a serious career. Which did he like better, I asked, painting or drawing? "Drawing is a racing yacht cutting through the ocean," he said. "Painting is the ocean itself."

My father showed him a photograph of the artist's painting where it hung in our living room. Brookmyer told him to lower it an inch. "You should look into a painting, not up at it," he said, "especially in a room where people are sitting down."

He took us to his favorite place to eat. I was just then old enough to order a real drink, and was sipping a Bloody Mary. "It's good," I said. "What would make it great?" he asked, and when I told him he signaled a waiter and asked him to bring Tabasco.

He was a kind man with whom it was hard to talk. So I listened. I followed, somewhat, his periodic sentences as they wound to their elegant ends. My visit was years too soon. I did not make the most of it. I should have pressed him about the difference between originality and creativity, about his feeling that confusion was caused by the lack of genuine feeling.

One morning he had business in town, and told us we should inspect his studio. Feel free, he said, to pull canvases out of the racks. Turned loose like that, I looked at everything he had done. It felt like meeting relatives. It was a lesson in revision and amplification, in devotion and experimentation. The irony everpresent: that my mother was the reason we were there. She was the one who, twenty years before, had directed my father, in New York on business, to the gallery that was showing Brookmyer's work.

We embarrassed him Christmas Eve. It was too much, he said.

On Christmas morning when we went to the main house before leaving for the city, there was a large sheet of heavy paper rolled and tied with red ribbon on the dining room table. It was an artist's trial proof, inscribed with Christmas wishes to us.

I was entrusted to hold it, rolled, in the front seat of the rented car. When another car cut suddenly in front of us, I struck out my arm reflexively when my father pressed the brake, and put a dent in the painting which was eased out, at no small expense, by a framer.

On a day early in the New Year, I looked through the catalogs my father kept in his basement. I found the transcript of a talk that Brookmyer had given in his youth, and entered in my diary this fragment of a quote about the importance of an artist's capacity to absorb "the shocks of reality" and to "reassert himself in the face of such shocks, as when a dog shakes off water after emerging from the sea."

I have heard that when you taught, you were considered an excellent teacher. Every so often my mother and I tried to teach ourselves something from a how-to book. Mostly I did things *around* her, the way nurses change the sheets with the patient still in bed.

When I turned fifteen, I asked if she would teach me how to drive. My mother wore pigskin gloves to drive, even though she drove a station wagon. She told me to ask my father for lessons. We made a date for a Saturday morning. I was ready before my father woke up. After a quick breakfast, we backed *his* car down the driveway. My mother appeared in the opened front door and called to my father that she needed his help. He called back to her that we would only be an hour. She yelled that she needed him now. She had been reading a magazine when we left, and had not looked up when we said good-bye. And there she was screaming for him as though she had opened a vein.

It was hard for me to concentrate as my father showed me the H of the gear box. I was not able to coordinate the clutch, thinking what might happen when we got home. I still can't drive a car you have to shift. Automatic is what I can manage. Isn't there enough to pay attention to *outside* the car? All I want inside a car is music. When a favorite old song comes on the radio, I can never hear it past the first few notes. The song, evocative, will take me to the place and time where I first came to hear it. I'll be taken over for the length of the song, and returned when it stops, having missed it, only knowing it was there because now it *isn't* there. The same thing happens when I think about you. Although the trajectory is different—it is not the past, a past we haven't shared, but the future I am taken to by how quickly you have left.

I would like to go for a ride with you, have you take me to stand beside a river in the dark where hundreds of lightning bugs blink this code in sequence: right here, nowhere else! Right now, never again!

A good day. The mound in the road was not cat, but tread.

A photographer sat me down in his studio and positioned umbrella lights. He was going to make a portrait. His instructions left me hopeless—I could not look at the camera as though it was my lover. The photographer changed his tack. He said, "Give me your best 'Fuck you' look." The camera, for an instant, was my mother. "Perfect!" the photographer said.

When we can't sleep, we sneak downstairs and into the chapel, take a front pew, and hope to hear the auditory ghost, the chord that sounds at night when moonlight hits the keys through the windows in the nave. I have yet to hear it, but Chatty says it started the night the actress in the thirties made her escape.

We love our lore.

I wish I was content to think of that hour—innocent hour over cups of tea—as part of my own, a story to pass along. But I am afraid it is like the sprinkling of rain that draws the roots of plants to the surface where the sun then dries them out.

What is enough? What is ever enough?

Across the road there is an apple tree.

Every so often a car will drive past, then come back around and park beneath its branches. People will get out and start to pick the apples, pausing to bite into one, a quality check. They'll hold out the fronts of their shirts, making hammocks for the apples, and pick and take until apples are spilling out the sides of their shirts, dropping as the people return to their car hunched over from the weight of them. I have seen a woman fill her pleated skirt, then lose every one of them, slipping on the fallen ones on the way back to her car, and drive off without even one in her hand.

In the chapel I write to you on the back of an Isaac Watts hymnal, "Have I been so long with you, and yet hast thou not known me?"

Late in the fall, the sunflowers that fill a corner of the former hockey field will look like brown showerheads ready to shower seeds at the turn of a handle till the gardener clears them for compost. "A cold compost" is what Warren tells me to put on my head for a headache.

I have taken to making bouquets, with an eye to successful still life. I know it is not your strong suit, but turns out it is mine. The counselors and guests have told me as much. One school of thought says a flower arrangement should feature one type of flower—a fountain of white tulips, say, or, in the bath, one fragrant tea rose in a bud vase on a commode. But I get good notices for odd combinations: lavender cosmos and purple flowering sage, bright yellow yarrow and orange day lilies, red rambling rose spiked with flowering chive. Desperate for a hobby on a college application, years ago I wrote, "Gardening." Because my mother used to make me rake the leaves! And suddenly it comes to me that my mother never cut flowers and brought them into the house. Frustration pulls weeds; it does not arrange bouquets.

In the Hostility Suite, Warren answers the phone. "Chatty?" he says, and holds out the receiver. He waits until she is beside him, reaching for it, before adding, "Phone call for Karen."

We are teasing each other.

Maybe it is the gentle weather, but I notice we can give and take it. Dinner one warm night was a barbecue outdoors. Karen wore shorts and, for the first time, a top that was tight, a stretchy sleeveless knit. Warren looked at her chest and said, "*That* was a well-kept secret."

And Karen, she's been reading her current events, she looked at the plate of hamburgers Warren was reaching toward; she said, "I forget how, but to produce the meat for one hamburger destroys an area of rain forest the size of a kitchen."

"That's not very big," Warren said, and helped himself.

I think of Karen, saying, "I finally solved my problem of how to talk with people," and Warren coming back with, "The hand puppets worked?"

Our own wobbly tries.

We sometimes forget why we're here. And when in a flash we remember, it is a feeling like something we're not fond of that has gone away but will be coming back. A quarrelsome mate off on a business trip.

Diminution. This is often a comfort, to be satisfied with

less. My grandmother told me that when I was born, she made my mother carry me straightaway up a flight of stairs. It is a superstition. You carry the infant up the stairs so the child will rise in the world.

"Are you sure?" I used to ask her, my grandmother, because it felt as though I'd been carried instead to the basement, my job to just break even, to rise to the place where the rest were pushing off. This is not a complaint, just the way it seemed to me. Whereas take a person like Chatty. At Scrabble today, she made the word *hepper.* We challenged her. She said, "That's Southern for 'assistant'—'He's mah hepper.'" She was playing with us, but Warren looked it up and found it really is a word, the name for a salmon in its second year. And Chatty got to keep her points.

I chose the F. That time I could have played the N or F?

"It is up to you," the counselor says. "And why is getting better up to you?"

"Because," I say, my answer practiced, "I am the one who cares the most." Even when I am not.

Remember last week's storm that blew up from the tropics? Karen and I walked the beach the morning after, what beach there was left to walk. We saw four people haul in a large piece of something that, out of the surf, you could see was the hull of a good-sized sailboat. A hundred yards ahead, another piece of wood was being examined by an elderly man. He showed us the splintered stern with part of the boat's name still stenciled on it in blue:—*Wood.*

Karen and I continued down the beach, guessing at the name of the ruined boat: *Driftwood? Hollywood?* Firewood now, more's the pity. Until the missing piece washed up at our feet, and all we had to do to complete the puzzle was bend down and turn it over, and—

Touch. *"Touch Wood."*

So it was to the objects in the world around her that the letter writer turned.

Please excuse the switch to notebook paper; I just ran out of the good stuff. And if my penmanship suffers, it is because I am not at a desk, but in a parked car, and using my knee for support.

The driver this time is polite. He has not tried to hurry me along as other of the drivers have. He brought along a book of the stripe I could hold up to the unidentified object that flies. He brought a Thermos. And has not asked me what time it is, but has only excused himself to use the facilities across the street.

It is rabbit hour, the time they come out into the open. I wish it never got any darker than this, the moment you can no longer tell that grass is green.

If you say that you think you need to stay on, the management here says, "Of course." If you tell them you feel you are ready to move on, these same people say, "That's right." I didn't tell anyone I was trying to leave—circle of well-wishers reaching to say good-bye, reaching so that arms tangle and heads knock, yourself caught in the cross-love.

I said I had to go to town to mail a letter, to get it weighed and buy the right stamps, being careful not to drop it on the ground before it is posted. That would bring bad luck. For us both.

I asked the driver, as soon as he returned, to cut around to back behind the residential homes; there's a corridor through the dunes where you can see the ocean waves and the saltwater pond, a sanctuary for birds. Terns are quarreling in a windswept, vine-hung pine. And—worthy of your brush—three egrets stop in different poses for a second, as if they were a single bird at three consecutive moments. Now they are in motion, alighting on the sand. The tide this time of year washes hundreds of tiny starfish up onto the beach. It leaves them stranded in salty constellations, a sandy galaxy within reach.

NOTES

Page 204: "The need for the new love . . ." is from "Wait," by Galway Kinnell, in *Mortal Acts, Mortal Words*, Houghton Mifflin, 1980.

Page 234: "Not every clocktick needs a martyr" is from the poem "Turning to Look Back," by John Woods, from *Keeping Out of Trouble*, Indiana University Press, 1968.

Pages 241 & 274: The gorilla who uses sign language is Koko. Incidents cited are either from the author's visit with Koko, or from documented exchanges and observations by Koko's teacher, Dr. Francine Patterson.

Page 260: The artists referred to are Alex Melamid and Vitaly Komar, whose conceptual art piece/poll was titled *The People's Art*.

Page 267: "He opens a book at random and consults randomness," is from the poem "Sortilege," by Eric Pankey, from *Apocrypha*, Knopf, 1993.

Page 293: "Drawing is a racing yacht . . ." is from Robert Motherwell in "Thoughts on Drawing," reprinted in *The Collected Writings of Robert Motherwell*, edited by Stephanie Terenzio, Oxford University Press, 1992.

Page 295: ". . . to reassert himself in the face of . . ." is from Robert Motherwell in conversation with the author and in "The Place of the Spiritual in a World of Property" (later titled "The Modern Painter's World"), and in *The Collected Writings of Robert Motherwell*, ibid.

Catherine Tatge's film, *Robert Motherwell and the New York School: Storming the Citadel*, for the PBS series *American Masters*, was also a valuable reference.

THE DOG OF
THE MARRIAGE

BEACH TOWN

The house next door was rented for the summer to a couple who swore at missed croquet shots. Their music at night was loud, and I liked it; it was not music I knew. Mornings, I picked up the empties they had lobbed across the hedge, Coronas with the limes wedged inside, and pitched them back over. We had not introduced ourselves these three months.

Between our houses a tall privet hedge is backed by white pine for privacy in winter. The day I heard the voice of a woman not the wife, I went out back to a spot more heavily planted but with a break I could just see through. Now it was the man who was talking, or trying to—he started to say things he could not seem to finish. I watched the woman do something memorable to him with her mouth. Then the man pulled her up from where she had been kneeling. He said, "Maybe you're just hungry. Maybe we should get you something to eat."

The woman had a nimble laugh.

The man said, "Paris is where you and I should go."

The woman asked what was wrong with here. She said, "I like a beach town."

I wanted to phone the wife's office in the city and hear what she would sound like if she answered. I had no fellow feeling; all she had ever said to me was couldn't I mow my lawn later in the day. It was noon when she asked. I told her the village bylaws disallow mowing before seven-thirty, and that I had waited until nine. A gardener, hired by my neighbor, cared for their yard. But still I was sure they were neglecting my neighbor's orchids. All summer long I had watched for the renters to leave the house together so that I could let myself in with the key from the shelf in the shed and test the soil and water the orchids.

The woman who did not want to go to Paris said that she had to leave. "But I don't want you to leave," the man said, and she said, "Think of the kiss at the door."

Nobody thinks about the way sound carries across water. Even the water in a swimming pool. A week later, when her husband was away, the wife had friends to lunch by the pool. I didn't have to hide to listen; I was in view if they had cared to look, pulling weeds in the raspberry canes.

The women told the wife it was an opportunity for her. They said, "Fair is fair," and to do those things she might not otherwise have done. "No regrets," they said, "if you are even the type of person who is given to regret, if you even have that type of wistful temperament to begin with."

The women said, "We are not unintelligent; we just let passion prevail." They said, "Who would deny that we have all had these feelings?"

The women told the wife she would not feel this way forever. "You will feel worse, however, before you feel better, and that is just the way it always is."

The women advised long walks. They told the wife to watch the sun rise and set, to look for solace in the natural world, though they admitted there was no comfort to be found in the world and they would all be fools to expect it.

The weekend the couple next door had moved in—their rental began on Memorial Day—I heard them place a bet on the moon. She said waxing, he said waning. Days later, the moon nearly full in the night sky, I listened for the woman to tell her husband she had won, knowing they had not named the terms of the bet, and that the woman next door would collect nothing.

JESUS IS WAITING

I didn't want the sunroof or the luggage rack, but neither did I want to wait the three months not to have to have them. So I took the white one anyway and put fifty thousand miles on it in just about a year.

Lincoln Tunnel to Baltimore, BWI: two and three-quarter hours; Holland Tunnel to D.C. (Connecticut Avenue exit): three and a quarter hours. In Virginia, anything over ninety is now reckless driving and reckless driving costs more than speeding does and they say no excuses, you have to show up in court, but don't believe it; I phoned in sick the day I was slated to appear and a clerk told me where to send the check. One more reckless driving ticket in Virginia and I'll have to find the place they have the safety class that, if you take it, knocks three points off your license. Or, I don't know, your life?

Maryland and New York are the states where I can push it.

No blue highways, nothing scenic.

In a tornado outside Baltimore, in a broken neighborhood off I-95, I asked the attendant in a Mobil station, "Where's anywhere else?"

The man didn't even point.

*　　*　　*

I write in pencil because a pencil is what is tied with string to the suggestion box. "We welcome your comments." I write, "I went to the other place first, but got pissed off in line and came here and am glad I did."

I had not fared so well at the one off Exit 7. The ice machine was broken. Yes, I got more Dr Pepper in the cup, but the Dr Pepper I got was warm.

I never eat in the place I stop for gas. I like to keep the odometer turning. Sometimes I will drive only as far as a local exit with a road or avenue in the name. Not a connecting artery. I will pull off into a community, find a cul-de-sac, stop the car, keep an eye on the trees that line the street. Maybe fill out a postcard bought at a rest stop, address it to the man who won't speak to me, ask him "Is one of the symptoms that you're thirsty all the time?"

Or is one of the symptoms a rash? Is one of the symptoms dry mouth? That it's hard to urinate? Maybe one of the symptoms is that you piss people off.

Taking it more slowly since the spinout on black ice. Where were the famed antilock brakes? Traveling under the speed limit on a flat stretch of road, and all of a sudden a wreck that takes the luggage rack off. No visible injuries—you can't see a sprain—but I had to make camp for days while the sunroof was checked out. There was a multiplex and a Mexican restaurant that used baked beans in their burritos. North Carolina, but nothing Carolingian.

The guy who sold me a map in the Exxon in Greensboro asked me who I was listening to the next hundred miles. Before he had stopped speaking to me, the man back home made me a tape for the road. It's the same cut over and over on both sides—"Jesus Is Waiting," by the Reverend Al Green. Apart from those, the words you hear the most are "Thank you."

On the New Jersey Turnpike, a box of animal crackers at the Walt Whitman rest area costs almost two dollars.

Here's something I didn't know: the drag you get from open windows uses more gas than running the air conditioner does.

The radio said Dorothy Love Coates died today. But I didn't know she'd even been alive.

A point of pride not to stop when tired. Drive a couple of hundred more miles. In St. Louis, they say when you hit Indianapolis, you're home. Home is a Days Inn or a Comfort Inn, unless there is more than one of those big trucks in the lot. In the morning, in the lobby, there are free doughnuts and coffee. I like handing the sticks and the sugar and the cream around. There's always a television going so we all have a place to look. Someone will always say to me, "Have a safe trip." I'll always say, "You too."

I keep meaning to pull off and visit an IKEA store.

Before I took to the road, a friend tried to get me to go to a department store with him. He said it was to improve the place where I lived. He said, "I want to know you are reading beneath *this* lamp." This fellow was dying. He knew it and I did not. I think he was tucking me in. He was making sure all of his friends had the right lamps, the comfiest pillows, the softest sheets. He was tucking us all in for the night.

In a motel off an interstate, a breakfaster warns me about

impetigo. But who in this century gets impetigo? The break-faster says to avoid standing water. Or maybe she says standing *in* water.

Avoid it, is the point.

Listening to Al Green, I didn't mind the smell of tar, a turn lane being paved. At a farm stand along a switchback road, I bought a bag of shiny red chiles. Wouldn't they be good for whatever there was to be good for?

It is the day before Thanksgiving. According to the radio, people travel to their destinations by car. One hundred percent if you count just me.

A good feeling when I see traffic cones. They weigh next to nothing and cannot hurt a car. That's not why I mow them down.

A point of pride—to drive like crazy in the passing lane, or, alternatively, to sit in the fast lane stuck in traffic and not to register any change in heart rate or respiration. I am often moved to tears when the lane I am in merges with another. I can well up where the New Jersey Turnpike becomes 95 and where 95 becomes 85 just outside Petersburg, Virginia.

On the day before a holiday, you feel you have a destination just by being on the road with so many people who do.

Have a destination, that is.

I write on a postcard, "Is one of the symptoms a fever of unknown origin?" I sign the card, "As ever."

*   *   *

I put a lot of money into tires. I don't rotate—I replace, with the best new radials. I am never late for scheduled mainte-nance. I learned the hard way to watch that they do not dilute the windshield-wiper fluid. Except for the iffy antilock brakes, if something goes wrong, it is not the car that's at fault. Bad form to blame something for the damage one does. I just mow them down—and drive on.

Countryside: a blue-lit blue spruce in the center of a pond with swans. City: a blue neon cellular sign, pigeons pecking crumbs on the sidewalk. Did someone stand toy soldiers in wet cement? A small brigade marches around the corner.

McDonald's has better french fries and their orange juice comes in a cup that fits the holder in the car. Burger King's orange juice comes in a carton, but their fish thing is better than the one at McDonald's. I don't know about the coffee at either place. I only know about the coffee if it's in a lobby and free. I saw a forensics special on the TV at a Days Inn—it examined the mystery of three hunters who were found dead at their campsite. Extensive testing revealed that there had been a newt in their coffeepot, and when they poured in boil-ing water, deadly toxins were released by the newt.

Driving togs are usually black jeans and a cotton turtle-neck, a wool-lined canvas jacket thrown across the front seat to put on when pumping gas. Do people still call them gas sta-tions? Filling stations? Where are the people who call them service stations?

If I had a gas station, would I name it Exxon or Hess?

For shoes: anything that slips right off. I drive barefoot unless there's snow.

The night before Thanksgiving, I turn onto an exit ramp for the Thomas Edison rest area. In the gift shop I buy a postcard with a picture of a dog trotting down Route 66. I ask if one of the symptoms is that you can't get a song out of your head, and sign it, "More as ever than ever."

The roads on Thanksgiving Day are as quiet as they were packed the day before. Destinations must have been reached.

I can still recognize a '67 Mustang.

I was not put on this earth to fill my own tank, but I have come to look forward to doing it. I like the smell on my hands from the pump, the restrooms never not out of soap. Each time I cross a state line, I visit the Welcome Center and ask for directions. What a laugh. Then back to the car, merging confidently into traffic, seeing how far I can go before racking up "Jesus Is Waiting."

It is Thanksgiving Day. I am driving the New Jersey Turnpike. Past the exit for the store where I once bought a hat made out of a Wonder Bread wrapper. Past the exit for the house where I was talked into playing a party game called "Empty Hands." Three more exits. Past them all.

The geographic cure, these bouts of driving, with the age-old bit built in: "Wherever you go, there you are." Maybe people should be trained like dogs. But people aren't dogs. Besides, a dog won't speak to you, either.

Is one of the symptoms restlessness? An inability to stay put?

The calluses on the palms of my hands show that I have put in the hours, hit the road early and often, stayed flexible and ready to leave on short notice, on even no notice; packed in the car are clothes, bottles of juice, a pass for bridges and tunnels and tolls, assorted useless maps, and the tape he made for me—"Jesus Is Waiting."

I never stop for the night before filling the tank.

In the back is a case with the word HELP on it. It contains jumper cables, flares, a flashlight, tire patches. I should add aspirin and a knife.

God, it's an ugly road.

And now someone is following me. He's driving a black car. It trumps the pickup that pulled up alongside me in Virginia, the guy turning on his inside light so I could get a look at him. This new guy isn't bad-looking, but he has a ponytail and there is no desire in his gaze.

In a pig's eye.

Soon I'll have a chance of a bridge or tunnel. In these last years I'm talking about, I've driven a tunnel only once. Since I have a choice, when I have a choice, I choose a bridge.

In the backseat of my car, a potted amaryllis blooms.

Sometimes, if I were not ready to get back in the car, I would phone a realtor from my motel. I would pick a name from the phone book, and ask to be shown houses. I would give the broker a price range. I would be taken to see Colonials, a saltbox, Cape Cods. I keep the business cards in a pocket of the case labeled HELP.

The drive is determinedly a drive. Mostly it is just about the sounds of the car, of driving, of the fade-in and fade-out of the radio, the removal from everything but the moving body in a vehicle, of the is-ness of passing from here to there, of not being where you were, of Jesus waiting. Call it a meditation. Call it *drone*. How else to approach Jesus than without history, without reason, without restraint? And buoyed by staying in motion away from everything, the mind become the traveling until wherever you stop, won't Jesus be waiting there?

Is one of the symptoms a loss of faith? Or faith in loss?

On the way back into the city, I stop to fill up. I would like to be scrambled and served with sausages at an all-night diner.

Is this what the world is?

I smell my fingers. Nice.

This time I use the telephone instead of sending a card. I leave him a message. I say I will be there in an hour. I say, "Can we take each other in?"

Back in the car I adjust the seat so I will have to sit up straighter. I take a mint from the glove compartment and twist off the wrapper.

I see myself in the rearview mirror.

I give the car some gas, and merge with the other drivers who are heading into the city where Jesus is waiting—or isn't.

THE UNINVITED

It was one and two and three and four and five o'clock in the morning. Whatever time it was, it was time to take the test. You did not have to wait until morning anymore; the instructions on the box said that for an accurate result you could dip the strip of litmus paper in a "clear stream of urine" any time of day. My waiting until morning was habit, a nod to the old days when "first morning's urine" was going to give you the answer. Though not at home. You had to go to a clinic then. Sometimes on the ceilings of exam rooms was a sign: "A woman can never be too thin or too rich, or too close to the end of the table."

I was fifty years old, and ten days late.

If menopausal, go on estrogen; if pregnant, go on welfare.

If I *was* pregnant, I did not know who to blame—my husband, whom I did not live with, or the man in the auditorium, whom I did not report.

I did what I had always done the night before taking the test: I watched *The Uninvited*.

"The cold . . . is no mere matter of degrees Fahrenheit, but a drawing of warmth from the vital centers of the living."

The Uninvited, made in 1944, stars Ray Milland and Ruth Hussey as the English brother and sister Roderick and Pamela Fitzgerald, who happen upon a stately empty house on a cliff in Cornwall when they are on vacation. The two are so won over by the place they decide to buy it and leave their London lives—he a composer and music critic, she a budding home-maker—for these "haunted shores."

"That's not because there are *more* ghosts here than in other places, mind you, it's just that the people who live here-abouts are more . . ."

I am courting ghosts at a place where ghosts are studied as a subset of the paranormal. I participate in experiments at an institute in the South. Last week I was placed in a private room and given a photograph to hold. I was supposed to try to "send" the image to a woman in another room down the hall. The photograph I held was a likeness of Frankenstein, a still from the movie. For nearly half an hour I stared and directed the thought: *Frankenstein, Frankenstein,* at the woman down the hall. A researcher came to get us and took us down-stairs to appear before the staff.

"Well?" the researcher prompted.

The woman from down the hall said, "I don't know, I kept getting Frank, Frank—*Frank Sinatra?*"

And I screamed, "That's a match!"—wanting so much the unexplainable in my life.

I had not been living in my house for months. I had accepted a job house-sitting, if you can call that a job, for a professor on sabbatical from a university in the South. He had hired a cleaning lady and a gardener, so all I had to do was occupy space and forward his mail. He would return for spring break, at which time I was to return to my house up North. Since it was winter up there, I returned for a night every three or four weeks; I had to check for burst pipes and whatever else could happen in my absence.

When I was back home, I read the local newspaper's weekly police blotter. It featured the usual thefts—houses closed for the winter are routinely broken into—as well as a range of conceptual crimes. Someone had turned up the thermostat in a beach house in the dunes. This person took nothing, but turned the temperature to ninety degrees, which, by the time it was discovered, had badly warped the floors. In another house, the owners discovered that someone had emptied the kitchen cabinets. Nothing had been stolen, but every item in the cabinets had been lined up neatly on the counters.

One kind of damage presented itself on my first visit home: the house smelled of mice, and when I lay still on the couch, I heard them scrabbling in the cabinets and behind the walls. There was no point setting out traps—I would be leaving the next day and anything caught would decompose in the weeks until my next visit. I could hear mice in a drawer. I yanked it open and found droppings like fat, dark grains of rice surrounding a diamond-and-sapphire pin my mother-in-law had given me when I married her son. When the marriage ended, I thought of giving the pin back to my husband; his parents had since died, and the pin had been a gift to his mother from his father. I thought about it, but I did nothing about it, and now the timeworn jewelry was in this sorry setting when it should have been safe in a tiny velvet pouch.

All of us should be safe in a tiny velvet pouch.

Well, I left the thing loose in the drawer.

And of course a pipe did burst, but luckily one outside, positioned to irrigate a cutting garden long since abandoned, the garden my husband's project, so I kept the water turned off except to flush a toilet when I would turn the relevant lever in the basement, go back upstairs and flush, then turn off the water again. Think of it as fancy camping, I told myself, and it was fine, this manner of thinking.

For instance, storm doors and windows had never been put up, so, like clocks not changed from Daylight Savings Time, wouldn't the absence of these fixtures be just right in a few more months?

Lightbulbs, that was a different matter. They were often burned out, however much they had not been used. So I just as often had to stand on one foot to change them in the kitchen.

"Important decisions have to be made quickly," says Pamela Fitzgerald.

"Anyway, how do you even know it's for sale?" says brother Roderick.

"Life isn't as cruel as that—it's *got* to be," says Pamela Fitzgerald.

Important decisions do have to be made quickly. Once the test stick is removed from its foil packet, once the "absorbent tip" is placed in the urine flow for at least five seconds, or dipped into a clean container of this person's urine, also for no fewer than five seconds, the result will be indicated in three minutes.

A decision will be made quickly, and not at all quickly forgotten.

There is a "sealed splashguard" on the test stick. Still, it seems smarter to collect the urine and place the test stick in the container. So the first decision of the morning is whether to go in a tumbler or a measuring cup. In crystal or in cookware?

*　　*　　*

At the video store in the town in the South, I rent *Topper* and *The Ghost and Mrs. Muir*—romantic, playful, companionable ghosts—but they don't compare with the ghost who sobs all night on the estate of Windward House where, from a cliff, young Mary Meredith falls (or is pushed?) to her death.

The night before taking the test the first time I had to take it, I watched *The Uninvited* on television, on the all-night oldies channel. I took it as a sign, its broadcast that night. The next morning, every minute of which I watched approach, I tested positive. It was a spring day in Southern California. It was 1970, and I was in college.

One week later, I signed a statement that would be sent to a committee of physicians. In it, I threatened to take my life if I were not allowed to terminate the pregnancy. A woman I barely knew had coached me to say this; she was the wife of a friend of a friend and had been moved to help a young thing she barely knew because she had been the young thing's age and it had not been easy for her. Or so I seemed to have thought.

I was a girl again.

I stood in the student union, studying the bulletin board.

What could have been better proof of girlhood reacquired?

It is the little terrier, Bobby, who first gets Pamela and Rick into Windward House. Bobby sets off across the lawn after a squirrel and squeezes in after it when the squirrel slips through an open window. Bobby chases the squirrel up the chimney, but refuses to mount the stairs, where his owners will find, behind the locked door of the studio, an unexplained chill and a despair that engulfs all who enter.

My own house is situated across the street from a cemetery. The lawn of "the Boneyard," as I call the place, is littered with dozens of chewed-out marrow bones. Neighbors would complain if the privet did not thrive and block the yard from view. The bones come frozen in packages of six; neighbor dogs get one apiece when they stop by to visit. They follow me across the lawn, back behind the backyard to where the growth has been too much to keep up with. The cold frame where seedlings made a dash for it is filled with weeds, and the rows of sunflowers and gladioli and irises are lost under grasses so long they bend and swirl into bedding for deer. The grasses have buried the rows of strawberries that my husband protected with net until the morning I went to pick some to serve with cream and found a box turtle caught in the webbing, dead. Like the "ghost nets" left behind by fishermen, seines that float loose to entangle porpoises and diving gulls.

That day I ripped off the net.

Let everything eat.

I did not call the police. Two years of working a hotline, and I did not report it.

We always offered to accompany victims to court. We offered follow-up support until a woman called to say she was moving and could a few of us come over and help her pack.

Some of the group never said the word *man*. Instead they said "potential rapist." There were men who wanted to donate money, but there was a faction among us who did not feel right accepting donations from future rapists.

Here is what I would have had to say, if I had been a caller: "Hello? Hello? Oh, man, I did not call the police because I had invited the man in. My clothes? I took them off myself."

The time I tried to keep it, I did not try for very long. Although one week did seem to me like a long time. I was sick enough to be in a hospital with an intravenous drip plugged into my wrist. There was an antiemetic I could ask for twice a day that made life tolerable for a little less than half an hour. Sometimes the body takes over to make a decision the mind can't make. This was one of the doctors. She said sometimes a woman thinks she wants a child when what she really wants is the father of the child.

Stella Meredith was only three years old when her mother died at Windward House. Now twenty, she lives with her grandfather, the Commander (Donald Crisp), in town. Stella, played by Gail Russell, meets the Fitzgeralds when they come to inquire about buying the deserted house on the cliff. Stella is rude to them, tells them the house is not for sale. But her grandfather arrives as she is ushering them out, and, keen to provide for Stella after he is gone, sells the Fitzgeralds the house on the spot. The grandfather does not mention the disturbances the new owners will find. Stella, meanwhile, has caught Roderick Fitzgerald's eye; later, he will readily accept her apology and invite Stella to dinner at her former home.

The act of taking the test made me feel sick. Before I could insert the test strip into the glass, I had to lie down and wait for the room to get steady. I wanted the hospital staple, Jell-O, cubed in a bowl on a tray. At home—a different story; was the problem sliced bananas or canned pears? The weight of diced peaches, the pits in the cherries? Waterlogged chunks of pineapple, fan-shaped mandarin oranges; they sank to the bottom or they rested on the surface—you had to know more about Jell-O than I did.

Mrs. Wynn used to make me Jell-O. She was a frequent babysitter, and, apart from my acquaintances in the movies, the only English person I knew. She was inventive, and once pasted the feet of paper dolls to either side of a Mexican jumping bean. She attached tissue skirts that covered the beans and then placed the dolls on a plate set on top of a chafing dish. In due course, the "fairies" had all been made to dance.

When I was sick, Mrs. Wynn performed a trick she called "the Passenger to Boulogne." She brought to my bedroom an orange and a wineglass and a penknife and handkerchief. She prepared the orange by cutting into the rind the best ears, nose, and mouth her skill could devise. She then smoothed out the handkerchief and stretched it lightly over the mouth of the wineglass; she set the carved orange thereon. When she saw that she had my attention, she moved the handkerchief backward and forward over the top of the glass, imparting to the orange a rolling motion and what she described to her woozy audience as the agonies of a seasick passenger making the Channel crossing. The performance, she explained, was supposed to end by draping the handkerchief like a hood over the "head" and squeezing the orange into the glass. In deference to my condition, however, Mrs. Wynn demurred, saying some people found it disagreeably realistic.

I thought I remembered a Mrs. Wynn from *The Uninvited,* but the devoted housekeeper the Fitzgeralds bring over from London is named Lizzie Flynn, not Wynn. She hectors and pampers Pamela and Rick; she makes them tipsy pudding. A superstitious woman, Lizzie Flynn is not long for Windward House. Soon she is spending nights in a farmhouse down the road where, presumably, no ghost can be heard sobbing until dawn.

On the hotline one night, I got a call from a local rock star. The woman was calling between sets to say that the man who had attacked her the week before was sitting in the audience.

Had she reported that attack the week before? No, she said, she had had a few drinks that night. Did she want me to call the police? No, but could I meet her at the club after the show?

We always went out in pairs, so I called another counselor, a resourceful dyke named Carolee. The bouncer waved us in. We stood in the back and watched the end of the show. The rocker was athletic, backlit, barely clothed. Carolee and I worked our way to the greenroom as the rocker came off the stage. I tapped my chest, and she came over and hugged me hard. With her arm around me, she walked me to where I could see the audience from behind a curtain. She pointed to a man alone.

"There's my rapist," she said.

Then, as was not uncommon, she wanted to know if she had put us to any trouble. I reminded her that I was already on call, and Carolee said she preferred this to the fight she had been having with her girlfriend. Lesbian fights are the worst, Carolee said—nobody ever walks out and slams the door because they're both women and want to talk about their *feelings*.

*   *   *

On the drive back home from the house-sitting job, I stopped off in West Virginia to meet my estranged husband. The large house sat on three hundred acres of horse and dairy farm amid gentle hills cut through by the Opequon Creek. His family staged fraught reunions every summer and lobbied for repairs needed to keep the place up. There were thirteen bedrooms and one bathroom, added in the 1920s. Each summer we all scraped and repainted the wraparound porch, taking breaks to chase off trespassers who pushed metal detectors across the grounds. My first time there, a charter bus wound up the drive on a hot afternoon. It advertised "The J. E. B. Stuart Singers," who dismounted—a busload of folks in period costume. They serenaded us with Civil War ballads. My husband—then-husband—allowed as how the family was used to this.

Over the years, the affable and ineffectual caretaker would phone to report break-ins and thefts. The great house was vacant except for reunions, encouraging thieves to back their trucks up to the wide front doors. They stole every piece of furniture. They were so unhurried as to remove and leave behind cheap replacement shades for the valuable antique lamps. Some of the thieves took time for a beer, and left crushed cans in the grand entry hall. By the time the family voted funds for an alarm, there was nothing of value left to protect.

The place had its ghost, of course. It was said she haunted the third floor, a well-defined apparition wearing a long white sleeping gown. I was told that the only people who saw this ghost ("the White Lady") were women who married into the family and of whom the White Lady approved. So one night I faked a rattled look and told my future husband that I had just seen a ghost when I went upstairs for more pillows. Years later, I asked this same man, now an ex-husband, if I could stay in his house to break up the long drive north and let some bad weather pass.

Was there a ghost who appeared to women *leaving* the family?

For extra class credit, we could volunteer for experiments at the parapsychology institute. These experiments took place on Saturday mornings. Downstairs, in the white clapboard house where the experiments were conducted, was a comfortable living room and library with worn, overstuffed chairs and dozens of psi journals. Across the hall was a dining room turned conference room with a rolling blackboard facing the large oval table. The research assistants were in their late twenties, conservatively dressed and courteous. My first time there, I was told to remain seated in the living room while an assistant went upstairs and turned on a computer. A photograph would appear on the screen. I was to concentrate on the image for a time, and draw it as best I could on the sheet of paper she gave me. All the assistant would say about the photograph was that there were no human beings in it.

I did as I was told.

I was about to begin sketching a cliff-dweller village along the lines of Mesa Verde when a more powerful image took its place. I roughed in the sides of a cliff, but instead of a village I drew a Niagara Falls–like waterfall.

Upstairs, the research assistant showed me the computer screen. It displayed a wide-angle view of the Vatican in Rome. We laughed it off, and she said it was only my first try. She said why didn't we take a peek at what the next volunteer would try to draw. She pressed a button, and my waterfall appeared onscreen.

"See?" she said, pleased. "I've seen this happen before."

She turned off the light in the room.

The grand chandeliers of Windward House supplement the light on the ceilings that is reflected off the water at the base of the cliffs.

Home on spring break, when I was already five days late, I went through closets and drawers to give my things away. Was this the beginning of the famed nesting instinct? Or its opposite? A friend had once opened a drawer in his kitchen and found four banana peels neatly folded by his pregnant wife. During the winter, mice carried cereal into the fingers of my gloves.

When I was six days late, I tried to fix the soaker hose ruined months before by a power mower. It fed a long stretch of privet. I found a length of replacement hose in the unlocked garage and battled it into place for more than an hour. When I turned on the water, I saw that the hose was a regular rubber hose without the tiny perforations of the soaker. I went inside the house and got a steak knife from the kitchen. I took it outdoors and stabbed the twenty-five feet of rubber repeatedly, making my own goddamn soaker hose.

Just when you begin to think you've dreamt it, it comes again.

This is Pamela Fitzgerald, talking to her brother about the ghost who sobs all night in Windward House.

Back in Los Angeles, when the woman I barely knew drove me to the hospital, we listened to somebody talking about old movies. But the movies being talked about, not one of them was as old as *The Uninvited.*

There was no blaming a poltergeist for the vase that flew off the mantel and shattered on the slate below. You had only to see that it was filled with top-heavy gerbera daisies to predict that the slightest stirring of the air, as from a person walking past, could cause the vase to topple over. As I sponged up the water and swept up the broken glass, I thought, What a relief, this loss.

The vase broke when I was seven days late. On the eighth day, I went to a lecture by a woman known as much for her compassion as for her clear soprano voice. She spoke of her work with the dying. She would bring her harp to their bedsides and sing.

"This is not ambient goodwill, not a bedside concert," she said. "It is palliative, prescriptive music. The harp invites the listener into the present so that something new can happen. Ideally, the music will make time stop—it will help unbind the dying from qualities of time that we are bound to."

She said she never sang the songs that people knew because to do so would be to hold the dying when the point is to help the dying let go. Chances are they have not heard "Rosa Mystica," or "Custodes Hominum," or "Dans Nos Obscurites," she said.

I asked her privately, when she had finished speaking, how the medical profession had first greeted her approach to the dying. She said she was invited to keep it to herself. She smiled and said, "Containment is also holy," a woman who could bide her time.

*   *   *

I had always thought women's clinics should replace their posters of "The Desiderata" and Erté's Nouveau nymphs with reproductions of Hans Holbein's *An Allegory of Passion,* with its caption from Petrarch's *Canzoniere*: *"E cosi desio me mena"*—"And so desire carries me along."

It is not always a matter of being careless, you know.

It is not always desire, either. Except as the desire to save oneself by doing what one is told to do by the person who has the knife.

An old friend from high school phoned on the ninth day I was late. She was in my town for the day. A tiny blond girl, she had left school for Japan where she put on ceremonial robes and apprenticed herself to elderly Japanese masters of the bamboo flute called *shakuhachi.* She was a quick study, and was soon quite the thing in performances throughout Japan. Back in this country, she told me she was recording "telepathic duets" with a partner on recorder two thousand miles away. She said that at an agreed-upon time, they would sit in meditation for an hour, then record an improvisation in their separate studios. Later, they would combine the two recordings into one piece.

Successful collaborations inspire envy in me. But "collaborate," someone once told me, also means "to betray."

I drove my crazy old friend to the train station that evening, and on the way home stopped at the all-night drugstore to buy the test.

When Stella first visits Windward House for dinner, a malevolent spirit causes her to faint. Pamela Fitzgerald calls for the doctor, who proves to be handsome, kind, and available. But will Pamela Fitzgerald be excluded from the happiness her brother and Stella share?

Crime around here has taken a new turn. People who live on the horse farms on the road to the beach report that the rails are disappearing from their split-rail fences. Charred rails are found in the sand. Imagine the kind of person who takes down someone's fence in order to make a bonfire on a beach.

Even when it was not my fault, I was lectured on the imperative of responsibility, a sitting dog being told to sit.

In the bathroom, I lifted the test strip out of the crystal tumbler. Without looking at it, I laid it on a saucer and left the room.

The next day, I took the train to the South to resume my house-sitting job. With time to kill in Union Station, I visited stores I would not otherwise have entered and underwent a kind of awakening, asking myself for the first time, Why don't I have shoe trees? Though I hadn't asked for help, a salesgirl at a cosmetics counter told me to comb my hair out wet. She said brushing stretched the hair, snapped it off. She sold me a comb, and I acted as though I had always known to use one.

You can do anything with ease if you act as though you do it all the time—dance, sunbathe nude, talk someone out of hurting you. What had prepared me to be good at that? I read in a psi journal that a superficially injured person often becomes hysterical, while someone hurt seriously may be more likely to conserve energy and get herself help.

*　　*　　*

The evening the man in the auditorium came to my place, I became steadily calmer until I was in a trance of self-preservation. I had missed a lecture just before we were to have an exam. The man to my right, always to my right, told me he had taken thorough notes; he said he was willing to share them with me if I wanted. He made a show of looking in his book bag. He looked again and said he must have left his notebook at home. He said he could drop it off for me that evening. He said it would be no trouble. I gave him my address, which he wrote on his hand with a felt-tipped marker.

Well, he had the book bag with him when he showed up at my place that night. I saw that he had changed from a T-shirt to something long-sleeved. He came in after standing out there for so long I felt I had to let him. He said he just wanted to drop off the notes. He sat in the armchair in the small living room furnished by the professor and his wife. There were no photographs of them, but there were, I remember, a lot of wood carvings from various foreign places. He dropped his book bag on the carpet beside him, but did not open it. I went to get him some soda or something. Was it just water?

In the crisis training I received in the women's group, we were told that our instincts were good, that if we sensed we were being followed, we were probably right.

I said, "How about the notes?"

He looked startled, then said, with exaggerated deference, "Of course. Don't let me keep the lady waiting."

He unbuckled the book bag.

I went to switch on a lamp.

When I turned around, he had the knife.

*   *   *

On the hotline one night, I took a call from a woman who had been raped by three men in a Turkish bath. "Why me?" she kept asking me. I told her it happens to anyone. I told her the stats for our city. I told her it was not her fault. Then it was revealed that she weighed nearly three hundred pounds, and that what she meant by "Why me?" was why they would want to rape *her.*

"What are you doing?" I said.

He had a close-trimmed black beard, I noticed. I have never understood how a man trims a beard. Is it the lawn-mower principle, where you raise the blade away from what you are going to mow?

He said, "You have a great mouth."

I said thank you.

He said he liked it that I was cordial. He said he didn't like it when a woman tried to run away, or push him away, and he had to use the knife.

Just when you begin to think you've dreamt it . . .

He tried and tried.

Said it was my fault.

I heard a dog bark outside. I didn't know the neighbors, but I knew their dog. He sometimes followed me into the house where I kept a box of biscuits for him.

"Stay," I said to the man from the auditorium.

He stopped slamming himself against me.

"It's enough that you're here," I said.

I saw his shoulders drop. He put the knife down. He put his arms around me. He said we would be lovers. He began to cry. I felt him begin to get hard.

The moment when Stella is saved from death on the cliffs is the moment the ghost stops sobbing, the moment Stella finds out who her real mother is, and what happened to her real mother when Stella was too young to know.

In spring, daffodils line the miles of the National Trust coastline of Cornwall. They flourish in my sorry northern yard, as well, passed over by deer as are the garish forsythia I failed to prune. It is the opposite of *ikebana,* the harmonious placement of a single bloom, and that is as close as I have ever come to making friends with disorder.

Given the number of times I have seen *The Uninvited,* you would think I would know to whom the title refers—to the ghosts or to the guests.

One of the assistants let me in when I arrived. Several handlers were already present, one for each of the dogs that would participate in the experiment.

The assistant signaled for a black Lab to be brought forward. The dog stood calmly. The assistant took a metal choke chain from her pocket. She moved to the dog's rear end. She stood above the dog and held the chain collar from one end so that it hung a few inches above the dog's hips.

"Keep her still?" the assistant said.

In a few moments, the chain began to move slowly from side to side, about an inch in each direction over the dog's hips.

"It's not scientific," said the assistant, "but it's about a hundred percent accurate in determining pregnancy. She'll have her sonogram to be sure, but if she wasn't pregnant, the chain would have swung north-south. Something to do with the magnetic field."

The assistant handed me the chain and said, "Would you like to try it?"

I said I would.

I gave her back the chain.

I got down on all fours.

REFERENCE #388475848-5

To: Parking Violations Bureau, New York City

I am writing in reference to the ticket I was issued today for "covering 'The Empire State'" on my license plate. I include two photographs I took this afternoon that show, front and back, that the words "The Empire State" *are* clearly visible. I noticed several cars on the same block featuring license plates on which these words were entirely covered by the frame provided by the car dealer, and I noticed that none of these cars had been ticketed, as mine had. I don't mean to appear insolent, but I am wondering if the ticket might have been issued by the young Hispanic guy I sometimes see patrolling the double-parked cars during the week? I ask because the other day my dog yanked the leash from my hand and ran to him and jumped up looking for a treat. He did not appear to be comfortable around dogs, and though mine is a friendly one, she's big, and maybe the guy was frightened for a moment? It happened as I was getting out of my car, so he would have known it was *my* car, is what I'm saying.

"The Empire State"—it occurred to me that this is a nickname. I mean, police officers do not put out an all-points bulletin in The Empire State, they put out an all-points bulletin in *New York,* which words are also clearly visible on my license plates. In fact, there is no information the government might require that is not visible on these plates. You could even say that the words "The Empire State" are *advertising*. They fit a standard definition: a paid announcement, a public notice in print to induce people to use something, the action of making that thing generally known, providing information of general interest. Close enough.

I have parked my car with the plates as they appear in the accompanying photos on New York City streets for five years, since I drove the car out of the dealership on the Island five years ago; it has never been a problem until now. (I bought the car without ever reading *Consumer Reports*. I checked with a friend who said the price I was quoted was a reasonable one, but that I should refuse the extended warranty the dealer was pushing. "I'm trying to do you a favor," the dealer said, pissed off.)

At the time I bought the car, I didn't know I would soon be back living in the city, and hardly ever needing it. I had thought I would stay the two-hour drive east. What is the saying?—"If you want to make God laugh, tell him your plans."

I haven't kept track of everything I'm supposed to do with the car, but your records will show that I paid the ticket for my expired registration the same week it was issued. I did better with the safety inspection, and FYI, I'm good through November.

It's not really about the money, the $75 the ticket would cost me. I wouldn't mind writing a check for that amount as a donation to a Police Athletic League, or a fund to help rebuild the city. I'm not like the guy at the film festival yesterday who asked the French director in the Q and A after his film was shown, "Are we going to get our money back?" I hadn't even wanted to see the film; before we went, I told my date what I did want to see, and he said, "They stole the idea from that other one, the one where they ate each other." And I said, "No, that was the plane crash; this is the two guys who had the mountain-climbing accident. It's a documentary." And he said, "What isn't?"

Then, after the French film, after the audience applauded for this *major piece of crap,* the date and I cut out and went to a place he had heard about in the East Village for tea. It turned out to be someone's exotic version of high tea, so instead of scones and clotted cream and cucumber sandwiches, we were each served a teaspoon of clear, rosemary-scented jelly with a single pomegranate seed inside! What came after that were these teensy cubes of polenta covered in grapefruit puree, all floating in a "bubble bath" of champagne. Then came a chocolate truffle the size of a tooth. The fellow and I were giddy. It was pouring outside, and when we left, after the tea ceremony, we didn't want to leave each other, so we walked another couple of blocks to see a second movie, one he wanted to see, and I didn't tell him I had already seen it because by that time I just wanted to sit next to him in the dark. "I wonder who that is singing," I whispered at one point in the sound track. He didn't know, but I did, from having read the credits the first time I saw the movie. "Kind of sounds like Dave Matthews," I said, knowing I was right. "Let's be sure to check at the end," I said. "I'd like to get it for you."

Music keeps you youthful. Like I'm not the target audience for the Verve, but this morning I put on that song that goes, "I'm a million different people from one day to the next—I can change, I can change . . ." and—what's my point? I was in a really good mood when I found the ticket on my windshield. Then how to get rid of the poison, like adrenaline, that flooded my system when I read what it was for?

There is a theory of healing based on animals in the wild. People have observed animals that barely escaped a predator, and they say these animals lie down and *shake,* and in so doing somehow release the trauma. Whereas human beings take it in; we don't work it out, so it lodges in us where it produces any number of nasty effects and symptoms. If you follow a kind of guided fantasy, supposedly you can locate a calm, still place inside you and practice visiting it over and over, and that's as far as I got with this theory. It's supposed to make you feel better.

Maybe I should sell the car. But there is something about being able to get in a car and *leave* when you want to, or need to, without waiting to get to a car rental agency if you even know where one is and if it is even open when you get there.

Like last week, after a guy grabbed my arm when I was running around the reservoir, when he was suddenly in front of me, coming from the trees on the south end of the track, and no one else was around just then and I couldn't swing around wide enough to get completely past him, and he grabbed my arm. I think it was my anger that made him finally release me, because that is what I felt, not fear, until I got back home with a sore throat from yelling at him to leave me the fuck alone. I was shaking like crazy, and it wouldn't stop, so I walked a block to where my car was parked, and I drove for a couple of hours toward the ocean. My right leg was bouncing on the accelerator from nerves for much of the way, but I stopped for coffee and when I started up again I steered with my knees, the way *real* drivers steer, with a cup of coffee in one hand, playing the radio with the other. So maybe I am a wild animal, shaking off the trauma of near-capture.

There were actually two men at the reservoir. And I thought it was odd that when the first one grabbed me, and

I reflexively swung my free arm around to sock him in the chest, the other man didn't stop me. Because he could have. He watched, and listened to me yell, so I don't know what the deal was. But I think it was worth paying the insurance and having to park the car and get this ticket to have the car there to use that day.

You could accuse me of trying to put a human face on this. And you would be correct. But is there anything wrong with that? Unless the ticket was issued by the guy my dog startled, I know it isn't personal. But I'm not a person who can take this ticket in stride with the kind of urbanity urbane people prize in each other. I feel I must question—and protest—this particular ticket.

I want what is fair. I don't want a fight. But the truth is, I'm shaking—right now, writing this letter. My hand is shaking while I write. It's saying what I can't say—this is the way I say it.

WHAT WERE THE WHITE THINGS?

These pieces of crockery are a repertory company, playing roles in each dream. No, that's not the way it started. He said the pieces of crockery played roles in each *painting*. The artist clicked through slides of still lifes he had painted over thirty years. Someone in the small, attentive audience said, "Isn't that the cup in the painting from years ago?" Yes, it was, the artist said, and the pitcher and mixing bowl and goblet, too. Who was the nude woman leaning against the table on which the crockery was displayed? The artist didn't say, and no one in the small, attentive audience asked.

I was content to look at objects that had held the attention of a gifted man for so many years. I arrived at the lecture on my way to someplace else, an appointment with a doctor my doctor had arranged. Two days before, she was telling me his name and address and I have to say, I stopped listening, even though—or because—it was important. So instead of going to the radiologist's office, I walked into a nondenominational church where the artist's presentation was advertised on a plaque outside: "Finding the Mystery in Clarity." Was this not the opposite of what most people sought? I thought, I will learn something!

The crockery was white, not glazed, and painted realistically. The pieces threw different lengths of shadows depending on the angle of the light in each painting. Sometimes the pieces were lined up touching one another, and other times there were gaps. Were these gaps part of the mystery the artist had in mind? Did he mean for us to be literal, to think: absence? He said the mind wants to make sense of a thing, the mind wants to know what something stands for. Okay, the artist said, here is what I painted that September. On the screen, we saw a familiar tabletop—familiar from years of his still lifes—and the two tallest pieces of crockery, the pitcher and the vase, were missing; nothing stood in their places.

Ahhhh, the small, attentive audience said.

Then someone asked the artist, What were the white things? He meant what were the white things in the other paintings. What did they represent? And the artist said that was not a question he would answer.

My mother, near the end of her life, announced that she was giving everything away. She was enraged. She told me to put a sticker on anything I wanted to keep, but every time I did, she said she had promised the thing to someone else. The house was all the houses I had grown up in. The things I wanted to keep were all white. But what *were* the white things?

After the lecture, I tried to remember what I had wanted to keep. But all I could say was that the things I wanted to keep were white.

After the lecture, a call to my doctor's receptionist, and I had the address of the specialist. I wasn't so late that he wouldn't see me.

When the films were developed, an assistant brought them into the examination room. The doctor placed them up against lights and pointed out the distinct spots he said my doctor had suspected he would find. I told him I would have thought the spots would be dark. I said, Is this not what most people would expect?

The doctor told me the meaning of what we looked at on the film. He asked me if I understood what he said. I said yes. I said yes, and that I wanted to ask one question: What were the white things?

The doctor said he would explain it to me again, and proceeded to tell me a second time. He asked me if this time I understood what he had told me. Yes, I said. I said, Yes, but what were the white things?

THE DOG OF THE MARRIAGE

1.

On the last night of the marriage, my husband and I went to the ballet. We sat behind a blind man; his guide dog, in harness, lay beside him in the aisle of the theater. I could not keep my attention on the performance; instead, I watched the guide dog watch the performance. Throughout the evening, the dog's head moved, following the dancers across the stage. Every so often the dog would whimper slightly. "Because he can hear high notes we can't?" my husband said. "No," I said, "because he was disappointed in the choreography."

I work with these dogs every day, and their capability, their decency, shames me.

I am trying not to take things personally. This on advice from the evaluator at the school for the blind where I train dogs. She had overheard me ask a Labrador retriever, "Are you *trying* to ruin my day?"

I suppose there are many things one should try not to take personally. An absence of convenient parking, inclement weather, a husband who finds that he loves someone else.

When I get low, I take a retired guide dog to the local hospital. Any time is good, but around the holidays is best. I will dress a handsome shepherd in a Santa suit and visit the Catholic hospital and bust in on the morning spiritual counseling. Once I heard a nun ask a patient if he was nervous about the test that was scheduled for him that afternoon, and the patient, a young man, told the nun he hadn't known there *was* a test scheduled, but now that he did, he could truthfully say that, yes, he was nervous. Then he saw "Santa" in the hallway outside his door and called, "My God! Get that dog in here!" And so we perform a service.

At work, what I technically do is *pre*-train. I do basic obedience and then some. If I am successful, and the dog has the desired temperament, a more skilled trainer will work for months to turn the dog into a guide for a blind partner. I don't know any blind people. I'm in it for the dogs. Although I remember the job interview I had before this job. I thought I might like to work in the music business, but my husband urged me in the direction of my first love: dogs. The man who would have been my employer at the record company asked me why I wanted to work there. I said, "Because I love music," and he said, "Maybe the love affair is best carried on outside the office."

"Are guide dogs happy?" my husband asked at the start. I considered this, and cited the expert who believes that an animal's happiness derives from doing his job. So in that respect, yes, I said, I would think that guide dogs are happy. "Then why do they all look like Eleanor Roosevelt?" he said.

I told him about the way they get to know you. Not the way people do, the way people flatter you by wanting to know every last thing about you, only it isn't a compliment, it is just efficient, a person getting more quickly to the end of you. Correction—dogs *do* want to know every last thing about you. They take in the smell of you, they know from the next room, asleep, when a mood settles over you. The difference is there's not an end to it.

I could tell my husband now about Goodman in the garden. I raised Goodman myself—solid black Lab—and, after a year, I gave him up, the way you do, for further training and a life with Alice Banks. Alice was a gardener. She and her husband relaxed on weekends tending beds of annuals and several kinds of tomatoes. When Alice and Goodman graduated from the program, Alice said I was welcome to stay in touch. It is always the blind person's call. We exchanged letters for several months, and in the spring, I sent her a package of things for the yard. Then I got a letter from Alice's husband, Paul. He said they had been weeding in the garden, Goodman off-duty and retrieving a tossed ball. When Goodman found himself in the tomato patch, Paul wrote, he picked something up in his mouth and began yipping with excitement, tossing the thing into the air and running in circles to retrieve it. Paul told me that Goodman had found one of the sachets I had made to keep away deer; it was a packet of cheesecloth stuffed with my hair.

That is how I like to be known.

It was something I learned from my husband, who trusted natural ways to keep predators away.

Today I am known as the Unusual Person. This is a test wherein I pull my windbreaker up over my head from behind and stagger around the corner and lurch menacingly down the walkway toward the dog-in-training. A volunteer will have the dog on a lead and attempt to walk the dog past me. We will see if the dog startles or balks or demonstrates curiosity; if the dog does startle, we'll see if he recovers quickly and continues on his way.

Before lunch I test half a dozen dogs. The first one walks

by without more than a glance—he is being raised in New York City. The suburban dogs are skittish when they pass, but only one barks, and on the second approach, she, too, is quiet and passes. I am not a threat.

I eat quickly and head over across the quad to the best part of this place, the Whelping Center. The broods are brought here a couple of days before their due dates and are settled in quiet kennels where there will be a quilt on the floor and a handful of biscuits waiting. Chicken soup for dinner. The women who work here are unflappable and funny and intuitive and have substantial personalities, though they are, some of them, elfin—if only *I* had been raised here, is what I'm saying.

I contrive excuses to bring myself often to the Whelping Center. Sometimes I scoot into a kennel and warm my hands under the heat lamp trained over the newborns sleeping inside a plastic kiddie pool lined with towels, their eyes not yet open, their ears leathery tabs. I feel, here, optimistic, yet hopeful. Jubilant, yet happy. This is the way I thought and spoke for an irritating year as a girl, annoying the teachers at the girls' school I attended. In school I was diligent, yet hardworking. The headmistress, I felt, was impartial, yet fair.

Jeanette will find me like this—sitting in the pen, eyes closed, puppies "nursing" on my fingertips—and say, "Don't just sit there, get busy." Ha ha, Jeanette. It's the command— "get busy" is—for a guide dog to eliminate.

I often time my visits to when the older puppies are fed. A Labrador eating looks like time-lapse photography. After the pups have been weaned and are on to softened kibble, their food is set down for them in bowls like Bundt cake pans, a kind of circular trough. They crowd in around it and the pan begins to turn. It spins faster as they eat and push, until the pups are like propeller blades. Then they'll move in the opposite direction, and the bowl spins the other way, as though they are in the southern hemisphere. One of the staff put a cartoon on the wall: "Why dogs never survive shipwrecks." It's the captain dog standing up in a lifeboat addressing the other dogs: "Those in favor of eating all the food now, say 'Aye.'"

A beauty came in yesterday—Stella, out of Barnstormer Billy and one-eyed Tara. Stella will have an *A* litter (we name the litters alphabetically), so in the time I have left I write down the names in a tiny three-ring binder: Avalon, Ardor, Able, Axel. Jeanette looks over my shoulder and says, "Like Axl Rose? You don't look like a headbanger."

Acre. I was looking in the dictionary, and after "acre" it said, From the Latin *agere:* to lead.

In the afternoon: stairs—closed and open, up and down, on a short lead.

It is astonishing to find out how quickly the wrong things come into your head. I don't mean the vain thoughts that are unseemly and irrelevant in surroundings such as these. I mean that I can pause outside a kennel to dip my shoes in bleach and be visited by the memory of shattering glass, the way the etched glass of the heirloom globe exploded. I had lit a candle in the old lamp but had not fitted it carefully; as it burned, it tilted until it touched the handblown glass, handily prefiguring the news, over dessert, that my husband was going to get on with it because how long *was* a person supposed to give the other person to come back?

Last night, Stella delivered early. Nine healthy puppies, and one—the smallest, a female—with a cleft palate. She died within minutes. Fran, the staffer present at the whelp, entered it in her log, her notation including the name she gave this pup: Angel. There are those of us who seek Fran out in the hope that something of her rubs off. Fran helped Stella deliver over a period of seven hours. At midnight, when there had been three quiet hours, Fran helped Stella to her feet and ran the ultrasound scanner over the dog's belly. Nothing showed on the monitor, so Fran left the kennel to get some sleep. Yet in the morning when she checked in on the mother, there were ten healthy puppies nursing. During the night, Stella had given birth to one more, a female, as though to replace the one who had died. I said why didn't we name her "After," or put a little French on it—"Après"—but Fran said no, she wanted to name her for Angel. Sentimental? I am not the one to say; before I gave up Goodman, I made a tape recording of his snores.

Maybe it was fatigue, or the sadness of losing the runt, but Fran snapped at me when I showed up for work. She asked a perfunctory question. I should have said I was fine. But instead I observed that this was the day my husband left for Paris with his new girlfriend.

"Like you have a right to complain," Fran said, incredulous. "Let's think back one short year."

I was stung, and flushed, and fumbled at the sink. Did I expect sympathy? Browbeaten, yet subdued. Subdued, yet humbled. I left the room before she could say I didn't have a leg to stand on, or the shoe was on the other foot.

Back in the lounge, I wiped at the antibacterial wash I had splashed on my jeans. What gets on my clothes here—if it came from a person I'd be sick. Last week I was in the infirmary when a Lab was brought in with the tip of his tail cut off by a car door. Yet he was so happy to see the veterinarian that he wagged his tail madly and sprayed us all with blood, back and forth, in wide arcs. The walls and cabinets, too.

There is much to learn from these dogs. And we must learn these things over and over!

In the way that we know things before we know them, I dreamed that I swam across Lake Michigan, then pulled myself up on a raft near shore; just then the light changed in such a way that everything underwater was visible in silhouette, and giant hammerheads shadowed by. This was the night before my husband told me about Paris, and even in the dream I remember thinking, If I had known what was in the lake, I never would have gone in.

It's a warmish day for December, so I take one of the broods for a walk on the grounds. It's a lovely old neighborhood. Down the road from the school is one of those classic mansions you admire until you notice it's a funeral home. Every day I drive past it to get here, and an image undoes me, though I can't say quite why: a pair of white gloves folded over the wheel of an old Ford Fairlane outside a funeral home in Georgia in June.

The sight of geese has this effect on me, too. The dogs scare them up from the pond. When my best friend and I were in the first grade, her father acquired a dozen German Embdens. He let them roam freely about the yard. Every evening when he came home from work, he would turn a hose on the droppings they left in the drive; the grass along both sides of blacktop was a stripe of vivid green. He was a little eccentric, and the first of my friends' parents to die.

Buddha, Baxter, Bailey, Baywatch. I throw in that last for Jeanette. Working a litter ahead. We don't name the pups until they are four weeks old and get their ears tattooed, but still, it's good to be ready.

Back in the lounge there are letters from a sister school in Canada that has taken several of our dogs who failed the qualifying exam—except we don't say "failed," we say the dog was *reassigned,* or *released* for adoption as a pet. Canada will take

a "soft" dog, one who maybe startles or is a bit less indepen-
dent. Maybe it is like William Faulkner not getting into the
U.S. Army Air Force and then going to fly for Canada. What's
with Canada?

Trying to smooth things over, I guess, Fran asks for a
hand in putting together the invitation for the Christmas
party. I make James Thurber look like da Vinci, but I stay
late—it's the night of the six-months-and-under class, the
babies—and work up a festive border. The party is a high point
for the volunteers who raise the puppies. They bring them to
the high school gymnasium we borrow, and dress them up in
Santa hats or felt reindeer antlers held on with chin straps, and
there are cookies for everyone, and in the center of the gym
floor there is a large cardboard box filled with wrapped gifts.
On the command, the volunteers walk their dogs, one at a
time, up to the box, where the dog is allowed to reach in and
select a present, then return in a mannerly way to his spot.
They get excited, of course, and invariably there will be a dog,
like Ivan last year, who will get to the box and jump in.

Everyone wants to know how you do it, how you raise a
puppy and train it for a year and a half and then give it up.
Because you don't just love the dogs, you *fall* in love with
them. A love affair begins with a fantasy. For instance, that the
beloved will always be there. But *these* love affairs begin with
yearning, for a future that won't be shared. Good training.
There is a Zen-like quality to this work, if you can find reward
in staying in the moment and in giving up what you love
because someone else's need is greater. Sounds good in theory,
but I counseled a volunteer who was coming up on the separation and she was crying and angry, and she said, "Just
because I'm not blind!" She said, "What if he never swims
again? Swimming's his favorite thing." I said, "You know

how dogs' paws paddle in their sleep?" Dreams: the place most of us get what we need.

There is another side to this; it makes a pretty picture. The folks who raise the pups and then have to give them up? When the dogs get old and retire, the raisers can get them back. They can take them back in their well-earned rest. Raise enough puppies over the years—a steady stream of dear ones returning home.

Fran doesn't hold a grudge. She says she liked the invitation, and we walk together to the office to have it copied.

There are people whose goodness brings them to do this work, and there are those of us who come here *for* it. Both ways work.

Although, metaphorically, I am still in the lake, priding myself on a strong Australian crawl while nearby a hammerhead waits. Never mind the fact that this ravenous shark, in real life, is found in warm seas. It is with me in the lake where I mourn my lost status as someone who doesn't cause problems, and prove again that life is one long medley of prayers that we are not exposed, and try to convince myself that people who seem to suffer are not, in fact, unhappy, and want to be persuaded by the Japanese poem: "The barn burned down. / Now I can see the moon."

Did I invite this? It is like sitting in prayers at school when the headmistress says, "Who dropped lunch bags on the hockey field?" and although you went home for lunch, you think, *I did, I did.*

2.

I picked up coffee in town, but skipped the doughnuts and scones; after fifty-two years, my body owes me nothing. I ran into a former neighbor at the deli. We were still dressed the same in barn jackets and jeans; we both worked at horse farms. Standing in line for coffee, she picked crumbs of rust off an old bulb digger that looked pornographic in her hand. My own rusted one was plunged to the hilt in a circle of tulips where I left it when I heard about Lynney.

Claire, the former neighbor, told me she hadn't known Lynne Markson was divorced. I said she wasn't, they weren't, who told her they were? She said, "I thought *she* did." She said they had run into each other in line at the Film Forum, and Lynne told her she only came into the city once a week now. Lynne told her the rest of the time she lived upstate near her husband. Claire said she thought that was an interesting slip: "near" instead of "with."

I told her it wasn't a slip, and the reason she was upstate started the week the dog showed up in my yard, the same week my husband moved out. I would find the dog curled under the forsythia in the morning, in a shallow dirt bed he had dug the night before. When I let my own dogs out in the yard, he would stand and stretch, then stay still while they sniffed at him. He was a beagle wearing a faded too-tight collar he would not let me close enough to remove.

He was terrified of people, so I was certain he had been abused. But he liked the company of the dogs; he made himself part of the pack. Each morning he followed my dogs from the front yard with its hill, where their tennis balls rolled away, down into the backyard, where the three of them pawed at holes in the garden rows, probably after the moles that ate the centers out of the melons.

My dogs are female, so of course I indulged the notion that he had selected my house to fill the male post just vacated by my husband, who had moved back to the city. I stayed at the beach with the dogs and filled out my share of paperwork to make the separation final.

The beagle was small enough to shimmy in under the cedar fence gate where rain had eroded a patch of dirt into a small trough. He had rolled in, shook himself off, and stayed. I put out a bowl of food for him twice a day, and kept a bucket filled with water in the shade from the wisteria. The only time I knew he left the yard was when I took my own dogs across the street to walk through the fields that end at Round Pond. He would trail us, letting their bodies brush his when they all chased rabbits and squirrels. He had the look of a harried executive; he carried himself, chest first, like a little mogul. So I called him Beagleman. "Get me Beagleman!" I would order my dogs. "I'll take a meeting in five minutes—*front* yard." And they would race off to get him and herd him into the front and we would file across the street, every day a parade.

I didn't bother to fill in the dirt beds that Beagleman dug, and that my own dogs copied. The yard was a yard—it had never been an even "carpet" of green. Mowing had always been my job, one I liked, but I did not go beyond that to what more was required: grading, fertilizing, sprinklers.

Starting early in the summer, I put Beagleman's bowl closer to the house. Then I sat on the outdoor steps without moving or looking at him while he ate. When he finished, I tossed a handful of crumbled cheese in his direction. He would follow the spray of cheese, eating a trail that led to my open hand where more cheese was offered. He would start toward me, then stop and pulsate and whimper. At that point I would toss him the cheese and try again later in the day.

In the evenings around six—this was in July when the sand at the beach is so hot—I would load my two dogs into the back of the station wagon and drive to the ocean for a swim. Beagleman would wiggle under the closed gate and stand at the top of the driveway as I backed the car into the street. He would be there when we returned at dusk, and fit himself under the gate when the three of us had passed inside.

After an early spring of taking the marriage apart, I was glad to have every day the same. I did not ask much of myself; it was enough to keep a cutting garden watered and shop at a farm stand for tomatoes and basil, and baby egg-plant to grill, and that white corn that needs just three min-utes in hot water with milk. It was enough to conduct classes for young beginning and intermediate riders at the farm, to keep my dogs and sometimes myself reasonably groomed, and try to win over the beagle. I was mindful of the symmetry—trying to establish this creature's trust, having dispatched that of my husband.

This took us up through August.

Then, just before Labor Day, I kept the cheese in my hand. And Beagleman ate it, his eyes on mine. I told him he was a very good boy. He ate from my hand several times that day. I got him to follow me inside and into the kitchen, source of the cheese. I introduced him to a wall of cheese in the refrigerator. He ate from my hand while I gently touched his chin with a finger. I rubbed under his chin while he ate, and it was only another day before he let me rub his muzzle. From there it was his ears, scratching them while he sat beside me. I cut off the collar that left a dent in the skin of his neck.

At the end of the summer, he let me brush him while he rested his head on my leg. Within the week I had him upstairs, and we celebrated by having a slumber party—the three dogs up on my bed in the dark, eating popcorn and watching a movie.

Beagleman seemed to be proud of himself. He walked with confidence, he no longer hung back. He was in the front seat of the car on every errand. At night he raced ahead of me up the stairs; I would find him on my pillow on his back, waiting for me to rub his stomach.

This lasted until the lawyers said we would have to sell the house. I would be moving, I would be renting, and no one would rent to a person with three dogs. That was when I heard that Lynne Markson wanted a dog.

Back then, they had the place on the North Fork as well as the apartment on Riverside Drive. I arranged for Lynne and her husband, Whit, to visit.

Beagleman liked Lynney right away. He showed no fear, and I was proud of how far he had come. He was less comfortable around Whit. I had predicted this; he was still skittish around men, probably because a man or men had hurt him. Whit was gentle and welcoming, so we said: sleepover, trial visit. Beagleman sat in Lynney's lap in the car on the way to the city.

A few weeks later, Whit takes Beagleman out for an evening walk. As they are about to cross Riverside Drive, Beagleman slips his leash and bolts into the street. Reflexively, Whit runs after him.

Lynne is at home when the confused doorman phones up to say her dog came back by himself. He tells her the dog walked right through the lobby and into the elevator, so he—the doorman—pressed the button for their floor and sent him up.

Lynne gets the dog inside, then runs out to find Whit.

She follows the sound of a siren, and finds him just as the ambulance pulls up.

Claire looked at me as though she had been watching a performance. Which she had. I could not tell the story enough times. An observant friend had remarked that "Those who can't repeat the past are condemned to remember it."

I realized I had left out the part about Christmas Eve when Beagleman got lost in Noyac. So I did not get to say, "If I had not driven back that third time—if I had gone to midnight mass instead." I did not tell Claire that Lynne does not blame the dog, or that the dog follows her from room to room and sleeps with his head on the pillow, in her bed, in the house where she lives near her husband, who lives in rehab.

Claire, my former neighbor, said she would write to Lynne if I would give her the new address. She said, "How's Lynney doing?" And I said, "It's *her* story now."

3.

I was the one who did the back and forth; he was the one who did the every which way. He would stop in the course of the walk and talk with a friend, or a not-even friend, someone he hadn't seen in a while, invite the person to breakfast or lunch, even if the person was more my friend than his. His invitation would be so open-faced that it would seem mean not to take it. Then he would want me to come along.

The people I stopped for when I walked the dog were strangers who wanted to pay the dog a compliment, or pay me one for having such a dog. An unusual mix that was hard to place, the dog was a maverick; she had attitude, she was willful and people responded to that. If she liked you, then you were worth liking. With the dog present, I could talk to people I could not have talked to without her.

The dog had been our second choice. My husband wanted the pretty one, and I had wanted to keep the runt. But we each picked the same runner-up.

I counted the blocks when I walked the dog, or the equivalent of blocks in the park. I liked to return the same way we had come. I walked the dog on the other side of the street, or the path, so she could have variety. But I liked things to be the same, to be where they were the last time I saw them, when I saw them for the last time.

4.

For sixty dollars charged to my MasterCard in advance, the psychic described a wooded area near a body of water—a pond? a stream? she couldn't be sure—with a view across an open field to a "civic-type building"—a post office? a school? she couldn't be sure—where, according to her vision as relayed to me over the phone, the lost dog had looked for food in the last twenty-four hours.

This was less useful than the woman down the turnpike who saw the leaflet left on her windshield. She phoned to say she had seen the dog drag a deer across the tracks a hundred yards away the day before. I found the dead deer beside the tracks where the woman said, part of its flank gnawed to the bone. The dog could not have felled the deer; it must have been hit by a train. Had an approaching train scared the dog from its food?

The leaflet is all over town.

The ex-husband made it.

He advertised a reward beside a picture of the dog. But he did not consult with me first. The reward would not buy you an ordinary dinner in this town. Whenever I come across any of his posters, I add a "1" before the amount.

Despite the reward, calls come in. I chase down all sightings, even when the caller says the collar is red, not blue. But there is never any dog of any kind with any color of collar in the spot reported by the time I am able to get there.

I check construction sites. Workmen eat lunch outdoors, and a hungry dog might try them for a handout, wouldn't she? Half a dozen calls come from builders on the beachfront. Once, when I got there, there was a deer swimming in the ocean. It appeared to be caught in the tide, and as I moved toward it—toward the deer—it managed to pull itself ahead of the surf, where it found its footing and limped ashore on a hurt front leg, to leap away when I moved closer. So I, who only wanted to help, was made to stand there watching the deer head for the dunes.

I went out again at night to lay down scent trails in the woods near my house, wearing the same shoes and socks I had been wearing for days. The moon was nearly full above a snowy field. When I had made my way into the woods, I turned and saw deer standing side by side, watching. I thought, Saints, guardian angels, my saviors, my friends.

We watched each other for a while, and then I went home, checking over my shoulder all the way for the deer. They never moved once—not that I saw.

There were three animal psychics.

I phoned them all.

The famous one you can't get to work with you anymore unless you're the president of something and your dog is, too. Still, this woman phoned me from the airport, she said, between flights. She gave me the names and numbers of the other psychics who found missing dogs. Where's the one who finds missing husbands?

I called the most psychic-sounding one first, who turned out not to be available until after the holidays. What holidays? Were there holidays?

I left a message for the next one, and the third psychic answered her phone and insisted we could go to work with no delay so long as I could describe my dog to her and recite the numerals of my credit card number.

The worst thought I had was, What if the dog was just here? Right where I was standing?

Every morning and every night there is a videotape I watch. The ex-husband made it when he was my husband. It was made when the dog had first come to us and seemed to be everywhere, shared everything, offering, offering.

I see the viewfinder swing wide across the lawn, one of those panning shots you always find in movies, where the idea is to get everybody in the audience ready for what will presently be revealed—but only if everybody will just be very very good, and very very patient, and will wait, with perfect hope, for the make-believe story to unfold.

THE AFTERLIFE

When my mother died, my father's early widowhood gave him social cachet he would not have had if they had divorced. He was a bigger catch for the sorrow attached. He was kind, cultured, youthful, and good-looking, and many women tended to him. They cooked dinner for him, and sent their housekeepers to his Victorian near the Presidio Gate. My brothers were away in college, but I, who had dropped out of school, spent a good deal of time at the house.

Some of the women who looked after my father banked their right actions for later, I felt. One woman signed him up for a concert series, but it was a kind of music he didn't much like, and he had been at a concert—chamber music—the night my mother died.

One woman stocked his kitchen with candied ginger and snail shells and bottles of good red wine. I would prop bags of Oreos and Fig Newtons alongside so my brothers would find something familiar when they came home.

One woman sang to him; another, when he asked if she could sing, said, "If I were to sing, it would sound like talking louder." A couple of the women courted me as the best bet. There were shopping trips, lunches in their gardens, suggestions for cutting my hair. I was not used to that kind of attention, and seeing through it didn't mean I didn't also like it.

One woman was impatient with his mourning, another seemed excited by it. She didn't wear underwear when she came to visit; I knew because I heard her tell him. He told me she sent him pictures of herself naked; he was midwestern enough to be stunned.

The woman I liked—for a while she came over every night. She would get to his house when it was still light enough to see fog blowing down the street from the bay window in the living room. He would make her a drink in the kitchen, stirring in the Rose's lime juice with a chopstick from the Japanese take-out place. He would carry it in to where he had seated her on the toast-colored Italian couch in front of the fire. The house was a hundred years old, but the furniture was futuristic.

She was futuristic. She was forward-looking, although the past was what they had between them. Jane Stein had known my mother in college. She had married a friend of my father's, and then had not seen my parents since. She still lived in the Midwest, but not with her husband anymore. I had looked her up the month before when I was in Chicago. When I found out she was going to San Francisco, I told my father to take her to dinner. On their second date, she arrived at the house with a black cashmere sweater for me—a "finder's fee," she said.

On their third date, the three of us went to dinner. Other of the women had wanted me along so my father could see them draw me out. Jane wanted me there because we thought the same things were funny. When my father complained about a nosy woman who detained him in the grocery store,

Jane said, "That's the trouble with people in general—you have to run into them."

When I hung back a bit walking to the car, she said, "Take up space!" and pulled me along by the arm. The next week, she didn't mind that I saw my father walk her to the front door in the morning.

One night: "I made a fool of myself on that trip," I heard my father say. "Staying in the places I stayed with their mother years ago—I was posing the whole time," he said, "playing the part of a man in grief, from St. Petersburg to Captiva."

He was telling her about the time he'd gone by himself to Florida, only a few weeks after my mother died. Jane and my father were in the habit of travel. Every night they returned to his house, he mixed her a drink with a wooden chopstick, and took her on the trips he had taken to China, and Switzerland, and Venice with his late wife. Jane told him she would have thought she would be more interested in hearing about the places she had not seen herself, but was, in fact, more interested in where they had gone in this country, especially the places that she knew, too, along the coast of Florida. "What year was that?" she would ask, then do the math to see what she had been doing at the time.

When it was time for her to leave for the night, or the next morning, my father would put an object in her hands for her to take; he would divest himself of yet another *thing*—a Waring blender, a toaster oven—he could not imagine using again. He gave her classical CDs, a copper omelet pan, several crystal vases, a Victorian planter, a set of good knives, sweaters if the temperature had dropped the slightest bit, a comforter, books, a pumpkin pie he had made—he gave her something every day. Most of it she gave to the women's shelter she was in town to advise. Then she would reappear, note all that had been given up or given away—the travel, the glass stirrer for drinks—and let him return to a place she'd never been.

On the last night she visited my father, she asked him if the two of them might go somewhere together. And he said, "Darling, I don't go to the *dining room* anymore."

"Is there a place you *could* go and be happy?" she asked.

My father said that maybe he could go back to Aspen. That was where he and my mother, and sometimes we kids, went every summer for a handful of years. None of us were skiers, and in summer the town hosted a music festival in a huge tent set up in a meadow. World-class musicians filled small hotels, and swam in the pools with tourists like us. My father knew a lot about classical music, so he was happy discussing the afternoon program with the First Chair Violin while my mother read on a chaise in the sun, and my brothers tried to land on me in the deep end from the high board.

This was when we had lived in a suburb of Denver, and went rock-collecting weekends in the foothills. The lichen-covered rocks we brought back in the car ended up in the yard framing native flowering plants. I got to stay in the car and drink Tab after a rock I picked up freed something I still have dreams about. The mountains had nothing for me, and I did not yet know that *water* was going to be my place on earth, not swimming pools at small hotels, but lakes, the ocean, a lazy-waved bay, ponds ringed with willows, and me the girl swimming under low-hanging branches brushed by leaves for the rest of my days.

I heard Jane ask my father if he was happiest when he was in Aspen. He said, "I was, and then I wasn't." She said, "You can *was* again." He said he didn't think so. And she didn't come back the next day.

In a note to me a couple of weeks later, Jane wrote from Chicago that she would miss us. She said she understood that my father's life had ended with my mother's death, and that what he inhabited now was a kind of afterlife—not dead, but not alive to possibility, to what else one might still choose, and "Who would choose to live less?" she asked.

I didn't mention the note to my father, but I asked him if he wished she still came over. He said she was a terrific person.

The women that followed included a self-styled libertine, and a beauty whose parents had called in a priest to exorcise her when she was a child. Some of the women were contenders—generous, brimming, game.

The woman he sees now seems decent and kind. I met her at his house this morning. She was clearing his garden of weeds, advising him on the placement of a eucalyptus tree.

She left before I did. My father waved to her from the bay window, and asked if I didn't think she looked a little like Jane Stein.

I said, "That was a long time ago," and he said, so I understood him, "*Nothing* is a long time ago."

MEMOIR

Just once in my life—oh, when have I ever wanted anything
just once in my life?

OFFERTORY

We did it twelve times—made love, all of us, to one another twelve times, the two of them doing everything two people could do to me twelve times. I was going to say only twelve times, but it wasn't "only," was it? It was wonderful.

I began, last night, at the beginning. The rule was I had to tell the truth, and I had to tell him everything. I could start where I liked. I told him the story every night; he asked for it, for some version of it, every night. Sometimes I left out a detail so he would prompt me, and thus participate after a fashion. "The inevitability of orgasm?" he might say, and I would say, "The way she moved her hip into me first."

Sometimes I changed their names. Names were not the details that mattered to him. What mattered was the most refined particularity of our actions, and the declarative nature of my narrative. He did not want me to use language that said anything other than what it was. For me, I mean. Well, for them, her. All of us.

"I want you to give me points on the body—nuanced, subtilized, exact," he said. "I want fine-grained diction in the reportage, and I want it to be plummy. I want the ring of inexpressible reality—yet lyric.

"Were there photographs?" he asked, knowing that there were.

"Tell me," he said he wanted to know, "who took the pictures of you?"

Sometimes I tried to tell a different story. But he liked best when I told him about the man and the woman together—together with me. I learned that the more *froideur* in my tone, the more heated, the more insistent he would become—until I would be unable to continue because his mouth would be stopped up.

"Don't let the game warden see you," said the man painting the dock. "Indians the only ones allowed to net fish."

The net I was sweeping through the shallow part of the lake was a child's butterfly net I had found in the sand. The dock painter who warned me against the game warden was the same dock painter who had told me that a black racer was a water moccasin. I didn't tell him I knew he was wrong, but let him think I was rash for reaching in after it.

People on the lake were ready with the rules, rebuked the fantasy daily. The vision had been: Swim with the dog, shoulder-to-shoulder, every morning, to the other side. But a hand-stenciled sign was posted when the season started: NO DOGS ON BATHING BEACH, though dogs were not the nonreaders leaving Band-Aids and cigarettes in the water.

The seven hundred dollars I had paid in dues covered plowing snow, but I would not be getting the benefit of winter. I had moved here for the lake, and then would not go in the lake; I'd be gone before leaves began to fall.

The former tenant said she had recovered here. From what, she did not say, but she said she had given herself five years to do it in. Well, was there anybody who wasn't here to get over something, too?

His letter was forwarded to me here.

"I believe I need another look at someone who writes such a charming letter," he said.

I had written to him after our meeting two years before. I had told him everything in that letter as though he had asked for me to. I had written him the whole time I was away, a woman he had met just once. And then he wrote me back. He invited me to see his new work. He had a show opening soon, he said, and the paintings were not, he said, anything like what he had done before.

He said he liked the way I described the place where I had been, where the small group of us lived, and got better. He said he liked the sound of the beach where we went when we were given a pass. He said he had tried to paint such a place, and maybe I would like to see it.

I had twenty years to go to get to be as old as he was, and then, if I got there, I'd have to go counting almost twenty years again. I was still in my thirties, but I was the one of us who was old. Anyway, he said he was nostalgic for my past.

I had a past, and my past contained a marriage and a job and friends. But I had long since dispensed with this past. I had spent the year before moving to the lake at a place where people recover from the bad things that seek them out. For the time I was there, I wrote to this man although, or because, I had met him only once, and because I felt our talk had been not an exchange of words, but of souls.

I read about a famous mystery writer who worked for one week in a department store. One day she saw a woman come in and buy a doll. The mystery writer found out the woman's name, and took a bus to New Jersey to see where the woman lived. That was all. Years later, she referred to this woman as the love of her life.

It is possible to imagine a person so entirely that the image resists attempts to dislodge it.

I lived in small rooms with heaps of bleached shells on distressed white tables and antique mantels. His place had the original brick arches between the large open areas of the loft. There were polished wood floors (slate in the kitchen and bath), and a frosted glass–and-steel screen hid the staircase to the upper bedroom. His paintings were hung in the enormous studio on the first floor, the range represented by portraits and landscapes following the early "systems" paintings. There were ordinary workday scenes supported by strict and intricate organization that a critic had commended as "art that conceals art."

Lying in bed early on: "We had rules," I reminded him. "I could fuck the wife anytime I wanted. I could fuck the husband if the wife was also present. The wife could, whenever she wanted, fuck either one of us—her choice: together or alone. The husband needed no rules, both we women felt, because, we also seemed to feel, we would have no idea where to start in the drawing up of them.

"They took me up," I told him. "I was young," I reminded him. As if he, of all we did, needed reminding!

"Which of you would make the first move?" he asked.

"The first time or any time?" I asked.

"Maybe the wife started it?" I said. "Maybe the first time she made a preemptive strike? Maybe she saw the way her husband was looking at me—I guess she made up her mind to beat him to it? You know, later on she told me that was exactly what she was doing."

"Tell me what you had on," he said, "the first time, and every time."

"The wife said any dress looks good in a heap on the floor by the bed."

He said he wanted me to tell him about myself and about the woman when the two of us were in bed before the husband came home, how we would not let him join us at first, but let him crouch beside the bed, his eyes at the level of our bodies on the mattress, first at the side of the bed, and then at the foot of the bed. And who had undressed first—had we undressed each other?

"Would you do anything—everything—they wanted?" he asked, although the real question was, Would I do everything with *him*?

Let him find out!

"It wasn't always like that," I said. "Sometimes we just let the cats sleep in the bed."

"Oh?" he said. "Did they come into it in some way? There was cat hair in the sheets? On the two of you? On the three of you?

"And did you like to be watched?" he prompted. "Did you like it more when she watched you with him, or when he watched you with her?"

"Don't forget the neighbors," I said. "The couple who watched at the window where the curtains didn't close all the way. The man I didn't mind, but I thought the woman wanted to take my place, and I felt she resented me for it."

"You had never done anything like this before?" he said.

"I saw no reason not to."

"It was the great experiment," he said. "Did you wait until evening? Often you couldn't wait."

"That's true," I said. "I was supposed to be available."

"Every day," he said, "they touched you every day? Even on Sundays—you made yourself available to Saturday night's predations?"

"All the better," I said. "The better it was, the better it was."

"You mean the more, the more of them?" he said.

"Repetition fueled us," I said.

In the bed where I described the couplings years ago, he would suddenly roll me over so that I was on top. He would tell me to lean over and show him how my hair had made a tent over the face of the husband or of the wife.

The enclave at the lake had begun as a German settlement. The original developer built cabins for his family, and more cabins for their friends. The row of mailboxes at the end of Valkyrie Drive still featured mostly German names.

After an evening in the city, downtown, I would drive myself at dawn up the parkway and back to the lake. Before going to bed for a couple of hours, I would walk the dog through the woods and up the small mountain that is the backdrop for the place. At a point near the top, on the edge of an overlook, are the two cedars the German founder planted to stand for himself and his wife.

There were motion-sensor lights throughout my yard, and the few nights I was there, all night animals set them off. My heart used to race at the thought of intruders, but then I would see the doe nursing a fawn not many feet from a window, or a procession of bucks crossing the front yard to drink from the lake. So I came to look forward to these sudden illuminations.

Replacing lightbulbs, taking out trash, watering plants: exigencies of the tiny life, a life that opened up inside me at night in a downtown loft on an ugly street in a city rebuilding itself.

It started up with us at the place we went for dinner after leaving his friend's opening at a gallery in Chelsea. I had strained to say something kind, and he had pointed out the flaws in the artist's logic; he criticized the concept as well as its execution, and was not wrong.

His voice, doing so, was—sophisticated. It was a young man's voice; it was dignified and persuasive, and made me feel like an accomplice. Under the words, his voice seemed to say, "You and I are looking at this together, and we see the same thing." When I could keep up with him, that was true.

We walked easily together; I leaned into him, my head almost to his shoulder.

He continued the analysis over dinner, and as we were finishing, he said, "What if one told every truth! Recorded the most evanescent reactions, every triviality, an unimpeded account of lovers' minute-by-minute feelings about the other person: Why didn't she order the braised beef the way I did? She raved about the sea bass, wrongly. I set my watch three minutes fast; she set it back."

Here he took us into the future—he reached across the table to stroke my hair. "And I'd say, 'What about her hair across the pillow? I had thought it would be finer.'"

His stance was not unlike the one I had proposed to him

in my letter, that we observe the Wild West practice: We put our cards on the table.

We moved into what he called "the precincts of possibility," of anything-goes, of nothing undisclosed.

He wanted to hear "cock" and "cunt," but I was more likely to want to show him what the man and woman did to me all those years ago. He had told me to say we did it twelve times. Did what? What we did, well, wouldn't that be up to me? Didn't it have to?

I told him what they did to me the first time, and the second, and the third through the eighth and ninth—some nights I teased him: "That's it. I can't remember the rest. Sorry. Only remember nine."

But he was persistent, encouraged me to continue, to say more, to remember, to get it right. And when I really could not remember what happened the tenth time, I made something up. I made up something I guessed would be what he wanted. For example, he wanted to know when the husband was with both of us at once, whose name did he cry out when he came? He asked for the tenderest time, the most violent time, the most nonchalant time, the classiest time, the first time and the last time, all twelve times.

"And everyone was the better for it?" he said with admiration. "You were each made to feel more yourselves?"

"Of ourselves," I said.

I was never more myself than when I was lying in this man's arms. But was I ever much *of* myself in them?

"Don't you ever get jealous?" I asked.

"Of course I do," he said. "I admit to ineluctable jealousy—comparisons, comparisons, real and imagined. And, as it happens, there exists in me—not pathologically, but all too humanly, I think—a species of delight arising from this knowledge. Darling," he said, conspiring, "are these conflicting sentiments and the mystery they point to not at the core of our alliance?"

The town whose main street ends at the river draws tourists who come to shop for antiques. The prices aren't bad, and the town is picturesque and you can walk off the train and be pricing iron garden chairs before you've caught your breath. Boaters wave from the river that is, at this point, miles across. But the Jet Skis are annoying, and dogs are not allowed on the restored promenade. I had been there just long enough for the owner of the delicatessen to know how I took my coffee, and to avoid the speed trap on the other side of the bridge.

There was a backup generator on the north side of my house. It kicked on on its own once a week at noon, startling me each time. It ran for a while to give the impression it would be in good working order when it was really needed. An engineer down the road explained it to me; he said that during a snowstorm mine would be the only house with lights and heat. He told me not to use more than two appliances at a time.

"You'll have all your neighbors coming over to get warm," he said to me, either believing the observation a comfort to me or a threat.

I filled the dog's water bowl about half the way full. I set it back on the porch. I could use a larger bowl, but I would rather the dog see me fill it many times in a day, see me think of her needs and move to meet those needs oh so many times each day.

Sleepy from the night before, I watched the kid from the next town mow my lawn in half the time it took me the times I did it. He charged very little. I would see him being careful out back where he would circle the maple tree not to nick the metal grave marker with the German name of a woman and the date of her birth and the date of her death. Ashes, I had guessed, but forgot to ask the owner.

That night in bed in the bed downtown, I said, "I know you don't know anything about ashes or lakes, but is it legal—can you put someone's ashes anywhere you want to?"

"There is no lake," he said, the words slurred against my neck. "There are only the two domains: this bed, and the bed of memory. Get rid of the lake," he said. "Two people can go anywhere they want to go right here."

I was never late.

By eight o'clock, he would already have ordered dinner for us. The sushi would be delivered in an hour, and left by the door.

Some nights we did not make it past the entryway before dinner arrived. Some nights he would close the door and then press me against it, or against a wall, and hold me there until we dropped to the polished wood floor together—we would not have said anything to each other. And we would stay there until we heard the brush of the delivery man outside.

When we finished dinner, he would put on music for us, something he had looped to play over and over again, a piece he had chosen or something he knew I liked, something we both liked to hear behind us.

Then he would be inside me again so quickly I was, each time, surprised.

Kissing my eyes, he said, "Did Phillip start like this?"

And that night the husband would be Phillip.

The first time I went to see him at the loft, I found something he didn't drink in the kitchen. I didn't like it either, and on subsequent visits I checked to see if the level of juice in the bottle was lower, if the juice-drinker had been to see him. This changed the night I told him about the twelve times. He asked me to come back the next night, and the next. Each time I looked, I saw that the level of juice was the same. That is when the place became a sanctuary for me, and which of us does not need sanctuary all the time?

I tried to remember what I had told him the time before. That Katherine—I was calling the wife "Katherine"—took me home after taking me to lunch at a grimy place in China Basin, a fishermen's supply shop that sold bait next to the coffee and doughnuts you could take out onto a dock and eat while oil tankers got overhauled.

"Did she want you to undress? Or did she want to undress you herself?" he wanted to know. He was twisting my hair as he spoke. He could not braid it with only one hand, so he twirled it around his fingers and let it spring loose again.

"Show me how she kissed you," he said.

I kissed him in a way I imagined Katherine might have done.

He said, "When you kiss me like that, my heart is so stolen."

Back at the apartment, he patted himself down.

"It must have slipped out of my pocket in the theater," he said, "when I reached over to button your coat."

I said, "Why don't you call the theater and ask them to check our row."

The book was a rare one. He had underlined parts throughout.

He returned to the kitchen to make the call, and—"Oh! Oh, look! I must have taken it out without thinking," he said of the book there beside the stove.

And when the phone rang, he said, "That must be the theater calling, to tell us the book has been found."

It was midnight when we removed the clear covers from the containers of densely packed sushi. He could not stand the green plastic fences that separated one kind from another, so I removed them and removed the ginger as well. I mixed soy sauce with the wasabi. I would have eaten from the containers, but he arranged the pieces in a pattern on good china.

We watched the late news while we ate the tuna and salmon. When he had cleared the plates and turned off the television, he asked me to put my black dress back on. He led me to the leather club chair near the bed. He sat down first, and brought me to him so that I faced him. He pushed the black dress up to my waist and pulled me somewhat roughly onto his lap.

"Did Phillip feel left out?" he asked, moving slowly inside me.

I told him that after a couple of weeks of going out with just Katherine, the three of us went to a party. I told him we drank and drank and then went to their house late. "Phillip got out his camera," I said, "and attached a different lens. He said, 'Show me what the two of you have learned about each other.' "

"Those pictures," my lover said, gripping my shoulders. "Where are they now? You have to get me those pictures.

"Ask Phillip for those pictures," he said, out of breath.

*   *   *

When he had me: the word "slown."

It was a thing between us—*slown*. One night I heard him say on the phone, "We were stoned, or I was stoned, and she said, 'You hear what you said?—you just said *slown*.' That was nice. It was nice, the way she heard me say it wrong and then went ahead and made it a thing between us—the word *slown*. 'Time has slown down.' It was like this woman was getting just as slown down as I was, even though she never touched the stuff. It was honor, it was allegiance. It had an effect on us—the word."

I listened to him talk to his friend, and, happy, went into his kitchen. I got silver polish and a rag from under the sink, and contentedly polished a pair of candlesticks.

Cast-iron bookends with embossed baskets of flowers on them—these are a morning's find on Main Street. The shops sell mirrors with milk-painted frames; I've bought several of them for gifts, but not for him. I am not allowed to bring him anything but myself. He has returned gifts to me the times I disobeyed ("We do not quite forgive a giver"), and I gave those things away.

Not lewd, not urbane, not leering or concupiscent, but *devotional*. That is how I felt about Katherine and Phillip, and about the man I offered them up to. He looked for jolting carnality, for physical imperatives. "Didn't more rules appear with a certain periodicity?" he wanted to know.

We were awake in the night, in the early morning, really.

I had been lying still, rubbing a finger on the mended spot on the sheet where hydrogen peroxide had made a hole when he rubbed at a spot of blood—not mine. He got out of bed to turn off the air conditioner, and wrapped himself around me when he returned. With no need of a segue from my hurried-off clothes on the floor, I said, "I can't remember—does the week in Acapulco count as one time?"

"I want *each* time in Acapulco," he said, as I knew he would.

I gave him a familiar travelogue just to see how long until he'd interrupt with "Cut to the chase—the beach, the waves, sunset, dinner, you're back in the house in bed."

I pushed him off me so that he could come back even closer.

"We chose a room with a skylight above the bed. It was smaller than the other bedrooms in the rented house, but we wanted to see the stars. Phillip would not be joining us for another day or two, so the mood was hen party, sorority house."

He moved steadily inside me, so wonderfully inside me as I spoke. When he asked me a question, he spoke into my mouth. I had to turn my head and tell him to repeat it in my ear.

He smoothed his hand down my silk camisole and asked me if I needed to be coaxed. "Did you reach for Katherine first?"

"Not then, maybe not ever," I said. "It was not a lack of desire," I told him. "I took an active part by setting desire in motion. To be in a condition of readiness is to participate fully," I said. "As I am now."

"Show me what she did to make you come that night," he said.

In showing him, I took him to the other side of himself.

A short time later, he pulled me down to the thick carpet in front of the tall oval mirror. He put a pillow beneath my head, and another under my hips. He said, "When Phillip arrived, did the three of you spend that night in the room with the skylight?"

In fact, I remembered pleading exhaustion that night, and sleeping by myself downstairs. But there was nothing for him in that. I gave him instead a scene from a live act I watched through a one-way mirror in a South-of-Market theater. Phillip had taken me there on a night when prohibitions turned into permissions. Neither of us had told Katherine.

I dressed for him on the night that made it a month since I had started meeting him at the loft downtown where he waited for me "all pins-and-needle-y," he said.

I had had to go to a dinner first, a benefit for something worth giving money to. The transition was too quick, the way it is when you fly to a place that you need train time to adjust to. On the way to the loft, I had felt tired by what went on there, by the bottomless pit of it, the ever-ratcheted-up attempts to hold his attention on me.

In the bedroom there was a movie playing. I recognized it as one of the red-boxed collection in his bedroom closet. We had watched this one before, the one in which the male star auditions Polish girls for his next film. Were they really in Poland in the film? Who could tell? What mattered was that these were girls who would do anything, anywhere.

I arrived during the scene where the two girls, maybe nineteen years old, are lying naked beside each other in a hotel room. The star opens one girl's legs, and then the other's, for the camera. Both of the girls have shaved, or have been shaved. Then the star pulls the first girl, the blonde, into a sitting position on the edge of the bed and, standing in front of her, forces his cock into her mouth. It is possible that the scene is, to some extent, unacted—the size of his cock forces tears into the girl's eyes.

When the actor is finished with her, he turns to the second girl, who has been watching him with the first. He turns her over so that he can fit himself into her from behind; at the same time, another man (he had been lounging in a chair earlier, naked) pulls her on top of him and enters her from the front. While this is going on, the first girl wipes her eyes and breathes with her mouth open as she watches the girl beside her on the bed. After a while, the second girl cries out in Polish.

"The thing about these films," he said, "is that this really happened. We're seeing something that really happened."

I tried to rally to the feel of his hand on my leg. But a part of me was still at the dinner, greeting guests in black tie.

"You know why I want to see you with another lover?" he said, watching the screen. "I want to see a secret you—I would trade possession of you for it."

He had offered to bring in women who modeled for him, and I had declined. I knew there was no one he would rather see me with than Katherine.

I thought of the photographs he had taken of me. He felt the results were not worthy, did not resemble the nature of what was. He said, "They do not convey the trance you occupy during those times, the trance both of us inhabit, one with the other, one on account of the other, during those times."

"So what is seen is not what is felt?" I asked.

He said, "No instrument carried from a prior place could be expected to capture the feelings effected there."

I had already found the photographs he'd taken of others in a portfolio in another part of the loft.

The moment I wished he would turn off the movie, he muted the sound and turned his attention to me. This quality of attention righted things between us.

Then we were all flesh, and all feeling in that flesh. We abided in it, joined and rejoined, distance collapsed.

"Harmony," he whispered.

I said the word back to him.

Harmony sought, harmony required, "No life lost to us," he said.

There is an almost unbridgeable gulf between what an artist sees and what an artist paints. I knew this from my studies, and from looking at things myself. There are artists—Mondrian was one—who went from representation to abstraction by painting dying flowers, chrysanthemums in Mondrian's case. With this man, it had happened in reverse. He had painted vases of dying asters, all the time getting closer to figuration. Early on, he gave me a drawing from this series, not the one I wanted, but the one he wanted me to have.

He told me not to bring him flowers, but I often brought flowers with me, lately cabbage roses. He seemed pained to receive them and did not really look at them until they started to decay. He could not wait to get rid of them so he could enjoy remembering them.

Renoir told Matisse he would pick flowers in the fields and arrange them in a vase, and then he would paint the side he had not arranged.

On the walls of the loft there were portraits of this man's

mother, drawn while she lay in her hospital bed; he drew her as she got smaller, up until the day she died there.

"No one tells me better stories," he assured me. I was aware of the point at which a compliment becomes a trap, because you are expected to keep doing the thing you are praised for; resentment will follow when you stop.

"Lie back," I said.

That night I had worn my grandmother's diamond earrings. I thought I might leave one behind in his bed the next morning. The moment this occurred to me, I thought, Why should he require an object to bring me to mind?

The music he had put on was a medieval motet. Two voices begin, and are joined by two more, then two more, until forty-eight singers are holding forth together. It has the hypnotic effect of chant, but it is song. I knew that if he ever heard this music out in the world, I would be the person he would think of. There it was again, thinking in terms of souvenirs, what you take away from a place to help you call it back.

Obediently, he lay back in the barely lit room. I kept on a sea green slip and joined him, sitting on the bed so as to force his legs apart. I stroked him slowly and said, "The time in the pool at night? There was something I left out before."

"This was in Laguna?" he said, as though he could have forgotten.

"Katherine and I drove down in a day. We left at dawn and took the Grapevine south—not much to see, but we wanted to make the best time. I wanted to watch the sunset from her sister's pool, or, if we were too late for that, to see the full moon from the pool. We only stopped at that place that has the oysters."

"I know that place—"

"That's the one," I said.

"Her sister lived in one of those heavily landscaped com-
pounds where several bungalows share a large pool. Night-
blooming jasmine was planted around this pool, so the air
smelled good when you swam after dark."

"You wear jasmine sometimes when you come to me," he
said.

"We both gave in to the drone of the drive, that line
down the center of the state. It was driving with a destination,
but with nothing required of us when we got there."

"The way you can drive in California!" he said. "I used to
love that about it."

I reached for a bottle of almond-scented oil. I poured a little in my hand.

"We didn't unpack at first," I said. "We pulled on bathing
suits from a duffel bag and wrapped beach towel sarongs
around them. Except that I had been unable to find mine, and
had packed a leotard instead, the Danskin kind with the
narrow straps, flesh-colored.

"There were only two other people in the pool. Two men
were doing laps in the deep end. Katherine and I stood in
water up to our breasts and held on to the edge of the pool
with our arms stretched out behind us. The water was heated,
and it swayed against us slowly from the motion of the swim-
mers doing laps."

"Time was slown way down," he said, his eyes closed.

"We stayed like that," I said, "until the men climbed out
of the pool and lay down on chaises spread with towels at
our end.

"Are you with me?" I asked.

"Darling," he said.

"Katherine churned the water around her, and when she did a handstand, I saw that she had taken off her suit. The men saw, too, of course. They were quite a bit older than we were, and wore plaid swimming trunks. What an awful word—trunks.

"Are you listening?" I asked. "Because one of the things I just told you was a lie. Can you tell me what was the thing that I made up?"

"You mustn't tease an old man."

"But really," I said, suddenly exhausted, "don't you have something like this on video? Maybe we could just watch that?"

My voice was raw, and when I coughed, he got up to get me a glass of water. On his way back from the kitchen, he stopped to play back messages left by callers during the night.

We were not much for dreams. But one I woke him up to tell him went like this:

"I'm driving on a bridge."

"Transition," he said.

"When my car breaks down."

"You have a breakdown," he said.

"And suddenly the water is rising."

"Feelings," he said, "rising," he said.

"Your car needs a tune-up," he said, and drew me back to bed, where the Nice Man made the Bad Dream stop.

Sometimes he would reminisce about another woman. When I was chilly because I suspected the woman had been to the loft the day before, he would say, "Oh, come on. Now, come on. What does that take away from you?"

"Dignity?" I said. "I find it humiliating."

"You said in your letter that humiliation brings the softness of heart that allows you to listen to God."

"If you believe in God," I said.

"Or in humiliation," he said.

And when I grabbed a stack of photos of another inamorata and made a spray of them across the bed, he refused to speak to me for nearly a month.

During that time I caught up on sleep and made the acquaintance of whatever turned up in the woods. I tutored some of the kids at the lake in drawing. I swam with the dog after dark. One night we followed a woman in a bathrobe down the lane to the little beach. She dropped her robe in the sand, and walked naked into the water. I didn't hear a splash, and I didn't see her again. But the robe was gone in the morning.

When the month had passed and we broached the borders of accord, we went to a screening of a documentary film about the life of an artist he used to know. Why this painter had had to go and kill himself was the least of the mysteries about him. He had had a lively sense of fairness; the film director interviewed a patron who had balked at the asking price of a new canvas, and suggested he pay the artist three-quarters of the price instead. The artist agreed, and shipped his patron the painting with one-fourth of the canvas cut out.

On the way to the theater we had reviewed the movie rules: He said there was to be no talking, no eating, no touching, and that if I needed to cross my legs I was to cross them in his direction. Before the lights dimmed, he had tucked his sweater up under my chin and around my shoulders. Soon, both his arms were around me. His lips brushed mine on the way to whisper in my ear. He said my composure was remarkable. He said, "It is your forbearance we have to thank for what could be a new tranquillity." He said he believed life could be, if we would strive for composure, "all affirmation."

"Are you happy?" he asked me. It was a serious question. He meant, Was I happy sitting beside him about to start up again?

I touched his face.

"Then let us go and consecrate the desecrated ground."

On the night his best friend died, he said, "Stay with me."

It was almost morning and we had not slept and had not let go of each other all those hours, and he said quietly, "Stay with me."

I said, "You know I will."

He said, "You know what I mean."

I did know. He meant not all the time, but *for* all time. He meant despite everything he would do that would make me want to leave.

I said, "I know what you mean, and you know I will."

The dog disappeared.

For days I did what a person does when her dog has disappeared. No one at the lake had seen her. No one found a collar. I showed up crying at the loft days later. He walked me into the part of the loft where he worked. I saw that he had hung a new painting. It was a scene of Central Park on a sunny summer day. I saw a dog, as I had described my own to him, painted into the park.

"She came here," he said.

I didn't know what my neighbors at the lake thought of me, out all night and coming home just after dawn, walking a dog and then not walking a dog, not showing up for potlucks or Flag Day. But I kept the lawn mowed and put a flag decal on my car.

He asked about the place on the lake but he never came to see it. He had done all the traveling he was ever going to do; that was the impression he gave. Now he traveled in time, taking me with him to where he had gone when he was a go-er. I was not so eager to go anywhere, really, so this didn't bother me, except for once when I thought we should drive to Maine. I wanted us to drift in a canoe across a calm, cold lake, and listen to loons.

He had been to a lake in Maine with someone else years before. He said his Maine had been a week at a famous fishing camp whose pricey guides took your family out at dawn and then fried your catch for lunch. What occupied him now was seeing how far a person could go in the realization of pleasure, without leaving home, two people in a bed.

"Where do you look first?" he asked, holding me from behind. "What do you look at first?"

He stood behind me after putting on a film. We looked at it together. In this one, a series of couples was glimpsed by a woman who made her way alone through a villa. There were no closed doors in this villa, so she kept finding men and women, or women and women, lying on beds or lounging in chairs naked. Those people were pleased, were excited, to have the woman see them. It seemed a good bet that one of those couples would invite the woman to join them.

His question was not rhetorical. He wanted to know what I looked at first. What anyone looked at first. His was a life of looking—he was an artist, and he said he wanted to see it all. I disappointed him. I did not know what I looked at first. The people onscreen were less interesting than what he was doing with me.

He kept the sound turned off. I was able to make him look away.

He said he wanted to see everything, but did he, really? Does a person want to know the thing he is asking you to tell him?

I wanted to get his voice on tape. I wanted to ask if he would mind repeating something he had said, this time into a microphone set on Record. The way he said "Darling," for example, with all seriousness. I would want to hear him say this over and over, the way he looked at the photographs he took of us in bed "to preserve our best behavior," he said, "against the times we are estranged and there is no one to divine our souls and pick us out from the rest."

The moment this would occur to me, I would feel a spur in my side, like the anxious spur of misalignment just before the two of us would subside into each other. I would kiss him roughly then, and he would kiss me back, and when we had fulfilled ourselves, we would fall asleep together. Waking later—I would wake up because he had—he would turn on the television and we would hold each other and watch the current events, "just lying still," he would croon, "while the world worlds up at us."

I had not heard from Katherine for many years when her forwarded letter reached me. She was coming to New York, and she said she wanted to see me. I did not think this was coincidence; I felt I had conjured her by talking about her every night. I was excited and panic-stricken. I wanted to show them off to each other, and that would be a disaster. The three weeks' notice had shrunk to a couple of days. I left a message at her hotel to hold for arrival.

Last night I found him looking at Raphael's *Alba Madonna*.

He held the book so I could see. "Why is she facing left instead of right?" he asked. "Why the triangular arrangement of figures? Why a river in the background? Why is she wearing red?"

"Because a human being made this?" I said.

"Because a human being made this," he said, pleased.

The window shades were up. I looked across the way to a window that was covered in sheer white fabric. The room was lit behind it so the woman in the room threw a visible silhouette. She was posing, or maybe doing a kind of yoga. Then a man joined the woman and she turned out the light.

"This dress is very beautiful," he said, his arms around me.

"An old gift from Katherine," I said. The seamstress had done a good job on the vintage navy lace. I had asked her to give it a lighter look by removing the silk lining from the knees down.

"I want to hear about your friend," he said, undoing the

hooks and eyes. "But first I want to fuck you on this couch," he said.

"You do give it a gentlemanly contour," I said, by way of welcome.

"Are these tears?" he asked, smoothing hair back from my forehead.

"It's better in French."

"What is?" he said.

I told him the part of a poem I was thinking about, one I'd had to learn in school in French as well as English: ". . . From hope and fear set free, . . . / . . . even the weariest river / Winds somewhere safe to sea."

"You're going to meet Katherine," I said.

"It's brilliant," he said, "liberating the past for a revival in the present."

His questions about Phillip had been abandoned some time back, but he started up again about Katherine and me. He suggested I bring her with me the next time I came to the loft. Well, of course he did. I said I thought we might do better in a gallery instead, with objects between us to look at, as we had. I knew he would be winning when I made the introductions. Katherine would be appreciative and intelligent and unimpeachably cordial to him. She might take a camera from her bag and take our picture, his and mine, then hand the camera to him to take one of her with me.

One kind of woman would phone him the next day. He would want to be helpful, and what would begin in passion and deceit would wind down to something ordinary. It would fill my mouth with stones. But maybe Katherine would do this, too? Would Katherine require his gaze?

"Tell me again—"

Call-and-response.

Such an extravagant sense of what is normal. Depends on what you're used to, I suppose.

All those questions, each one of them a version of just the one thing: Was I better served in another's embrace than in his own?

"We might clear a space," I said. "You can't fill every hour."

"Is that what we've been doing?"

I never wanted to tell him.

He wanted his suspicion confirmed, although it would be ghastly to have it confirmed. I watched his salacity turn to fear. All the nights I had drawn out the exchange, holding back information, scornful of his boyish need to know, yet protective of that boyishness, too—his insatiable urging, wanting the savor of the way women are with each other, what they say to each other, him begging for female truth.

"May I count on you to utter the next sentence?" he would say.

I never wanted to tell him. I said, "I'll show you what she did to me," and he said, "But you can't show me, I'm not a woman—you have to tell me."

He was eager for the thing that would undo him. He had disallowed my earlier squeamishness, insisted I tear it apart. Okay. I would give him some female truth. What would have made me seem compliant when we started was assault by the time I told him.

I told him in just one word.

I said, "The answer to your question is: Precision. I can tincture it with more patently sexual language, but really, that's what you're after. Katherine was precise. I mean what you think I mean."

He looked me over to see if I was playing.

A thrilling calm settled over me.

He propped himself up on an elbow.

"Look at that," he said. "The single word that brings an inquisition to an end."

I leaned back on the couch and let my breath out. I held his hand and thought, What now? Not asking him, but myself.

Because it was up to me!

I would not introduce him to Katherine; I would not give him the chance to tell me she was more beautiful than he had imagined. Let him reside in his failure of imagination; I had been generous. I had more. But it was mine.

I led him from the couch back to the desecrated ground. I lay down next to him. I wanted to console him—I sent a herd of words and the dust rose and it was not enough.

He had told me to say we did it twelve times.

Well, maybe it was twelve times, and maybe it wasn't any times at all.

You want the truth and you want the truth and when you get it you can't take it and have to turn away. So is telling a person the truth a good or malignant act? Precision—that was easy. He had asked for it! There was more to tell; there would always be more to tell. If I chose to tell him.

In the meantime.

I was never more myself than when I was lying in this man's arms.

We lay quietly, holding each other. Time was slown way down. Finally he said, "Did you ever wear a linen dress on a summer day? A wheat-colored linen dress whose hem fluttered in a breeze? And did you pin up your hair on both sides so that your long hair funneled down your back in that breeze?"

I did not know who he was describing, but I said yes, I had dressed like that in the summers when I was young.

"Darling," he said.

I knew he was not entirely with me, and I had a shopworn thought: To be able to reverse the direction of time! But wouldn't we have to go through the same things in reverse?

"Darling," he said again.

So here we go, careening along in the only direction there is to go in, our bodies braced for transport—"Unimprovable," he says.

NOTES

Page 329: The harpist who sings at the bedside of the dying is the musicologist and thanatologist Therese Schroeder-Sheker.

Page 348: The expert who defined animal happiness is Vicki Hearne.

Page 360: "Those who can't repeat the past are condemned to remember it" is from Mark O'Donnell.

Pages 377–78: The mystery writer is Patricia Highsmith.

Page 387: "We do not quite forgive a giver" is from Ralph Waldo Emerson's essay "Gifts."

Page 395: The artist is Ray Johnson, in the film *How to Draw a Bunny*.

Page 400: The lines quoted are from "The Garden of Proserpine" by Algernon Charles Swinburne.

*With special thanks to Gordon Lish,
editor of my first and second books,
for the conversation of thirty years.*

ABOUT THE AUTHOR

AMY HEMPEL is the author of *The Dog of the Marriage, Tumble Home, At the Gates of the Animal Kingdom,* and *Reasons to Live,* and the coeditor of *Unleashed.* Her stories have appeared in *Elle; GQ; Harper's; Playboy; The Quarterly; The Yale Review; O, The Oprah Magazine;* and *Vanity Fair.* She is a Guggenheim Fellowship recipient and she teaches at the Graduate Writing Program at Bennington College. She lives in New York City.

Reasons to Live

Certain stories originally appeared in the following periodicals, sometimes under different titles and in slightly different form: Tendril, Mademoiselle, California, *and* The Missouri Review. *"In the Cemetery Where Al Jolson Is Buried" originally appeared in* TriQuarterly *and has been reprinted in* The Editors' Choice: New American Stories. *"Going" and "Why I'm Here" originally appeared in* Vanity Fair. *"San Francisco" originally appeared in* Harper's.

At the Gates of the Animal Kingdom

"The Most Girl Part of You" was published in Vanity Fair *and reprinted in* New American Short Stories, Vol. I. *"Du Jour" was published in* The Mississippi Review. *"Rapture of the Deep" and "The Day I Had Everything" were published in* Grand Street. *"At the Gates of the Animal Kingdom" appeared in* Columbia. *"The Harvest," "The Lady Will Have the Slug Louie," and "To Those of You Who Missed Your Connecting Flights Out of O'Hare" were published in* The Quarterly. *"And Lead Us Not into Penn Station" appeared as "Litany" in* 7 Days. *"Murder" was published in* Mother Jones *and was reprinted in* Louder Than Words. *"In the Animal Shelter" appeared in* Tampa Review. *"Under No Moon" appeared in* Zyzzyva. *"The Rest of God" was published in* The Yale Review. *"The Center" appeared in* Witness. *"Tom-Rock Through the Eels" was published in* Taxi. Flower Lore and Legend, *by Katherine M. Beals, from which a verse of the Mary Clemmer Ames poem is excerpted, was originally published by Henry Holt and Company, Inc. Grateful acknowledgment is made to Wesleyan University Press for permission to reprint an excerpt from "Approaching Prayer" by James Dickey from* James Dickey Poems 1957–1967. *Copyright © 1964 by James Dickey. Reprinted by permission of Wesleyan University Press.*

Tumble Home

"Weekend" appeared first in Harper's; *"Sportsman" appeared first in* GQ; *"The Annex" in* The Yale Review; *"The New Lodger" in* The Quarterly; *"Church Cancels Cow" in* The Alaska Quarterly Review; *"Housewife" in* Micro Fiction. *Parts of "Tumble Home" appeared first in* Epoch, Elle, *and* Salmagundi.

The Dog of the Marriage

"Beach Town" was previously published in Tin House *and appeared in* Bestial Noise *(an anthology published by Tin House). "The Uninvited" was previously published in* GQ. *"Reference #388475848-5" appeared in* Ontario Review. *"What Were the White Things?" appeared in* Bellevue Literary Review. *"The Dog of the Marriage, Part 1" was published as "Now I Can See the Moon" in* Elle *and reprinted in* Labor Days. The Mississippi Review *first published "The Dog of the Marriage, Part 4." "The Afterlife" was previously published in* Playboy. *"Matinee"— now part of "Offertory"—appeared in* Fence.